JC 423 POL

THE POLITICS OF RADICAL DEMOCRACY

Edited by
Adrian Little and Moya Lloyd

EDINBURGH UNIVERSITY PRESS

© in this edition Edinburgh University Press, 2009
© in the individual contributions is retained by the authors

Edinburgh University Press Ltd
22 George Square, Edinburgh
www.euppublishing.com

Typeset in Sabon
by Servis Filmsetting Ltd, Stockport, Cheshire, and
printed and bound in Great Britain by
Biddles Ltd, King's Lynn, Norfolk

A CIP record for this book is available from the British Library

ISBN 978 0 7486 3399 9 (hardback)

The right of the contributors
to be identified as authors of this
work has been asserted in accordance
with the Copyright, Designs and Patents Act 1988.

Chapter 8 is an abridged version of 'Friends and Enemies,
Slaves and Masters: Fanaticism, Wendell Phillips, and the
Limits of Democratic Theory,' *Journal of Politics*, Vol. 71,
No. 1 (January 2009), Copyright Southern Political Science
Association, published by Cambridge University Press,
reproduced with permission.

Contents

Acknowledgements

The editors would like to thank the staff at Edinburgh University Press for their assistance in the production of this volume. In particular, we would like to acknowledge the advice and forbearance of Nicola Ramsey in supporting the project and enduring the delays in the production of the final manuscript.

The initial idea for the book was developed around a panel established at the Second Annual Workshops on Political Theory conference held at Manchester Metropolitan University in September 2005. Some of the chapters emerged from papers presented at the original workshop while others were later commissioned. We would thus like to thank the conference organisers, Jules Townsend and Joseph Femia, as well as Pablo Ghetti and Jon Simons, both of whom contributed immeasurably to the debate in the workshop itself.

Adrian would like to thank Holly Marshall for her support of a sometimes absent partner during the production of the book. During the final stages of the book preparation, she gave birth to Jude and Milo Little; while they didn't make the production of the book any easier, they provided much respite when the editorial processes were difficult. Adrian dedicates the book to Holly, Jude and Milo.

Moya would like to thank Andrew Thacker, yet again, for his love, patience and encouragement during the writing and editing of this book, not least given his own writing and editorial commitments. Special thanks are also due to Daniel, who has rapidly become accustomed to his mum disappearing into her study to write and who rarely complains about it. This book is dedicated to them both.

Notes on the Contributors

Alan Finlayson is Reader in the Department of Politics and International Relations at Swansea University. His research is concerned with the interaction between political theory and political analysis and he has published work in both fields, including *Making Sense of New Labour* (Lawrence and Wishart, 2003) and *Contemporary Political Thought: A Reader and Guide* (Edinburgh University Press/New York University Press, 2003). More recently he has published a number of articles concerning rhetoric and politics and is currently overseeing a research project, funded by the Leverhulme Trust, involving the theoretical analysis of the historical development of rhetoric in British politics.

Adrian Little is Associate Professor and Reader in Political Theory at the University of Melbourne, and Head of the School of Political Science, Criminology and Sociology. His most recent books are *Democratic Piety: Complexity, Conflict and Violence* (Edinburgh University Press, 2008) and *Democracy and Northern Ireland: Beyond the Liberal Paradigm?* (Palgrave, 2004). He has published widely in the fields of social and political theory and Northern Irish politics in journals including the *Australian Journal of Political Science*, *Theoria*, the *British Journal of Politics and International Relations*, *Irish Political Studies*, *Contemporary Politics* and the *Journal of Political Ideologies*.

Moya Lloyd is Professor of Political Theory at Loughborough University. She has published widely in the areas of contemporary political theory and feminist theory, focusing for the last few years on the work of Judith Butler. Her most recent books include *Beyond Identity Politics: Feminism, Power and Politics* (Sage, 2005) and *Judith Butler: From Norms to Politics* (Polity, 2007). She is currently working on a new project on politics and affect.

James Martin is Reader in Political Theory at Goldsmiths, University of London. He is the author of *Piero Gobetti and the Politics of Liberal Revolution* (Palgrave, 2008), *Gramsci's Political Analysis* (Macmillan, 1998), co-author (with Steve Bastow) of *Third Way Discourse* (Edinburgh University Press, 2003) and editor of several works including *The Poulantzas Reader: Marxism, Law and the State* (Verso, 2008), *Palgrave Advances in Continental Political Theory* (Palgrave, 2006, with Terrell Carver) and *Antonio Gramsci: Critical Assessments* (Routledge, 2002).

Joel Olson teaches political theory at Northern Arizona University (joel.olson@nau.edu). He is the author of *The Abolition of White Democracy* (University of Minnesota Press, 2004) and is currently writing a book on the fanatical tradition in American politics.

Andrew Robinson is an independent researcher connected to the Centre for the Study of Social and Global Justice (CSSGJ), University of Nottingham, UK where he was until recently a Leverhume Early Career Fellow. He is the author and co-author of many articles on a variety of topics and has published in *Thesis Eleven*, *Theory & Event*, *Capital & Class* and *Utopian Studies*. He is currently working on topics around the concepts of exclusion, oppressive discourse and hegemony and contemporary politics.

Andrew Schaap is Lecturer in the Department of Politics at the University of Exeter. He is author of *Political Reconciliation* (Routledge, 2005) and has recently published articles in *Australian Journal of Political Science*, *Political Studies Review*, *Philosophy and Social Criticism* and *Constellations*. Andrew is currently editing a book entitled *Law and Agonistic Politics* (Ashgate, forthcoming).

Birgit Schippers teaches social and political theory at St Mary's University College Belfast. Her areas of interest include feminist theory, citizenship and democratic theory, and identity politics. She is currently working on a book concerning Julia Kristeva and feminist philosophy.

Simon Tormey is Professor of Politics and Critical Theory and Director of the Centre for the Study of Social and Global Justice (CSSGJ) at the University of Nottingham. He has published numerous books and articles, including most recently *Anti-Capitalism: A*

Beginner's Guide (Oneworld, 2004) and *Key Thinkers from Critical Theory to Post-Marxism* (Sage, 2006). He is interested in radical movements, radical theories and contending understandings of global justice.

Mark Wenman is Lecturer in Political Theory in the School of Politics and International Relations at the University of Nottingham, and a Fellow of the Centre for the Study of Social and Global Justice (CSSGJ). His research focuses on post-Marxism and contemporary theories of pluralism, and has been published in journals such as *Contemporary Political Theory, Philosophy and Social Criticism* and *Political Studies.*

Introduction

Moya Lloyd and Adrian Little

Radical democracy emerged in response to the crisis that affected Western left-wing thought throughout the second half of the twentieth century. This crisis was the product of a number of factors, including a mounting disaffection with the capacity of socialist, and in particular, orthodox Marxist thought to explain developments in the industrialised world; the appearance of various social movements (including feminism, gay and lesbian rights, and environmentalism) that challenged the centrality of class-based politics; the expansion of multicultural protest; the events of 1989 that signalled the demise of Communism; the break-up of the Eastern bloc; and the spread of both capitalism and liberal democracy (or, perhaps better, liberal capitalism) to ever-increasing areas of the globe. The theory of radical democracy – or rather theories, since there is no single version – developed as a way to address the challenges posed by these developments. So what is radical democracy?

The first version to note takes its co-ordinates from debates on the US left. As Barbara Epstein comments, here, '"radical democracy" has come to replace "socialism" as the point of reference for what used to be called left politics' (1995: 127). This shift, initiated in large part by Stanley Aronowitz's 1994 essay, 'The Situation of the Left in the United States', advocated replacing the term 'socialism' with that of 'radical democracy' as a better way to capture the breadth and heterogeneity of 'left' struggles, post-60s, against what was perceived to be the universalising tendencies of socialist thinking. While many followed his lead – though not Epstein – their use of the term 'radical democracy' frequently differed.[1]

A second, alternative, way to characterise radical democracy, therefore, is as a 'post-Marxist' political and theoretical orientation. This, however, only introduces further variation. 'Post-Marxism', as Iris Young defines it in *Inclusion and Democracy*, refers to those inspired by socialism 'who continue to be critical of capitalist economic

1

processes and who argue for radical democracy, but who also criticize some aspects of historic Marxism' (2000: 182). Here she highlights work by Claus Offe, Jean Cohen and Andrew Arato, Jürgen Habermas, Nancy Fraser and herself. All contend that the 'radical anti-capitalist pursuit of justice' is best conceived of as a 'project of democratizing' the state, civil society and the 'corporate economy' (Young 2000: 183). Arguably, however, those listed might be better thought of as the critical theory tradition of radical democracy rather than simply 'post-Marxist'. For this latter label needs to be able to encompass one group of thinkers ignored here by Young. These latter, perhaps best exemplified by Ernesto Laclau and Chantal Mouffe in *Hegemony and Socialist Strategy: Towards a Radical Democratic Politics* (1985), are also post-Marxist.[2] Instead of drawing inspiration from the Frankfurt School of critical theory, however, they blend a *critical* indebtedness to Marxism/socialism with insights drawn from French post-structuralism, and particularly its theories of language. For analytical clarity, therefore, in what follows, a distinction will be drawn between critical theory (sometimes referred to as deliberative democracy in recognition of the dominant paradigm within that field) and post-structuralist accounts of radical democracy, both of which, to compound matters, are themselves internally variegated.

What though do these two traditions of post-Marxist radical democracy share? According to Aletta Norval, there are two specific features: a critical stance towards liberal democracy and, paradoxically at first sight, a commitment to certain elements of the liberal tradition 'while attempting to further democratise it' (Norval 2001: 587; see also Norval 2004 and 2007). At its simplest, this means that radical democrats (echoing Rousseau and Marx) favour participation and enhanced opportunities for popular control (self-government) over the limitations of representative democracy. It indicates that (like Marx) they are attentive to the inequalities of power that undermine the capacities of individuals or groups to access or exercise the formal or abstract rights characteristic of liberalism. It implies, too, that they conceive of democracy not in terms of the aggregation of pre-existing interests but as the means by which those interests, and the identities associated with them, are articulated. Against classical critics of liberalism, however, it also suggests that they regard certain liberal norms or ideals – specifically equality and freedom – as vital to the continued extension and intensification of democracy. In this latter respect, as Norval comments, 'contemporary radical democrats deconstruct rather than reject the liberal tradition' (2001: 588). We will return to this point later.

Critical theory and post-structuralist accounts differ, however, in a number of significant respects, some of which will be traced in greater detail in forthcoming chapters. We want to highlight just two of them here. First, and perhaps most importantly, critical theory radical democrats emphasise the possibility of rational consensus, achieved through deliberation according to normatively grounded procedures, where their post-structuralist counterparts stress dissensus, disagreement, agonism and/or antagonism, or, in other words, the ineliminability of contestation from politics. Second, those within the critical theory camp privilege 'reason over power' (Young 1996: 122); it is the force of the better argument for deliberative democrats that ought to carry the day, not the fact that the person or group articulating it is powerful. Post-structuralist radical democrats, by contrast, view democratisation and power as intimately entwined. Democratisation *is* the very struggle to occupy the place of power left empty, as Lefort notes, by democratic revolution (1988: 17); the site of hegemonic practice.

In this edited collection, it is specifically the post-structuralist form of radical democratic theory that concerns us (though, as noted earlier, some contributors situate their discussions of post-structuralist radical democracy in relation to the critical theory/deliberative form). When we speak in this volume of radical democracy, therefore, unless otherwise specified, we mean its post-structuralist variants.

Although, in the UK, 'radical democracy' is most closely associated with *Hegemony and Socialist Strategy*, and perhaps more recently with Mouffe's 2000 book *The Democratic Paradox*, it would be a mistake to confine the term to describing the work of Laclau and Mouffe, either together or singly, or the writings of those directly inspired by them. If we take radical democracy to encompass (amongst others) the following features, then, clearly, it incorporates other thinkers:

- that democracy is understood as a fugitive condition or open-ended process, and thus perpetually amenable to disruption and renewal;
- that the political is apprehended as ontologically conflictual or contestatory;
- that civil society rather than the state is construed as the principal, even exclusive, site of democratic struggle;
- that democracy is not a form of government or set of institutions but rather a moment marking the practice of politics itself; and

- that radical democratic politics is oriented towards the contestation of prevailing regimes of cultural intelligibility (and thus exclusion).

Those deploying some or, in many cases, all of the above ideas include, for instance, Judith Butler; William Connolly; Bonnie Honig; Claude Lefort; Jacques Rancière; and Sheldon Wolin, though not all would characterise themselves explicitly as radical democrats.

Many of these writers are discussed in detail in the ensuing chapters. Thus, for example, most contributors engage critically with the writings of Laclau and/or Mouffe. In addition, Little, Lloyd and Martin, amongst others, explore the contribution to radical democratic theory of Rancière; and Schippers and Lloyd that of Butler. Robinson and Tormey draw on the work of Deleuze to argue for an expanded notion of radical politics. In addition, two chapters seek to extend the purview of radical democracy: Wenman's considers what Michael Hardt's and Antonio Negri's work on globalisation might add to an understanding of the sites of radical democratic practice while Olson's explores how the philosophy of Wendell Phillips offers democratic options foreclosed in the work of both deliberative and radical – or agonistic – democrats.

The broad characterisation of post-structuralist radical democracy offered above might be further qualified by exploring the ontological presuppositions underpinning the work of different thinkers; whether they focus, that is, on lack or abundance (Tønder and Thomassen 2005). The former strand is exemplified both by Laclau, who creatively deploys ideas drawn from the psychoanalytical writings of Jacques Lacan, and by Lefort, who conceives of democracy as constituted by 'the *dissolution of the markers of certainty*' (1988: 19). The latter strand, informed mainly by the writings of Deleuze, underpins the work of Connolly and of Hardt and Negri, all of whom emphasise modes of becoming and the irruption of the 'new'. There are important implications for the nature of radical democratic politics depending on which ontology is deployed: one stresses its hegemonic character; the other focuses on pluralisation (Tønder and Thomassen 2005: 7). Without over-stating the differences between the two versions of post-structuralist radical democracy – arguably they share much in common – the distinction bears on an important question for those studying them, namely, what is radical about radical democracy? This returns us to an issue touched on above: the relation between radical democracy and liberalism.

That many post-structuralist radical democrats conceive of their enterprise in terms of the democratisation of liberalism is incontestable. Butler, for example, characterises her own account of radical democracy in terms of 'expanding the democratic possibilities for the key terms of liberalism, rendering them more inclusive, dynamic and more concrete' (2000a: 13). Similarly, Mouffe, reflecting back on her work with Laclau, proclaims that 'What we propose [in *Hegemony*] is a type of "radical liberal democracy"'. Moreover, she continues, 'we do not present it as a rejection of the liberal democratic regime or as the institution of a new political form of society'; rather 'political liberalism' is necessary to 'pluralist democracy' (Mouffe 1996a: 20). The radicalisation of liberalism, it appears, involves its democratisation. What though does it mean to democratise liberalism?[3]

If we construe liberalism as a set of political values and democracy in terms of political equality and popular sovereignty then there are a number of ways we could interpret this claim (see also Laclau 2005a). First, we might read the idea of liberalism's democratisation in terms of the extension of its core values to ever greater sectors of the population. Certainly, this is how the history of liberal rights has been recounted. A discourse that began as 'the language of the group – the white male bourgeoisie' has been repeatedly resignified in order to advance the claims of women, former slaves, workers and sexual minorities and so as to support calls for an increasing array of rights: civil, political, social, economic, cultural, sexual and so on (Kennedy 2002: 214).

Although it is certainly the case that radical democrats share a commitment to the liberal democratic values of liberty and equality and seek to see those values extended in more egalitarian directions, as Tønder and Thomassen remind us, they do not (necessarily) adhere to a 'liberal *interpretation*' of those values (2005: 4, emphasis added). Instead, they see the terms of liberalism as fundamentally political, which means infinitely contestable and perpetually susceptible to reformulation. One consequence of this is that rights are not regarded by some radical democrats as the best means for articulating the values of equality and liberty. In fact, rights, it might be said, pose something of a problem for radical democracy, raising questions as to whether they ought to be rejected because of their embeddedness in liberalism or whether they could be opened up to a more radical democratic future. (See Schaap, this volume and Chambers 2004.)

An alternative option is to see the democratisation of liberalism in terms of the performative constitution and reconstitution of the 'people' or *demos*. Instead of emphasising liberal values, here priority is placed on the side of democracy and, in particular, 'the people'. This 'populist' position (to borrow from Laclau) privileges the idea of the people as the key political actor in democratic politics (2005a: 259). Democracy, in this sense, might, as Wolin observes, be best thought of as 'a project concerned with the political potentialities of ordinary citizens'; with their capacity to become 'political beings' (1994: 11). Radical democratic theory, however, does not simply assume the 'fact' of the demos (as a pre-existing body with a shared identity) as the basis for democratic politics. It argues, instead, that the demos (the democratic 'we') is produced, albeit contingently, through democratic politics – when the excluded demand to be included (Schaap 2006: 258). Jacques Rancière's work provides several examples of this process. Let us take the case of suffragist and socialist Jeanne Deroin, who, in 1849, 'presents herself as a candidate for a legislative election in which she cannot run' (Rancière 1999: 41).

According to Rancière, Deroin's act exposes the contradiction of excluding women from *universal* suffrage: 'She reveals herself and she reveals the subject "women" as necessarily included in the sovereign French people enjoying universal suffrage and the equality of all before the law yet being at the same time radically excluded' (1999: 41). At this moment, when, that is, 'those who have no right to be counted . . . make themselves of some account' (Rancière 1999: 27), the demos is reconstituted as sex-inclusive. As Jane Bennett remarks, the point for Rancière is that the demos 'does not pre-exist its act of disruption, but is constituted by its very refutation of the order's claim to have already accounted for all parties to the polity' (2005: 140). Deroin, to use language more familiar from Butler's work (see Lloyd, this volume), performatively (re)constitutes the democratic body in the moment of enacting her demand.

Finally, the democratisation of liberalism might be tied to pluralism, even to what Connolly terms 'the pluralization of pluralism' (1995: xix). A central feature of radical democratic writing is its emphasis on difference over identity; that is, that identity is always potentially disrupted by the differences within it that it cannot subsume. This has both ontological and axiological effects. Radical democrats contend that there are always multiple, competing, identities in existence in society at any one time, which belie any claim to a 'stable' or 'universal' identity, as well as competing interpretations of equality and liberty, which foreclose the possibility of fully realising either. Pluralism is the (ontological) condition of possibility and impossibility of democratic politics. It 'implies' the conflict and disagreement that keep alive democratic contestation (Mouffe 1996b: 254).

Radical democracy, however, does more than merely note the 'fact' of pluralism: the empirical presence in liberal society of comparatively settled interest groups with diverse conceptions of the good life (Mouffe 1996b; Connolly 1995). It also evinces a normative commitment to it, though what this normative commitment entails is conceived somewhat differently by different authors. For some, pluralism as an 'axiological principle' involves celebrating and enhancing the differences that characterise modern democracies (Mouffe 1996b: 246). For others, such as Connolly, the celebration of social pluralism needs to be supplemented by an ethical responsiveness to what Deleuze calls the 'wild, free or untamed differences' (1994: 50) that burst onto the social and political scene time and again. This is what Connolly calls 'pluralisation': the emergence of new 'positive identities' out of 'old differences, injuries, and energies' (1995: xiv). The democratic goal here is to negotiate the tension between the recognition of existing identities (pluralism) and the emergence of new ones (the drive to pluralisation). So, where Mouffe aims to turn enemies into adversaries, through the production of 'radical democratic citizens', Connolly argues for an ethos of critical responsiveness towards movements of pluralisation. In sum, radical democracy is always plural democracy but plural democracy in a state of perpetual renewal.[4]

It would be a mistake, however, to see these different ways of conceiving of the democratisation of liberalism as somehow mutually exclusive. As will become clear in the chapters that follow, they are often seen as different dimensions of the same process; a process that is always contingent. This is why democracy, as we understand it in this book, is viewed as an elusive condition; what Jacques Derrida terms 'democracy *to come*', democracy as a promise that can never entirely deliver (1994: 64). Democracy is not primarily a system of government (parliamentary or presidential) or a means of legitimising the state (Rancière 1999: 99). It is a moment of disruption and a practice of political contestation.

The chapters

Radical democracy, we have suggested, is distinctive in claiming that democratic practice is a practice of contestation and disagreement. In chapter one, Alan Finlayson takes up this issue and considers how the practice of disagreement might itself be conducted. Counter-posing radical democracy to what he terms 'aggregationist' and 'accommodationist' theories of democracy, and later to proceduralism, he argues, innovatively, that radical democratic politics is an essentially and ineradicably *rhetorical* politics. Focusing on the 'rhetoricality' of politics (Norval 2007) emphasises the variety of styles (polemical, parodic, emotive, scientific), as well as the range of strategies (metaphor, analogy, catachresis), mobilised in attempts to persuade others to a particular way of thinking. It thus contrasts sharply with the highly attenuated sense of argumentation assumed by deliberative democrats.

In chapter two, Moya Lloyd critically examines Judith Butler's contribution to radical democratic theory. Lloyd begins by considering the place of universality in Butler's thought. Although radical democrats, in general, are wary of *a priori* universals, they do not unconditionally reject universality. Rather, they seek to reconceptualise it as both vital to democratisation yet ultimately unrealisable, and Butler is no exception. Lloyd then analyses the case of same-sex marriage in order to explore an aporia in Butler's work, generated by the latter's apparent *a priori* assumption that the state is not a viable site for restaging the universal. The worry for Lloyd is that this assumption denies the significance of the specific historical context in which particular democratic struggles occur; times when the state might be a key site for democratic activism.

An issue raised throughout this book concerns the extent to which radical democracy involves simply a reworking of liberalism as opposed to its (complete) democratic transformation. In chapter three, Andrew Schaap ponders this question by exploring the relation between popular sovereignty and human rights set out by Mouffe and Habermas, and their implications for representing political claims. By way of illustration, he considers the problem of Aboriginal sovereignty. In a compelling argument, Schaap concludes that where the Habermasian assumption of co-originality operates peremptorily to prevent challenges to the terms of political association, the alternative offered by Mouffe, although more attuned to agonism, remains ensnared within liberal ideology. As such, he contends, and here there are parallels with Olson's claims in chapter eight, that it is similarly unable to recognise as legitimate (and democratic) claims that challenge the prevailing political order.

We return in chapter four to the work of Judith Butler. Here Birgit Schippers assesses the significance of micro-politics for Butler's understanding of radical democratic practice. Like Schaap and Lloyd, Schippers is thus keen to examine the *politics* of radical democracy, not just its theoretical contours. To this end, she focuses on two inter-related forms of micro-politics: 'talking back' (or linguistic resignification) and transformative bodily practices (or corporeal resignification). Although applauding her radicalism, Schippers nevertheless contends that what these two examples reveal are the limitations, from a democratic perspective, of Butler's project: its neglect of the anti-egalitarian tendencies rife within civil society and associational politics; its failure to attend to the numerical dimension of democratic politics; and its abandonment of the state as a site of democratic transformation (see also Lloyd).

The theme of civil society addressed briefly by Schippers is the focus of James Martin's chapter. Much has been written about civil society in recent years, particularly within the critical theory or deliberative traditions of radical democracy. According to Martin, however, such accounts misunderstand the peculiarly spatial character of the political and, as such, the nature of civil society. That spatiality, encapsulated for him in the idea of 'perverse duplicity', is better represented by Laclau's notion of 'dislocation'. This allows for an apprehension of civil society as a democratic domain but one characterised by hegemonic struggles for power and, thus, by antagonism. Martin argues decisively that what is needed, therefore, is a re-politicisation of conflict based on 'a politics of civility' (Balibar 2004); the goal of which is not to resolve difference but to develop (ethical) strategies aimed at converting antagonism to agonism.

Towards the end of his chapter, Martin reflects briefly on the notion of global civil society, a theme picked up by Wenman. His aim is to develop a theory of radical democracy able to address globalisation, and particularly what Hardt and Negri (2001) identify as the new forms of power associated with it. Critical of Mouffe's approach to world politics, Wenman turns to Laclau and, in particular, his idea of hegemony. Developed in the context of domestic politics, however, this notion assumes the idea of an 'historical bloc', a concept inappropriate at global level. In an original turn, Wenman argues what is required is an understanding of hegemony as 'event', centred on the hegemonisation of 'empty signifiers' such as human rights or global justice. He ends by exploring briefly how the media might be pivotal in generating such global 'events'.

In different ways, the next two chapters raise what they perceive to be a specific limitation with the accounts of radical democracy espoused by Laclau and/or Mouffe; namely, their tendency to fall back on liberal (or liberal democratic) notions of 'reasonable' politics. (See also Vázquez-Arroyo (2004) on Connolly.) They thus link back to concerns expressed by Schaap in chapter three. In chapter seven, Robinson and Tormey present a provocative, Deleuzian-inspired critique of Laclau and Mouffe that centres on two perceived deficiencies with their thought: first, its statism and second, its defence of (what Deleuze terms) despotic signification. Their central charge is that Laclau and Mouffe assume a single mode of doing politics: one based on representation. This mode not only preserves the framework of liberal democracy rather than radicalising it. It is also contradicted empirically by the many radical social movements (and they catalogue a wide range of examples) that conduct their politics in ways other than those outlined by Laclau and Mouffe. 'Horizontal' movements, that is, who practise everyday, immanent, anti-representational politics. The chapter ends with a brief sketch of their 'horizontalist' alternative to radical democracy.

In chapter eight, Olson explores fanaticism from the perspective of radical (or agonistic) democracy. Despite its accent on conflict, radical democracy, he contends, struggles to understand fanaticism because it operates with too narrow a conception of agonism, namely as contestation *within* a shared liberal framework. As such it cannot see struggles over the framework itself as democratic struggles. To rectify this shortcoming, Olson, in a creative move, turns to the work of nineteenth-century orator and abolitionist Wendell Phillips and the latter's idea of 'talk' (an example of rhetorical politics of the kind favoured by Finlayson). Here Phillips deploys a friend/enemy distinction, not dissimilar to that used by Mouffe. Where Mouffe aims to produce a 'conflictual consensus' by converting enemies into adversaries, Phillips's strategy is to encourage enmity in order to reshape public opinion into a new democratic common sense. From this Olson concludes, persuasively, that in conditions of irreconcilable discord, fanaticism may aid democratisation.

In the final chapter, Little examines radical democracy through the case of Northern Ireland, once thought of as an example of intractable conflict. Northern Ireland, at least since the signing of the Belfast Agreement in 1998, has often been analysed in terms of liberal democratic consensus-driven models of democracy. Little argues convincingly that this is a mistake. The repeated suspensions of the democratic institutions and outbreaks of disagreement that have marked the post-Agreement period are better interpreted through the 'paradigm of radical democracy', with its emphasis on democracy as a fragile, contingent and always incomplete project. Although radical democracy has undoubted strengths as an interpretive frame, particularly for divided societies in the midst of political transformation, and as a critique of liberal democracy, Little argues it needs to be clearer in its critique of democracy (including its exploration of popular sovereignty and rule of the people).

Notes

1. The variety of positions taken by leftists in the US on the question of radical democracy can be glimpsed in Trend (1995).
2. Young tends to refer to these as agonistic theorists.
3. In fact, when some critics talk of radical democracy they talk of it as radicalising (rather than democratising) liberalism (see Little, this volume), which of course begs the question, not really addressed here, of whether democratisation and radicalisation are the same.
4. And, of course, one of the ways in which this renewal occurs – in which pluralisation takes place – is through the (re-)composition of the demos (Bennett 2005: 141).

1

Rhetoric and Radical Democratic Political Theory

Alan Finlayson

Introduction

The simplest definition of radical democracy is this: it is the theory and practice of democratic political contestation. While many contemporary theories of democracy emphasise the aggregation or accommodation of various identities and interests, radical democracy emphasises how these are permanently contested in ways that transform them as they combine and recombine in the white heat of political action. And where other theories of democracy emphasise the consultation or the participation of citizens in political decision-making, the theory and practice of radical democracy emphasise that this is a process of conflict and disagreement rather than one of consensus and resolution.

Such contestation is something many political theorists seek to avoid, preferring to ground a political system in advance, specifying the proper location of sovereignty, its extent and the rules to which it must defer. In liberal theories this often entails ensuring that the state is neutral as to the kinds of life people choose to lead so that it can be the object of stable consensus. The distinctiveness of theories of radical democracy lies in their rejection of these principles of consensus and neutrality and their recognition of the ongoing historical reality of contestation within social life and over the state.

Radical democrats argue that the location of sovereignty cannot be specified in the way liberal theory desires. Sovereignties are not the initial foundation upon which a political architecture can be constructed. They are the outcome of political actions. As such they are objects not of consensus but of ongoing political contestation. The boundaries of sovereignties ebb and flow and the forms they take are subject not only to addition and subtraction but also to multiplication and division. For many political theories the stable containment of sovereignty is essential for the production of justice. For radical democratic theory the possibility of redefining, relocating and reinventing sovereignty is definitive of democracy. Radical democrats are critical of other democratic theories on the grounds that, because they are based on a misunderstanding of what sovereignty is in relation to the contemporary state, their attempts to give to that sovereignty an ultimate foundation that is objective and neutral, blind them to their own projects of collective transformation which they imagine to be beyond the reach of democratic critique. Radical democrats understand that persons are always, inevitably, acting upon each other as they are themselves acted upon; that they cannot help but always be attempting to direct the conduct of others, be directed, resist such direction or be resisted; and that such action is crystallised and amplified in state and social institutions. Only if we understand this can we begin to understand the different ways in which it takes place and incorporate it into a democratic political theory.

In explicating this perspective on radical democratic theory this chapter begins by characterising a stand off within democratic theory as that between what we will name 'aggregationist' and 'accommodationist' theories. Each is concerned to devise an approach to politics that can command rational consent, ground sovereignty and avoid prescribing to individuals how they should live. But neither succeeds in this endeavour. Consequently, they find themselves in conflict with each other – a conflict that is currently being played out very clearly in the politics of contemporary societies, particularly, but not exclusively, those of Europe and America.

After exploring this 'crisis' of democratic theory the chapter examines the proposition that a procedural theory of democracy might be the solution. However, it is argued that the main theories of procedural deliberation are wedded to an ideal of sovereign consensus that leads them to propose a democratic procedure quite unrelated to actual democratic life. Turning to a consideration of the nature of the contemporary state and the consequently constitutively agonistic condition of modern politics, the chapter explores how agonism can best be understood through the terms of rhetorical theory and practice. Politics necessarily involves an ongoing practice of artistic persuasion that cannot be eliminated by philosophical or legalistic claims, however refined, and that practice is rhetoric.

The crisis of democratic theory

Contemporary theories of democracy in the West, be they philosophically normative or more generally social theoretic, are dominated by two rival orientations: the aggregationist and the accommodationist. The first of these emphasises that individual human beings are primarily defined by their capacity to formulate an independent and individual life-plan and to make rational choices as to their own interests and how to satisfy them. In short, the person is a purposive rational actor. Their choices are definitive of who they are and this gives rise to some form of inviolable rights-claim. It is a violation of their basic humanity and rights, and therefore wrong, to interfere with these choices. Furthermore, it is often argued that just and good outcomes will emerge as the unintended result of innumerable individual choices, decisions and actions. And for these reasons constitutional liberal democracy with limited government is the best political system both morally and practically. It makes possible an effective aggregation of individual interests underwritten by the rule of a minimal law that guarantees basic rights and limits interference within individual lives by the state.

In contrast, accommodationist conceptions of democracy, generally speaking, regard persons as individuals wedded to, or embedded within, some more or less substantive outlook on life; perhaps one that is shared within a particular community and that gives rise to obligations as well as rights and to a general and meaningful orientation in life that is not reducible to purely individual rights and interests. This substantive outlook may be at variance with the philosophy of purposive rational choice that underpins aggregationist democracy. For this reason the latter may, in the very attempt to be neutral with regard to the moral, economic and social choices of individuals, in fact promote a particular and partial course of action that violates the standards and legitimate expectations of those with alternate outlooks and lifestyles. The aggregationist may imagine that his or her philosophy proposes no substantive content to the lives of human individuals who are to remain free to determine what it is they want to do. For this reason he or she believes it to be perfectly pluralist. But the accommodationist counters that while advocates of aggregation may propose no specific content to the lives of citizens, they do in fact prescribe the form a life will take: namely that of individuated rational choice. This, the advocate of accommodation will suggest, presupposes an awful lot about human existence and in the name of

15

neutrality proposes a constitutional system that in fact embodies a partial moral outlook.

The accommodationist, then, will argue that people certainly do make choices but that they do so within the context of what the later Rawls (1993) called a 'comprehensive doctrine'. This is an irreducible component of human experience that comes, conceptually speaking, before the formation of any state. But the accommodationist does not embrace one of these doctrines and propose that it be the guiding philosophy of political society. The accommodationist is a liberal holding to the view that the state cannot be properly consented to if it fails to operate in a way that refuses to privilege any particular pre-political perspective over others. Thus, rather than embrace one doctrine over another we must build on whatever minimal overlapping consensus there might be, and establish a 'thin universalism' on top of which a just and legitimate polity may be founded.[1] The challenge is to ensure that varied communities may flourish, and that fairness and justice are accorded to all the pre-political perspectives of the various communities within a polity. This requires, in most matters, state neutrality with regard to the various comprehensive doctrines but also that it help establish and maintain an accommodation between them (or, in Rawls' (1993) words, a *modus vivendi*).

Accommodationism, then, is a critique of a form of liberalism but does not reject liberalism as such. Rather, its critique is that the liberal state is not liberal enough; that it represents to too great a degree a particular moral or cultural outlook.

Recognition of the potential for partiality and particularism within the state or government is a definitive feature of contemporary political theory and politics. For the accommodationists it leads to the conclusion that we must try ever harder to make state and government neutral and always be alert to the ways in which it may come to possess specific attributes or interests. For them the state ought actively to take definitive and positive steps to ensure that it really is neutral between comprehensive doctrines.[2] That might mean adapting the political system so that it is culturally neutral by for example: willingly providing information in multiple languages (as does Canada with regard to the French-speaking region of Quebec); adapting legislation at the edges where it might have a particular and prejudicial effect on a particular belief-holding group (such as the exemptions from some British animal welfare laws that are granted to both Jewish and Muslim slaughterhouses), or trying to remove from itself any accoutrements that are too tradition-specific (such as the swearing of religiously particular oaths when becoming a member of a legislature).

This sort of view can be extended into a radical liberal argument that the state needs not only to make itself neutral but should take an active role in fostering a similar neutrality across society: it should promote accommodation and equality between social groups; intervene and regulate to ensure equal recognition and participation within the political system. That can include ensuring an appropriate education in toleration for all or perhaps legislation to promote equal treatment and restrict public activities that might offend particular groups in an extreme way. It may even entail various ameliorative or constructive measures intended to end numerous forms of cultural marginalisation, oppression and domination (see Young 1990; 1996; 2000). In this way the ideal of state neutrality as expressed in non-prejudicial and equal treatment of all, leads to an active role for the state in promoting neutrality and equality by engendering a transformation of persons and practices across the social terrain governed by that state. For such a radical liberalism, collective or state action is required to achieve not merely the accommodation of varied interests but a modification of those interests in order to ensure their accommodation.

The paradox of such radical liberalism is very real: in the name of political neutrality, freedom for all, toleration, and equality between traditions, the radical liberal state will intervene into social and individual life, limit the freedom of individuals to manifest intolerance, be intolerant towards the prejudiced and not treat certain outlooks (those that are sexist or racist for instance) as in any way equal to the philosophy of radical liberalism. It is a paradox that such liberal political theory is not happy to recognise: that it is attempting simultaneously to advance the claim that the state must be neutral with regard to the best form of life, and a substantive notion (in the form of a commitment to tolerance and equality) of what that best form of life might in fact be – all the while advocating the deployment of state power to bring it about.

Into this paradox have marched the forces of political reaction, where they have happily camped at great political profit to themselves. The political Right in the UK and the US choose derisively to call such radical liberalism 'social engineering'. And there is something to this charge in as much as radical liberalism has ceased to conceive of politics as limited to what Oakeshott (1991) called a 'civic association' and has begun to develop it as some kind of 'enterprise association'. That is to say, political society is conceived not as an association of more or less civil but separable individuals but as a body dedicated to the attainment of a particular goal (in this case the goal of equality and toleration).

However, in advancing this critique of accommodationism and radical liberalism the aggregationists do not assert that the state as currently constituted is neutral and just. Far from rejecting the claim that the state represents a party in its own right and with its own interests they embrace it, explaining the partiality of the state or government as inevitable given the self-interested nature of purposive rational actors. This is the argument of the theorists of 'public-choice' and the advocates of 'neo-liberalism' for whom it follows that the state must be reduced radically in size and power, leaving individuals free to pursue their own interests however they conceive them. This project also has its paradoxes. For it too has been pursued through the deployment of state power at national and international levels. For instance, in countries such as the UK and Australia, the state agencies of welfare and education have been so constructed that they invite or demand of individuals that they become the kind of purposive, rational, self-capitalising and entrepreneurial individual demanded by a particular version of contemporary neo-liberalism (see Finlayson 2003). And, of course, international state banking and financial institutions are used to induce nations to act in line with neo-liberal cultural and political assumptions.

The accommodationist and aggregationist perspectives are both critiques of the liberal state (or, to be more specific, of the post-war American and European liberal welfare state). And this dispute, at least as it plays out in US and UK politics, is often portrayed as between liberals and conservatives. But both operate within a shared liberal problematic. The fundamental question animating the liberal tradition is this: how can political society be in our rational interest? If we imagine individuals to be in possession of 'pre-social' or 'pre-political' attributes (the capacity to choose, a 'comprehensive doctrine', certain interests, natural rights and reason and so forth) then the question arises of why one would risk damage to these on entering into the obligations found within political society. Why would a rational person so consent? The history of liberal political theory, from its imaginary contracts to the veils of ignorance behind which they are signed, is a history of attempts to establish a conceptual foundation that would answer this question, assign the correct place to sovereign powers and their Right and thus ensure sovereignty can be consented to because it doesn't challenge in any substantive way the sovereignty of individuals and their cultural communal affiliations.

While different in important ways, aggregationist and accommodationist political theories operate on the basis of a shared problematic concerned with the arrangement of sovereignty in relation to individuals, communities and states. The mainstream of contemporary politics in Europe and America presents us with a choice between a politics for which selfish individuals are sovereign and must be left to their own devices and a politics in which, in the name of sovereign reason, our actions will be ruled in or out until we become 'better people'. For the former, the latter is a conceit. Radical liberalism, the neo-liberal will say, dissembles. It appears to promise liberty within a neutral state while in fact instantiating a political game that is ultimately rigged in favour of its particular presumptions and that legitimates the use of the state against those who won't play properly. But for radical liberalism, of course, it is this neo-liberal perspective that dissembles and that permits a particular and specific interest to pretend to the rank of universal interest all the while ensuring only the self-interest of some. Both sides claim that the other has usurped sovereignty and sought to make the state into a vehicle for its own ideologically motivated project. And both sides are correct.

These two broad political churches duly do battle, advancing competing claims about the correct location of sovereignty, making rival assertions of the primacy of liberty or equality and delivering varied specifications of the content of rational interest. Some claim that the specific conceptions of freedom, equality and justice they propose are already the basis of any rational political system and that all they advocate is the bringing to fruition of what is necessarily implicit in political association – another way of grounding their project in a natural law, natural right or natural reason. Others seek to make their politics yet more neutral, accepting each and every charge of partiality and striving to become ever 'thinner' until they erase themselves in an excess of self-abasement.

From the liberal stalemate to deliberative procedure

In search of a way out of the stalemate between these aggregationist and accommodationist perspectives some theorists have reconnected liberal thought with its historic interest in the freedom of thought and discussion; with that part of the optimistic, enlightenment tradition for which reason and progress could be attained by all people if only they were permitted to live in a condition of rational freedom governed by liberty of speech and argument (Kant 1991c; Mill 1985; see also Laursen 1986). From this perspective we can, as it were, dispense with the substantive claims that underpin accommodation and aggregation, and avoid imposing a series of metaphysical presumptions upon society, by relocating legitimacy and consent from substantive outcomes or ultimate groundings to decision-making procedures grounded in the norms of public deliberation. Properly organised, it is argued, procedures of debate and deliberation will provide opportunities for varied persons to experience recognition of their perspective, feel able to consent to decisions in which they have been involved and, ultimately, be transformed by an experience of the universality intrinsic to communication. They will thus be enabled to think at the level of public reason.

This is the approach of the theorists of so-called discourse-ethics, and of deliberative theories of democracy more generally (Habermas 1996; Gutman and Thompson 1996; Dryzek 2002). In contemporary theories of deliberation the process is generally imagined as a kind of hermeneutic conversation: a co-operative, mutually enriching dialogue oriented towards understanding between persons who respectfully listen as well as talk to each other, leading to awareness of a level of reason and interest beyond our limited personal perspective: an enlargement of mentality. Failure naturally to come to rational conclusions is understood not as the result of the innate weakness of those unable to practise true philosophy but as symptomatic of consciousness kept immature and unenlightened by illegitimate instrumental forces. The task of critical philosophy is that of exposing these illegitimate instrumental forces so we may be free of them; identifying all the things that might disrupt or distort free communication and purging deliberation of them so that we may be reconciled with a higher knowledge already implicit in human being: a principle of rational order contained within our structures and categories of cognition or within the ideal claims intrinsic to language itself.

Despite claims to be post-metaphysical, then, discourse ethics and deliberative democratic theory posit a pre-political orientation towards rational understanding which subsists within inter-subjective communicative networks that can be fixed in place by procedural frameworks for deliberation made manifest via the law. Constitutionally authorised procedures of argumentation will give empirical form to these implications of communication and call into being around them a speech community able to become a tribunal of public reason that can then verify this same constitution and the procedures employed in its formation. Thus conceived, the deliberative procedure does not create justice. It exposes or makes available a justice that was already there. It is not constitutive but revelatory. And in the name of this justice proponents may specify in advance the forms that deliberation will be permitted to take.[3]

When the ideals of deliberative democracy are put into practice they tend to take the form of a jury. This is a very specific way of imagining public involvement in political decision-making: quasi-legal rather than political; employing citizens as spectators rather than participants. Jurors watch rival arguments formulated within strict criteria and are then enjoined to make a dispassionate judgement between them. There are at least three main reasons for thinking that political activity must necessarily exceed this juridical model of deliberation.

First, where courts are asked to establish the facts of past events, and to evaluate their meaning and significance, political arguments, although profoundly shaped by the past, are always also about the future: what we might become or the possible consequences of our present actions or inactions. In that they connect to imagination and the projection of hopes and fears for the future, such arguments always exceed the boundaries that reason places on expectation. In a free polis, freedom in part consists in this unreasonableness, a yearning for what Ernst Bloch called the 'not-yet' (see Geoghegan 1995).

Second, and relatedly, where a legal jury is supposed to make an evaluation of the case presented, free from a partial interest in it, a citizen is by definition partial and interested in the outcome of a decision concerning the organisation or purpose of the state of which they are a citizen. Sometimes political theory seems to consider the highest virtue to be the ability to disassociate ourselves from our particular polis and to judge its doings as if they had nothing to do with us, and likes to think that this vacation from mentality is really its enlargement.

Third, and as we shall discuss in more detail in a moment, political deliberation takes place in antagonistic conditions where what is in dispute is not only a substantive matter but the very criteria by which we identify problems and issues and evaluate possible courses of action; where histories, traditions, perspectives and schemas of value and interest meet and, as a consequence, the criteria for objective evaluation proposed by each are found wanting by the other. Where the legitimacy of a legal procedure rests on the fact that it can be seen to maintain fidelity to an established and recognised procedure, and that it stays within the boundaries that mark out the extent of its jurisdiction, revision of the rules and relocation of the boundaries is an essential element of political procedures precisely because they take place when the given procedures and criteria have been found not to be inclusive of all parties, persons and phenomena and to have an 'outside' or an 'other' that has had the temerity to try and make itself known.

We cannot proceed (and we cannot move beyond the stalemate of aggregation and accommodation) without understanding the social-historical reality of this situation: the vertiginous variety and ambiguity of a 'modernity' in which sovereignty is displaced or 'decentred' and the interaction of state and society takes place on a shifting frontier (while each has forces deep in the terrain of the other). Aggregationists respond to this situation by reinventing sovereignty as a property only of individuals, facilitating the spread of a political and moral subjectivism circumscribed only by the injunction that all interest must be self-interest. Accommodationists seek to limit the number of relevant unified traditions and communal doctrines so as to legislate for the careful and restricted maintenance of a limited plurality: an effective inducement to treat politics as merely a series of efforts to win recognition as a proper tradition. Radical liberalism goes further by instructing us not only that we are all minorities but that we have a right to this minority status which should be jealously as well as zealously exercised. Deliberative theories acknowledge the rise of a determinate ambiguity within contemporary social formation and the co-presence within them of contrary modes of interest and knowledge formation but, attributing this to an isolable deformation, seek to identify in the transcendent implications of shared communication a new location for real sovereignty. All these varied theories, then, strive in a similar way to identify an ultimate ground on which to build a secure polity to which all can rationally consent. This is a strange thing to want to do.

The state of the state

The founding of a polity, and the arrangement of power within it, is not a conceptual issue. It is an historical fact. Forms of political organisation are created out of or on top of the ruins of other political formations and those circumstances enter into such political formations in ways that, although discontinuous and opaque, are nevertheless, to some degree, specifiable. As Rousseau understood of Locke, to imagine fully formed rational individuals negotiating a social contract is to imagine something that can only take place long after some form of social life and organisation has been established and we have already become certain sorts of social being.

Imagining or inventing the theoretical grounding of a state or polity, understood as a neutral institution or the expression of a genuinely universal interest, is a rather quixotic enterprise. Real states already exist. We do not have to endorse every word of *The Communist Manifesto* to see that they are very often and in many respects 'executive committees' to help manage the affairs of some particular social interest: an economic class, an ethnic group, a national community, a sectoral financial interest, a gender or, perhaps most likely, some complex and ever-shifting alliance of fractions of all of these and others. Furthermore, and importantly, in this they are also thoroughly contested. The state is a site of contestation concerning the partial interests it will most represent and over the rationality it must employ when calculating what to do and how to do it (see Finlayson and Martin 2006).

If we start from the recognition of this fact then the liberal problematic begins immediately to recede in relevance. That problematic is concerned either to rise to the heavens in order to find the universal viewpoint or to dig away all the cities that actually exist in order to find the level ground on which it hopes to prove they all truly stand. But the genealogy of actually existing political institutions and modes of power, of the varied justifications on which they rest, the desires and demands they embody, the rituals and rites that sustain them, cannot be ignored or bracketed off by political theories without the latter losing all sense.

The contemporary state is not what liberal political theory must imagine it to be: a single sovereign authority, set to judge between our rival feudal claims (see Foucault 2003: chapters 1 and 2; Foucault 1980: 121). It is involved in a vast range of activities oriented towards the collective organisation and reorganisation of aspects of social and economic existence. It monitors water supplies, maintains transport networks, watches for outbreaks of disease and intervenes directly in the training of the young. It is an ensemble of functions and practices (juridical, military, communicative, logistical and so on) drawing on numerous forms of expertise (informational, statistical, financial, medical, actuarial, psychological to name but a few), operating through varied institutions, departments and bureaucracies that employ numerous ritualised forms of legitimation and differing ways of organising both coercion and consent. Contemporary governmental politics is thus not at all confined to matters that reduce to questions of authority and right. It is spread across dimensions of social activity where it exercises not only a prohibitive power that threatens punishment but a productive bio-power over the functions of life (see Foucault 2002; 2003; Rose 1999; Burchell, Gordon and Miller 1991). Furthermore, the state is not the sole source of power and its exercise, and does not take on all social functions even in the most extreme instances. It is necessarily dependent on distinct forms of expertise and knowledge creation, ordering, classifying, organising and verifying and it is sometimes in conflict or contradiction with other forms of power from the religious and spiritual to the economic and fiduciary.

This is not to suggest that the state no longer exists or that there are not concentrations or convergences of powers in particular places or upon particular activities. Nor is it to argue that sovereign powers or disciplinary authority have disappeared. For this reason questions of the proper limits of state coercion are entirely appropriate, alongside a variety of other questions and areas of inquiry. But given this extensive context, it makes little sense to try and address these questions via concepts of 'pre-political' or 'pre-social' attributes. We are already parts of numerous histories, the outcome of prior forms of political organisations, of past and ongoing struggles, and of multiple forms of power already at work within, upon and between us. The state is a mobile arrangement, a partial crystallisation, of multiple forces of varied kinds and political theory, analytic, normative, explanatory or critical, must seek to specify that crystallisation at any particular time.

Once we realise this, our list of pressing political questions necessarily needs adjusting. If politics is a game then it is one that has already begun – we are already players and resignation is not an option. The issue of whether or not this or that action is properly legitimated in accordance with the rules is a part of the game and not a preliminary to it. In contemporary societies evaluation of state, governmental and political activity by reference to a principle of Right now takes its place alongside evaluations of what is merely 'right' in the sense of efficacious. But the evaluation of states by efficacy alone is no straightforward activity. Assessment by efficacy necessarily raises the question of the system of measurement used: efficacious by what standard and for the attainment of what goal? Rather than eliminate judgements of the Right or the Good it pluralises and displaces them. The more peoples that are integrated into the interdependent and complex structures of a global social and economic order, the harder it is immediately to provide a simple answer to these questions and the more an aggregationist polity comes to look to some like just one culturally specific form amongst others, legitimated by traditions and rituals unique to it.

Political modernity thus induces an experience not of 'incredulity towards meta-narratives' (Lyotard 1984) but of their proliferation: meta-narratives that not only prescribe differing methods and goals for social organisation but rival schemas for judgement and evaluation. Consequently the objectivity and integrity of a social order in political modernity lacks, in Claude Lefort's phrase, a 'transcendental guarantor' (1986). Political modernity and its objectivity is not founded on any past, present or promised consent to such a guarantor, thick or thin, Kantian categorical or Kantian constructed. Although Right (and right) are meaningfully and sincerely invoked they do not of themselves ground or found the polity. It is founded politically (see Valentine 2001).

The claim here is not that in 'modernity' the social order floats free of all moorings and its subjects occupy a condition of permanent solipsistic self-founding. Rather, political modernity is characterised by a proliferation of grounds that may complement or contradict each other, may find between them overlapping consensus or constitutive antagonism. This is an historical condition of 'dislocation': the exposure of social organisation to its contingency because it has expanded geographically, encompassing multiple traditions; deepened bureaucratically as states and governments have become involved with ever more realms of social organisation; and intensified intellectually as ever more disciplinary formations respond to these changes by making them sources and objects of expert knowledge. Instead of a single source of sovereign authority, a king on a throne talking to God and passing His word on to the loyal subjects, contemporary social formations experience the paradox of multiple sovereignties contending against each other. Since sovereignty is meant to be, by definition, singular and unitary this is an impossible situation when viewed from within the frame of much mainstream political theory. This might be one reason why such theory has retreated from what it has chosen to call the 'non-ideal world' the better to live in an 'ideal world' of true theory. Some have escaped this fateful delusion, but only by turning this fragmentation into an ideal coming close to imagining that all is for the best in this best of all possible worlds. For them, our contemporary experience of contingency, complexity and 'difference' should be celebrated as an exciting, vertiginous and exotic experience of 'alterity'. This certainly has the merit (not to be underestimated) of being a lot more fun. But here we propose something rather more prosaic.

Political theory must recognise the contingency and complexity of contemporary social formations in order to begin considering the interaction of very real social, cultural, political and, as De Landa (1997) or Bennett (2007) might add, geological and biological histories. Where these discontinuous histories rub up against each other, politics emerges as exactly the opposite of what Liberalism construes it to be: not what proceeds from or towards an experience of consensus and grounding but what takes place when the objectivity of a universal is exposed as already a particular; when a stable objectivity is rejected or resisted by those with an alternative; when the premises or grounds on which conceptions stand are brought into question, interest is ambiguous and rational adjudication or bartering between perspectives is no longer possible. For much political theory this is the 'end' of civilisation in the sense of finality or of *telos*. But for radical democracy it is its beginning.

Beyond the liberal paradigm: rhetorical radical democracy

Contemporary theories of radical democracy are often associated with theories of semiotics. Sometimes, a theory of meaning as derived from an open system of differences is regarded as a kind of ontological commitment of radical democratic theory. But the textbook presentation of radical democratic theory as the political theory of Saussurean structuralism obscures the extent to which the theory of meaning or of language found in the work of, say, Laclau and Mouffe or Judith Butler is primarily a theory of political speech action. For Laclau and Mouffe political action takes place upon a terrain made up of sedimented, differentially defined discursive practices. These practices exceed the capacity of social institutions to contain them. Consequently the totality can only be represented by means of an act of naming, a catachrestical speech act that is constitutive, for Laclau, of hegemony (see Laclau 2005b: 69–72). Butler, in conceptualising the formation of identities in terms of performatives sustained by the possibility of their own repetition, shows how the intrinsic possibility of the failure of citation makes it possible for signification to be converted into re-signification and thus made the object of a political practice (Butler 1993; Chambers 2007b; Chambers and Carver 2008. See also Lloyd and Schippers, this volume).

Both catachresis and re-description are well known rhetorical figurative techniques and, as both Laclau and Butler recognise, rhetoric is a far from merely ornamental feature of politics; it is, rather, constitutive (see Laclau 2005b: 14). But where Laclau tends to reduce rhetorical action to catachresis and Butler to concentrate upon re-signification, and where they both tend to divert to considerations of psychoanalysis and theories of subject-formation, we will here consider rhetoric more fully and directly as a way of thinking about the conduct of disagreement within contemporary societies.

Rhetoric is today often considered to be merely an art of eloquence. But classically, rhetoric was much more – it was a theory of civic discourse, of how to argue within the conflicted realms of the political or legal assembly (see Kennedy 1991). These are realms of contestation, brought into being precisely because the stable framework of facts and adjudications on which we might otherwise rely has been ruptured. Consequently, one must 'invent' a persuasive argument and combine appeals to emotion or to character with quasi-logical argumentation. Rhetorical 'invention' involves furnishing primary assertions, statements that are 'indicative' and that, as Ernesto Grassi remarks, have an 'evangelic' character – revealing and showing (2001: 20). For Aristotle this involved, perhaps above all, enthymemes: the flesh and blood of rhetoric, the body of persuasion.

Enthymemes are commonly understood simply as logical syllogisms in which one statement is left out or suppressed, or as deductions based on premises that are probable rather than certain. But this definition neglects the fact that the enthymeme is deployed in the context of actual argumentative exchange and in front of an audience. As such, it is not so much a logical statement or proposition as an invitation for people to consider things in a certain way (see Burnyeat 1994); to become involved in the conceptual process by formulating the absent (but implied) premise. In this way the enthymeme invokes a 'common sense', inviting us to take a particular premise as so obvious it does not need to be explicated, at the same time as it constitutes that common sense. For instance, when a charitable campaign urges us to donate to help victims of a natural disaster who are 'human beings just like us' or who 'could be your mother, father, brother or sister' it invokes a premise about the obligation to help fellow human beings. When a member of a racist political organisation tells a crowd of supporters that there has been an increase in immigrants and an increase in crime he invokes as common sense the premise that immigrants cause crime. And having thus defined the situation, characterised or named a reality, we are invited to deduce the inevitable from it. If globalisation is like a tidal wave then, of course, we must devote all our energies to preparing for and adapting to it rather than think of how we might stop it or divert it from its unstoppable path.

Rhetoric, then, is fundamentally about the formation of conceptual images that start us thinking about an uncertain or contested thing in a particular way. It proceeds through 'plausible analogies', explaining actual or possible situations and experiences as 'like this' or 'like that'. It 'inclines', inviting sympathy and identification (Hampshire 1999: 64). As such political rhetoric shapes arguments not only out of words but moods, feelings and aspirations. It appeals not only to the mind but to the visceral affections implicated in all experience (see Connolly 2002; 2005a). In referring contexts and events to other contexts and events, things unknown to things already known, political rhetorical argument draws on a range of schemes and figures: the transformative re-description of events and phenomena (*paradiastole* in the classical canon – see Skinner 2002); the naming of things with no name (*catachresis*) but many other kinds of metaphor that invoke and reorder our 'system' of 'commonplaces' (see Richards 1936). Political dispute comes in varied registers: polemical, parodic, paranoid, satirical, ironic, authoritative, emotive and sentimental, as narrative and as exhortation, as scientific explication and instruction. And in contemporary societies it is far from confined to those who possess or seek elected office and is expressed through media other than that of speech and too often ignored by theorists and analysts of politics: it is cinematic, novelistic, televisual (see Chambers 2008).

This extent and variety of political argument cannot be grasped by the schools of deliberative democracy. Employing a normative conception of a speech that 'embodies norms of freedom, equality and publicity [that] would produce (under further ideal conditions of full information, absence of time constraints and so on) an outcome that everyone in principle could accept' (Bohman 1998: 402) it will find most of the techniques of actual political argument to be suspect. Dryzek (2002), for instance, acknowledges the place of rhetorical modes of argument because through them deliberation may reach across communal frames of reference. But he still regards these as 'insurgent discourses', incomplete and 'insufficient to warrant any particular collective decision' (2002: 168). The rhetorical conception, by contrast, perceives this reaching across and reordering of communal frames as an intrinsic aspect of political activity: imaginative and probabilistic reasonings that invite or reject pictures of the world, conjuring and moulding the images on which we may subsequently deliberate where the outcome of this rhetorical deliberation authorises collective decision, not the benchmarks laid down by hermeneuticists.

To be sure, persuasion is not obtainable only through the arts of rhetorical argument. Persons can be persuaded through threats or inducements. Violence and bribery are well-known and oft-used tools of political ordering and disordering (although both Machiavelli and Hobbes knew that even these needed to generate some measure of consent). Just as common, if not more so, is simply the giving of orders that persons accept because of the place they occupy in a social hierarchy. A venerable tradition would like to include rhetoric alongside these means of obtaining the 'compliance' of others.

Because it does not derive a theory of political communication from a larger theory of political truth and reason, rhetoric seems to be a kind of secondary theory of technique or practice rather than a proper philosophy. This, indeed, is the thrust of the Platonic critique of rhetoric: that it masquerades as a form of knowledge when it is really a knack or a series of tricks. And in a sense Plato is absolutely correct. Rhetoric requires and stimulates understanding of the shifting and unstable world of the democratic polis and proposes strategies for operating within it. And these strategies, directly and by implication, are indicative of a democratic ethos that Platonists of many kinds dislike. For to attempt rhetorical persuasion is already to accept that those whom we seek to persuade need to be persuaded and that they are capable of being so persuaded; that no single authority may impose conceptions uniformly upon others; that citizens must persuade each other rather than simply order or instruct them; that others' consent is required and must be won, not presumed or stolen. These are not implicit or immanent 'validity' claims from which the legitimacy of a state may be derived. They are actions and bearings that instantiate it, sometimes paradoxically so: persons can speak and argue in such a way or in such a place that it immediately begins to reorder the previous organisation or 'distribution of speaking places' (see Rancière 1995).

Plato's poorly portrayed interlocutor Protagoras had the very un-Platonic idea that political skills might be taught to just about anyone. For Protagoras, the conclusion to draw from the proposition he makes, in the *Theaetetus*, that 'each thing is such to me as it appears to me, and is to you such as it appears to you' is *not* that nothing can be said or that each should just be left to themselves, but that, as we find him saying elsewhere, 'on every subject there are two speeches or arguments opposed to one another' (see Gagarin and Woodruff 1995; Farrar 1998). Recognition of the socially embedded nature of truth-claims and perceptions leads one to recognition of the *fact* of argua-bility which is the core around which the democratic practice of contestation can be developed or even embodied (as it is, for example, in the structure of many legislatures such as the British Parliament with its division into government and opposition benches).

Rhetoric does not seek to overthrow all philosophy. It comes into being when a philosophy has already begun to be overthrown. And it does so because the justifications that hold in the domain of a philos-ophy do not and cannot automatically apply in all contexts. The justifications relied upon by the religious observer, the secular moral philosopher and the revolutionary theorist no longer function without question when they meet each other and fall into dispute. They lose what appeared to be their apodictic form and for just this reason such arguments, in this political moment, *become* rhetorical. Where some choose to regard this as a demeaned status, radical democratic theory urges us instead to see thinking politically as a dis-tinctive form of thought which does not involve forgetting our com-mitments and beliefs, nor suppressing them but, rather, participating in the political *agon*. That thought is enthymematic, artistic and per-suasive: rhetorical. In contemporary societies where sovereignty is fragmented, where there flourish multiple interpretations and multi-ple schemas by which we might adjudicate between them, only a full-blooded rhetorical practice can make manifest, sustain and stage the agonism between them. Only rhetoric can attain what Stuart Hampshire called a 'smart compromise' in which 'the tension bet-ween contrary forces and impulses, pulling against each other, is per-ceptible and vivid, and both forces and impulses have been kept at full strength' (1999: 39). The alternative, and we find this all over con-temporary politics and political theory, is to bemoan the absence of a transcendental guarantor and insist on its being brought back to centre-stage. And this, as we have seen, is to reject democracy and politics altogether (see also Rancière, 2006).

Conclusion

I have presented a particular way of conceiving of the diversity of liberal political theories; a way that enables us to perceive their com-monality of both ambition and error. I have also presented a particu-lar way of conceiving of the constitution of power and government, of diversity and conflict within contemporary polities; a way that enables us to see that persons are always already involved in these processes and that theorising a way out of them makes no sense. I have presented a way of conceiving of political debate and deliberation that emphasises the inapplicability of schemes of evaluation and assessment that come from outside of the political contest itself; and that thus enable us to see the ineradicably rhetorical nature of all political dispute. And finally I have suggested ways in which this rhetorical disposition accords with a certain democratic and egalitarian spirit precisely because it takes up the argument rather than hides it behind a claim of toleration. And in so presenting I too have, of course, been rhetorical. I have sought to 'define the situation' of contemporary liberal politics and political theory in a very particular way, combining a presentation of unattributed – but nevertheless recognisable – political theoretical claims with reference to their instantiation in actual political life. Thus, I hope to indicate the presence of political philosophy in its 'non-ideal world' and the extent to which non-ideal politics cannot be reduced to a play of prosaic interests but is also always caught up in the ideas (and ideologies) that constitute interests in the first place.

There need be no doubt that a certain sort of philosopher will observe in these remarks a series of normative claims; that they will demand justification and, scenting a performative contradiction, wish to stake a claim to victory. I invite such a response. I want such a philosopher to want to win and to show their case at its best. Democracy is not reducible to majority rule or to any kind of aggregation of interests. The radical conception of democracy envisages a multitude of plural and pluralising points that engage with each other, acting on and being acted upon, in a process that causes them to be reordered, renamed and redefined. And for this reason, democracy is not best maintained by the demarcation of an impregnable boundary between that which is private and that which is public, in order to defend each from incursion by the other, confining belief to a private realm where it pays for its protection from the public with its own powerlessness. The attempt to institute just this order is characteristic of contemporary politics in the liberal democratic states. Rather, democracy survives only by each of us embracing our commitments as possibly commitments that others ought to share. But we also recognise that others do not share them and will not be brought to share them so long as we assume they must necessarily reason, desire and hope in the way we do. It is up to us to give them reason, act on their desires and shape their hopes – and for them to do the same with regard to us.

When the well-grounded and universal beliefs and commitments on which our political ideals rest are contested and, in the context of the political arena, revealed precisely as commitments to which we must now have a conscious relation, then politics is already in process. It will not halt in order to hear how well it has been scored by the arbiters of judgement. This worries the philosopher. But we have, some time since, left the olive groves of our Academy. If we stop now to look we shall see that we have already entered the *Ecclesia*.

Notes

1. See, for example, Haddock, Roberts and Sutch (2006).
2. See, for instance, the discussion of Kymlicka (1996), the proposals of Parekh (2000), the critique of Barry (2001) and the review of Modood and Favell (2003).
3. See the explication of Chambers (1996), the discussion of Dryzek (2002) and the critical remarks of Young (1996) and Sanders (1997).

2

Performing Radical Democracy

Moya Lloyd

Power is not stable or static, but is remade at various junctures within everyday life; it constitutes our tenuous sense of common sense, and is ensconced as the prevailing epistemes of a culture. Moreover, social transformation occurs not merely by rallying mass numbers in favour of a cause, but precisely through the ways in which daily social relations are rearticulated, and new conceptual horizons opened up by anomalous and subversive practices. (Butler 2000a: 14)

It may seem perplexing in a book exploring the politics of radical democracy to have two chapters devoted to the work of Judith Butler, for she is hardly known as a democratic theorist. Indeed, a quick search through the indexes to all her single-authored books reveals the sum total of only one reference to democracy in all nine texts (2004a: 226).[1] Even extending the remit a bit wider to include references to the writings of, say, radical democratic thinkers such as Laclau and Mouffe fails to yield much more. They appear in the indexes of just two books (*Excitable Speech* and *Bodies that Matter*).[2] Yet in this chapter, I will argue that Judith Butler *is* a radical democrat and that she develops her account of radical democracy, in part, out of a critical engagement with the work of Laclau and Mouffe, particularly that of Laclau. Moreover, to make my case, I will be drawing amongst other things on some of the very texts that appear to offer little indexical evidence of Butler's interest in radical democracy. In part I am able to do so because the indexes to Butler's books are highly parsimonious: democracy – as both a theory and a practice – appears more often than they suggest, though still not on the scale to warrant identifying any of her books as a piece of democratic theory *per se*. The more important factor, however, is that the concept that I suggest is central to Butler's understanding of radical democracy, what I term universality-to-come (echoing, of course, Derrida's idea of democracy-to-come), becomes increasingly salient in these writings over time.

There are two areas that concern me in this chapter; I have examined the broad terms of Butler's discussions of radical democracy elsewhere (Lloyd 2007a and 2007b). The first relates to the idea of universality-to-come. I am interested here both in the contours of this concept and in how Butler differentiates her approach from that of Laclau, whose own contribution to advancing the debate on radical democracy has been identified by some commentators in terms of its concentration on the universal (Critchley and Marchart 2004: 4). The second area concerns the transfiguration of 'daily social relations' alluded to at the outset of the chapter. Here I focus on same-sex marriage. As an issue it illustrates very clearly, I propose, a deconstructive aporia at the heart of Butler's account of radical democracy: a blindness to the state as a possible mechanism for universalisation that is in tension with Butler's characterisation of radical democratic struggles as struggles to resignify the universal (and, most particularly, the human as a universal). As I demonstrate below, an account of radical democracy that does not conceive of the possibility of operating through the state in the advancement of democratic demands is an account that risks abstracting from, and thus neglecting, the specific contexts within which political contestation actually occurs. To contend *a priori* that the state cannot facilitate democratic demands is not a radical claim *per se*. The radicalism of any political strategy can only be evaluated *in situ*. For this reason, I will argue that it is necessary in the light of shifting political circumstances in the US to re-evaluate Butler's assertion that radical sexual politics is best served by rejecting same-sex marriage.[3]

Competing universalities

Butler develops her account of radical democracy, as noted earlier, in part out of a critical engagement with the work of Laclau and Mouffe. Tellingly, she rejects Laclau and Mouffe's emphasis in *Hegemony and Socialist Strategy* (1985) on the production of democratic identities as such; queries what she perceives to be their positing of transcendental 'a priori conditions of political articulation itself (across all time and place)' (2000c: 272) as the basis for democratisation; and worries about the hermeneutics of their reading of new social movements as pivotal to democracy. Where she does draw intellectual sustenance for her account of radical democracy is from Laclau's discussion of universality, though as will become clear, hers is a qualified approval of his position.

Over the last thirty years or so, feminists, post-colonialists, communitarians and post-structuralists have expended considerable energy endeavouring to demonstrate the limited and partial nature of what passes for the universal. The fall of Communism, the rise of various nationalisms and the shift towards multicultural politics (itself fed by the appearance of a constellation of different political movements representing diverse groups) have all contributed in various ways to the problematisation of the universal. Butler was once a vociferous critic of the universal, contending that it was not just 'violent and exclusionary' but also 'totalizing' (2004b: 339). Yet within only a few years, she was arguing that an open-ended sense of universality was not only useful for but essential to the radical democratic transformation of society. It is not the reason for this apparent change of heart that concerns me here, though needless to say it should not be construed as signalling a return to old-style notions of the universal as predicated on some pre-existing characteristic of humanity.[4] It is how Butler characterises the relation between universality-to-come and radical democracy that is of interest.

In *Contingency, Hegemony, Universality*, Butler engages in a debate with Ernesto Laclau and Slavoj Žižek about, amongst other things, the status of the universal. Echoing Laclau (I will set aside Butler's debate with Žižek on this occasion), Butler argues that the 'open-endedness that is essential to democratization implies that the universal cannot be finally identified with any particular content, and that this incommensurability (for which we do not need the Real) is crucial to the futural possibilities of democratic contestation' (2000b: 161). The unrealisability of the universal is precisely what keeps democracy alive. Democratic political struggles arise as a means both of contesting the exclusionary nature of particular universals and of endeavouring to render 'key terms of liberalism', as she puts it, 'more inclusive, dynamic and more concrete' (Butler 2000a: 13; see also Butler 1997a: 160 and 2001: 419). Such struggles are politically potent, then, when they compel a less exclusionary rearticulation of the fundamental assumptions of democracy itself. Butler thus shares with Laclau the idea of the impossibility of a fully realisable universalism – or to use different language, the incompletion of the universal. Significantly, she differentiates her account from Laclau's in two ways.

First, she returns to Hegel to argue that 'the relation of universality to its cultural articulation is insuperable' (2000a: 24). The universal, she claims, is always already thoroughly cultural, shaped by the customary practices through which it is enacted – a 'given syntax' and 'a certain set of cultural conventions' (Butler 2000a: 35). She thus rejects Laclau's conceptualisation of the universal as being formally empty. Rather the 'universal in culture', as she calls it, always depends on 'decidedly less than universal conditions' for its expression (Butler 1996: 44–5). Second, although seeming to endorse Laclau's claim that it is the incommensurability between the particular and the universal that is central to democratisation, Butler distances herself from what she perceives to be his *a priori* assumption that the political field is divided between 'modes of resistance that are particular and those that successfully make the claim to universality' (Butler 2000b: 165). The point is not that she queries the inter-imbrication of universal and particular suggested by Laclau but that she rejects the idea that they are logically incompatible categories (Butler 2000b: 162). Here she draws on Linda Zerilli's discussion of Joan Scott's work on post-revolutionary French feminist politics to make her case (Zerilli 1998: 16).[5]

When Scott explores the universal in relation to feminism, one of the paradoxes she identifies is that of a possible 'undecidable coincidence of particular and universal' within one idea; in this case the term 'sexual difference', which 'can denote the particular in one political context and the universal in another' (Butler 2000a: 33). It can thus stand for women's specificity (a particularism) or for something that is common to all humanity (a universal). Examining the 'particular in its particularity' might reveal, in other words, that 'a certain competing version of universality is intrinsic to the particular movement itself' (Butler 2000b: 166). What sustains democratisation for Butler is not a clash between universal and particular, as Laclau maintains but, in a context of deep pluralisation, a clash between particular cultural universals.

The inevitable question raised by this formulation is how best to mediate between competing universals. What kind of radical democratic politics is involved here? The short answer is one of 'establishing *practices of translation*' amongst conflicting universals so that a non-transcendental commonality can be forged (Butler 2000b: 167; see Lloyd 2007a for a fuller discussion). What does this involve? According to Butler, when a disenfranchised group make a universal demand they commit a performative contradiction: they lay claim to something (a right, an ontology) from which they are constitutively excluded (1996: 48). At that very moment, 'an invocation that has no prior legitimacy can have the effect of challenging existing forms of legitimacy', and open up a new, more universal, form (Butler 1997a: 147; see also Rancière 1999). The limited reach of the existing universal is divulged and the universal is thus challenged. In appealing to the universal, the disenfranchised, that is, expose the extent to which the universal rests on particular, exclusionary assumptions about who qualifies as a person having the right to appeal to the universal.

It is not just that those demanding universal rights do not already have them; the real problem is that they are not recognised as possible subjects of said rights in the first place. They thus signify both the limit of the human and thus 'the limit to universalizability' (Butler 1996: 46). The 'assertion of rights becomes', for Butler therefore, 'a way of intervening into the social and political process by which the human is articulated' (2004a: 33); a way of challenging the norms defining who counts as human. And so, a radical democratic politics, oriented towards universality-to-come, is intrinsically tied to 'struggle[s] with the norm' (Butler 2004a: 13): norms defining the human, norms establishing sex and sexual difference, norms defining whose life counts. By disrupting that which is settled and 'known', radical democratic politics opens up space to 'rethink the possible' (Butler 1999a: xx); to contest, in other words, the normative violence that determines who counts. (For more on normative violence see Lloyd 2007a.) What, however, is the relation between struggling with the norm and cultural translation?

The aim of cultural translation is neither to posit an alternative set of *a priori* universal assumptions about the human nor to attempt to assimilate the excluded to an existing (heteronormative, racially or ethnically framed) conception of the human. There is equally no point in endeavouring to impose a view of the universal on a culture resistant to it. Rather, cultural translation involves an encounter between competing conceptions of the universal, articulated in different languages, that produces a transformation in how the universal is thought. It is a difficult and laborious process. It requires that each of the competing universals *'change in order to apprehend the other'* (Butler 2004a: 38), to give up some of their foundational assumptions. This, in turn, demands of radical democratic subjects if not a commitment to, then at least a willingness to undergo, epistemological uncertainty. Drawing inspiration from the work of Chicana feminist Gloria Anzaldúa, Butler commends subjects to 'put our own epistemological certainties into question, and through that risk and openness to another way of knowing and of living in the world to expand our capacity to imagine the human'. And, reading her at her most radical, democratic transformation for Butler can and will occur only when such subjects 'exist [. . .] in the mode of translation, constant translation' (Butler 2004a: 228); when they can let go of the comfort of knowing already what the human is – giving up, in other words, the limiting religious, racial or heteronormative frames that presently define the human in order to generate a wider, more uncertain, yet less restrictive conception (Butler 2004c: 89–91).

So, to sum up, radical democratic politics for Butler: is inherently contestatory and dissonant; operates through practices of cultural translation designed to rework the universal 'from myriad directions' so that it becomes more capacious (Butler 2004a: 224); is staged through the appropriation of claims to equality, freedom, justice and rights by the disenfranchised; and is constitutively open-ended. Radical democratic universality is thus always a universality-to-come. Moreover, no *a priori* assumptions can be made either about the process or the conditions of democratisation (articulating the universal and particular), or about its agents (new social movements). Democratisation is always already culturally articulated: dependent on historically embedded subjects and available political vernacular. For all the strengths of her account, however, when it comes to Butler's discussion of specific examples of radical democratic politics at work, particularly with regard to sexual politics, she introduces a questionable *a priori* assumption of her own: that civil society is the most appropriate locus for radical democratisation and the production of universals-to-come. (For an exploration of the place of civil society in radical democratic thought see Martin, this volume).

Restaging the universal – demanding 'love rights'

Earlier in this chapter, I suggested that as a radical democrat Butler might be understood as arguing for the radicalisation of liberalism – that is, the extension of liberal notions of equality, freedom and so on to more and more areas of social life. I also hinted that she conceives of radical democratic politics in terms of everyday-ness. Finally, I suggested in the introduction to this chapter that democratic politics had been present in her work from at least *Gender Trouble* onwards. I now want to return to some of these claims. My first contention is that Butler does rather more than seek to democratise the explicit values of liberalism (liberty, equality, justice). In her efforts to argue for an extension of the norms that 'sustain a viable life' to all persons (Butler 2004a: 225) she argues for the necessity to democratise the 'fundamental categories' that organise cultural and social life so as to make them 'more inclusive and more responsive to the full range of cultural populations' (Butler 2004a: 223–4). This is what is required in order to instantiate a 'radical democratic transformation' of society (Butler 2000b: 147). Although it is not possible to specify all the fundamental categories Butler has in mind in this statement, it ought to be clear from her work to date that it includes sex, gender and sexuality.[6] Her critique of heteronormativity (begun in the essays leading to the publication of *Gender Trouble* and continued unabated since) should thus be read, I am suggesting, as an effort to democratise what is understood by sex and sexual difference. Similarly her interventions in the debate surrounding same-sex marriage should be understood as part of an endeavour to develop a more radically democratic formulation of intimate relations.

One of the third-generation rights, or 'love rights' as Robert Wintemute terms them (2005), that has dominated much gay and lesbian campaigning across the globe has been that of same-sex marriage.[7] This is certainly true of the United States where it has been at the forefront of debates *within* the gay, lesbian and queer movements since the 1990s. In what follows, I want to explore Butler's somewhat late entry into this debate. Before I do so, however, a little context is appropriate.[8]

In 1993 the Hawaii Supreme Court ruled, in the case of *Baehr* v. *Lewin*, that refusing to issue marriage licences to members of the same sex seemed to be in violation of the equal protection clause of the state's constitution. An evidentiary hearing was ordered at which the state was to be granted the opportunity to show that there were 'compelling state interests' in denying same-sex couples the right to marry. Before that hearing was over, not only had Congress passed and pro-gay President Clinton signed the Defense of Marriage Act (1996), which stipulated that 'the word "marriage" means only a legal union between one man and one woman as husband and wife' ('DOMA', in Baird and Rosenbaum 2004: 290) but the people of Hawaii had voted in favour of a constitutional amendment *prohibiting* same-sex marriage (1998). What was widely perceived to be a decision paving the way for the legalisation of same-sex marriage in Hawaii (*Baehr* v. *Lewin*) turned out to be the start of a battle that divided the gay, lesbian and queer movements as activists contended over whether state-sanctioned same-sex marriage was the right strategy to pursue.

Since then much has happened: the Massachusetts Supreme Court in *Goodridge* v. *Department of Public Health* (2003) ruled in favour of same-sex marriages, thus legalising them; in 2004 the mayor of San Francisco, Gavin Newsom, started authorising same-sex marriages on the grounds that failure to do so was discriminatory under the terms of the Californian Constitution, only to have his decision over-turned that same year by the California Supreme Court (with some four thousand marriages voided as a consequence); and in 2006 President George W. Bush attempted, unsuccessfully, to fulfil his election promise to amend the US Constitution via the Marriage Protection Amendment. Had it succeeded, this amendment would have secured the heteronormativity of marriage in law.[9]

Given the characteristics of radical democracy outlined in the intro-duction to this book, from a theoretical perspective at least, one might expect a radical democrat – or, at least, a radical democrat who con-ceives of the expansion and contestation of rights as a radical move (and I will return to this below) – to embrace the campaign to extend the right to marry to gays and lesbians. First, it seeks to extend a uni-versal right, indeed a human right, to a constituency denied it.[10] The campaign for same-sex marriage might be understood, therefore, as not only endeavouring to secure equal civil and human rights for gays and lesbians but also as a means of contesting the nature of, and thus of rethinking, marriage and sexual citizenship in non-heteronormative terms. Next, the demand appears to involve a performative reconsti-tution of the *demos*. Just as in the case of Jeanne Deroin, the excluded (gays and lesbians) seize the very language of entitlement that de-recognises them (in this case, that of marital entitlement) and claim to be covered by it, effecting what Butler terms a 'performative contra-diction' (Butler 1996: 48). To paraphrase Rancière, we might say that gays and lesbians reveal themselves as necessarily included in the pop-ulous enjoying marital rights while being at the same time radically excluded from that populous. In the process, they restage it. Next, we might also read this campaign as evidence of what Connolly calls 'plu-ralist *enactment*' (1995: xiv); that is, part of the forging of a new plu-ralising identity. Here the demand for same-sex marriage is one that disturbs established identities, challenging them to revise the terms of their own self-recognition, and one that shatters the terms of normal-ity that define the current state of pluralist existence.

Moreover, with reference to Butler's own discussion of universal-ity, there seems to be evidence to support the case that this campaign is a radically democratic one. Given that the right to marry is predi-cated upon a heterosexual subject (and, even then, only some hetero-sexual subjects), the campaign discloses the extent to which the hegemonic universal is haunted by, indeed depends on, the particular. If the radical democratisation of social relations involves the contestation and resignification of the universal in a more inclusive manner, then the gay and lesbian demand to wed *appears* to do precisely that: to extend a right to more and more people regardless of sexual orientation. Also, there are competing universals at stake in the political debates that have raged: between those who consider the universality of marriage rights as indelibly tied not just to heterosexuality but to heteronormativity and those who see the right to marry as a human right that ought to be open to *all* humans, including gay and lesbian humans. It does not seem too far-fetched to contend that at issue in this political spat is one of translation as Butler describes it: where translation discloses the 'alterity within the norm' (1996: 50) and, in so doing, divulges the limited reach of the universal. Yet, as Butler's interventions in the debate around same-sex marriage make clear, she is profoundly sceptical of it as a goal. First, I want to consider what it was that was deemed problematic about same-sex marriage from a movement perspective and second, how this squares with the account of radical democracy Butler articulates.

The trouble with same-sex marriage

The critics, many of them queer theorists and activists, who began developing their critique of same-sex marriage in the 1990s focused on a number of arguments, all of which Butler more or less reprises in her own work (see Warner 1999 chapter 3 by way of comparison). Before we consider them it is important, I think, to point out that these arguments were articulated as part of an immanent debate within the gay and lesbian movement, directed at those in its mainstream who had embraced same-sex marriage. As such, their purpose was to attempt to (re-)galvanise a more radical gay and lesbian and/or queer sexual politics. So, what was the gist of this movement-based rejection of same-sex marriage?

The first claim levelled was that the campaign sought to naturalise and thus to normalise marriage and, in so doing, was merely seeking to assimilate the 'shiny, new gay citizen' (Butler 2004b: 150) to an existing *straight* norm. Such assimilation reinforced another problematic feature of marriage: its construction as the necessary site for the attainment of particular rights and benefits: for instance, the rights to adopt, to inherit, to gain executive control of medical decision-making, to various tax advantages and to spousal support.[11]

Next, it was charged, the campaign was less to do with 'recognition' than with 'regulation', as Claudia Card comments (2007: 24; see also Butler 2004a: 102–30). That is, because marriage is a state-sanctioned contract designed to organise intimate life it is never – and never can be – simply a private arrangement between two consenting adults. It requires, as Michael Warner, one of the foremost queer critics of same-sex marriage, points out 'the recognition', indeed the enforceable recognition, 'of a third party' (1999: 117): the state (sometimes via one of the organs it authorises to conduct marriage ceremonies). Seeking to extend marriage to same-sex couples would thus further bolster the power of the state to police intimate life, in the process allowing it to determine who counts and, as just observed, who gets what in the way of privileges. Because marriage is a form of 'selective legitimacy', sanctifying 'some couples at the expense of others' (Warner 1999: 82; Card 1996), it is not only able to deny the legal benefits attaching to marriage to those who reject it but it also guarantees that the intimate relations of those who refuse marriage are less valued – less legitimate – than those of their married (gay or straight) peers (Butler 2000b: 175–6 and 2004a: 109). In this respect, same-sex marriage entails a failure of universalisation.

Perhaps the most trenchant criticism, however, had to do with the impact of the focus on same-sex marriage on gay and lesbian politics in general, and on queer politics in particular. As Warner notes, although the issue of same-sex marriage was raised in the 1970s, lesbian and gay groups did not make its legalisation central to their political demands until the 1990s. In fact, for the most part the movement regarded marriage as a deeply problematic institution: oppressive, patriarchal and a way of mainstreaming gays and lesbians (Ettelbrick [1989] 2004). Instead, it sought to find ways to affirm gay culture and identity and to validate alternative expressions of desire and of forms of relationship and of family life. From the 1970s to the 1990s, as Warner remarks, what dominated was 'an ethical vision of queer politics centred on the need to resist the state regulation of sexuality' (1999: 88; see Butler 2000b: 176). This was an anti-nomian politics centred on politicising sexuality. And, of course, *Gender Trouble* can be seen as articulating this trend with its critique of heteronormative constructions of sex, gender, sexuality and desire. Focusing on questions of who may marry and, when allied to questions of kinship, of who is entitled to conceive and raise children (Butler 2004a: 130) as the mainstream lesbian and gay movement has done signals, therefore, that a major reorientation of gay and lesbian politics has taken place, one that troubles both Warner and, more recently, Butler.

As noted earlier, Butler reiterates the critique of same-sex marriage advocated by the likes of Ettelbrick and Warner. How, though, does this critique fit with her account of radical democracy? At best, it seems, same-sex marriage symbolises a 'contested zone' of gay and lesbian democratic politics (Butler 2000b: 161): one that divides the movement. Is there a policy, however, that from a queer perspective might capture more fully the radically universal and thus democratic potential of gay, lesbian and queer politics than same-sex marriage has done? Clearly, one fault-line in the marriage campaign identified by Butler (and others) concerns the yoking of marriage to a set of entitlements. One option she (like others) considers is thus to delink marriage and the said bundle of rights and privileges: to open up rights to adoption or reproductive technology to those in non-heteronormative and non-marital alliances (see also Card 2007 and Ferguson 2007). That way, marriage would not be the pre-condition for said privileges. Instead they would simply accrue to individuals independent of the type of relationship they were in.

The more important element of Butler's argument in my view, however, concerns the site of democratic struggle. It is the fact that same-sex marriage is 'a project of litigation' (Warner 1999: 85) that bothers her. As the opening paragraph of *Antigone's Claim* makes clear, Butler is resistant to 'contemporary efforts to recast political opposition as legal plaint and to seek the legitimacy of the state in the espousal of [political] . . . claims' (2000e: 1). And same-sex marriage is no different. Her reasons are clear: litigation confers additional legitimacy and regulatory power on the state and leads to the view that the state is the 'necessary venue for democratization itself' (2000b: 176). This is why in contrast to some other queer critics, Butler, I would suggest, is critical not only of same-sex marriage but equally so of other forms of legal partnership arrangement: because they rest on state-approved and thence regulatory and normalising legal contracts (2004a: 109).

Against this juridical emphasis, she proposes that 'the only possible route for a radical democratization of legitimating effects' is to displace marriage and allow a 'return to non-state-centred forms of alliance that augment the possibility for multiple forms on the level of culture and civil society'. It is, in other words, more radical and democratic to refuse marriage – indeed, to let the norm of marriage shrivel and die – and to support the alternative relationship (both intimate and kinship) forms that *already* exist in civil society. That way, she suggests, 'the hope would be, from the point of view of performativity, that the discourse [of marriage] would eventually reveal its limited reach, avowed only as one practice among many that organize human sexual life' (Butler 2000b: 177). This political stance reinforces the contention noted in the epigraph to this chapter: that radical democratic transformation is facilitated by the restaging of quotidian social relations, which themselves lead to the emergence of 'new conceptual horizons'. The presence of a multiplicity of non-marital relations in civil society itself suggests that there already exist alternative ways of thinking about – of conceptualising – sexuality, sexual alliances and kinship relations to the ideal touted by the pro-marriage lobby (gay and/or straight).

To wed or not to wed: that is the question

At the heart of Butler's scepticism about same-sex marriage is the belief that this policy will not, indeed cannot, bring about social change in the sense of securing the democratisation of intimate relations. Central to this, as noted, is Butler's critique of the place of the state in this campaign. In this section, however, I want to cast doubt on her interpretation of same-sex marriage given the way that the US political context has changed since the 1990s when the internecine debate concerning same-sex marriage emerged within the gay, lesbian and queer movement to now, towards the end of the first decade of the twenty-first century, when the opposition to same-sex marriage from all quarters (including, in particular, conservative forces) has intensified; from a time when Michael Warner could write that 'the only people arguing against gay marriage, it seems, are those homophobic dinosaurs – like [Representative Henry] Hyde, or Senator Jesse Helms, or the feminist philosopher Jean Bethke Elshtain' (1999: 83) to a time when an increasing number of US states have acted – and are continuing to act – to ban same-sex marriage.[12]

The critique I advance will draw on Butler's own theorisation of radical democracy. My purpose is not, however, to advocate same-sex marriage *per se*; I remain ambivalent about it as a radical political project. What I seek to expose, rather, is a tension at the heart of Butler's account of radical democracy with respect to the state, which compels her to view it *ipso facto* as a hindrance to democratisation, a position that consequently produces a certain disabling inattentiveness on her part to political context. In short, I will suggest that Butler's

critique of same-sex marriage needs amending in the light of the political developments that have taken place since gays and lesbians first
began demanding the right to marry. Not only has the 'marriage issue
been used to reentrench homophobia' since then but, as Claudia Card
observes, it has also given new life to the forces of conservatism determined to preserve the sanctity of heterosexual marriage (2007: 33).
Before I consider same-sex marriage in terms of the current US political context, I need to demonstrate that the theoretical resources are
present in Butler's work to show that marriage is potentially resig-
nifiable. I thus return to the idea of performative contradiction and the
radical democratic potential that, according to Butler, inheres in it.

One of the examples that Butler cites, and cites frequently, is Paul
Gilroy's discussion in *The Black Atlantic* (1993) of the relation
between slavery and modernity. Butler is interested in Gilroy's
Hegelian contention that, far from being excluded from modernity as
so often claimed, the enslaved have been 'able to appropriate essential concepts from the theoretical arsenal of modernity to fight for
their rightful inclusion in the process' (Butler 2001: 420) and, as such,
historically slavery operated as a force of modernisation. As Butler
parses it, when slaves took up the terms of modernity (equality, justice
and so forth), they revised them, a process that had '*radical* consequences' for the development of a non-ethnocentric understanding of
modernity. From this she concludes, in an argument that proved
pivotal to *Excitable Speech*, that the role of 'reappropriation is to
illustrate the vulnerability of these often compromised terms to an
unexpected progressive possibility', the creation (in this particular
case) of a 'more radically democratic modernity' (Butler 2001: 421,
my emphasis; and Butler 1997a: 160–1).

For all its structural similarity to the case of slavery and modernity,
however, Butler disallows same-sex marriage this radical outcome.
Yet, gays and lesbians in demanding a right from which they have
been constitutively excluded are performing a contradiction not dissimilar to that performed by slaves.[13] Going further, in so doing they
recompose the demos, extending its terms to include some of those
conventionally denied entry to it. For all this, however, their performative contradiction apparently does not, in Butler's eyes, produce
the same kind of radical resignification that slaves effected with
respect to the core ideals of modernity. Theirs opened up a different
future for ideals like freedom, justice and equality; theirs unsettled
the polity (Butler 1997a: 161). By contrast, same-sex marriage she
suggests does not. The question is why?

There is ample evidence throughout her work, and here *Excitable Speech* is exemplary, to demonstrate *both* that Butler regards rights discourse as having potentially radically democratising effects, because of its amenability to resignification, *and yet* sees the turning of such rights into justiciable or legal rules (their positivisation) as a problem.[14] It appears as if the radical democratic moment in the restaging of rights discourse is the moment when a rhetorical or symbolic claim is made on specific rights. At such times, Butler interprets them admitting 'a sense of difference and futurity' into the polity (1997a: 161). By contrast, Butler views, almost without fail, the demand to have such rights recognised in law as an invitation to the state to increase its regulatory and normalising powers and thus as working against democratisation. This exposes, I propose, a tension in her account of radical democracy. In the first instance, the appropriation and recycling of rights discourse suggests the possible constitution of a newer, more encompassing universal. Not so the second instance, for state recognition of such rights, it seems, is not an appropriate means of instating a universal. For the state is divisive: a means of policing and controlling particular sectors of the population.

Given this, one might wonder what place rights (symbolic or legal) have in radical democratic politics. In what sense(s), if any, is it sufficient simply to lay claim to a particular right *without* the eventual prospect of that right being codified in some way? Is it enough just to make a claim on legitimacy without requiring its conversion into something enforceable? The plot only thickens when we recall that Butler is opposed to marriage because it is the only way to access particular rights. She does not, on this occasion at least, appear to doubt or to contest the need for such rights. This only begs another question, however: that if rights (of adoption, inheritance and so on) are to be meaningful politically then how are they to be secured, if not by the state? And if, paradoxically, it is the state that is to guarantee these rights, then what is it at such times that prevents it from fortifying its own power?

Let us assume, for a moment (and perhaps against our better judgement), that rights have a place in radical democratic politics (see also Chambers 2004). In this context, is there any way of viewing a right to same-sex marriage as contributing in a radical democratic sense to the transformation of intimate alliances? That is, is there a way that it might aid in the articulation of a more inclusive universal? Taking my lead from Butler, I want to suggest there is. It concerns the way that positing a less exclusive universal requires struggle with the norm. I want to return, therefore, to the theme of heteronormativity, which Butler did so much to challenge in works such as *Gender Trouble* and *Bodies that Matter*. I want to suggest that in reading same-sex marriage as operating simply to assimilate gays and lesbians to an existing norm, Butler downplays the extent to which same-sex marriage has the potential in the present context to contest – and resignify – the *heteronormativity* of that norm.

Heteronormativity is a regulatory practice made up of/operating through institutions, modes of understanding, norms and discourses that posits heterosexuality as natural to humanity. In this normative regime, sex, gender and desire are assumed to be connected in a specific way: that gender follows from sex and that desire follows from sex and gender. Clearly if any institution symbolises heteronormativity, it is marriage. Masculine man weds feminine woman in order to reproduce a version of the mommy-daddy-me family so beloved of psychoanalysis. It is evident that one of the effects of the demand for marriage between two people of the same sex in a context *where that is prohibited* is to expose the heteronormativity of marriage. It makes visible, that is, the fact that marriage is predicated on heterosexual norms and that so too are the benefits accruing to it (the rights mentioned so often above). To demand that gays and lesbians be allowed to marry partners of the same sex when same-sex marriage is largely impossible, as it is presently in the US (and where it may yet become unconstitutional), poses both a direct and, possibly, a necessary challenge to this normative gender order. It threatens to subvert it by divulging the heterosexual presumption underpinning marriage and, consequently, in making it visible opens it up to deconstruction. The heterosexuality of marriage can no longer be tacitly assumed or taken for granted.[15]

In Butler's terms it is, of course, the very performativity of marriage that facilitates this process of subversion – the fact that the saying ('I do') is a doing but a saying and doing that are themselves always already citational (based on repetition). Recall that in her discussion of hate speech, it is the citationality of language that Butler regards as creating the space for a 'counter-mobilization' – when a term or practice is appropriated and made to resignify in mutinous fashion (1997a: 163). The call to legalise same-sex marriage – to resignify it beyond the heteronormative frame – is surely, given Butler's terms, a potential example of a counter-mobilisation. If marriage is, after all, reiterable in an insurrectionary fashion, as Butler must allow given the parameters of her own theory (and as seemed to be the case when in a succession of two-minute ceremonies same-sex couples lined up to be married in San Francisco's City Hall in February 2004), then what is to stop gay marriage in certain contexts contributing to the 'democratic cultivation of alternative sexualities' (Warner 1999: 90) that queer thinkers and activists like her press for? Why not draw a similar conclusion to conservative thinker Stanley Kurtz when he argues that:

> Once we say that gay couples have a right to have their commitments recognized by the state, it becomes next to impossible to deny that same right to polygamists, polyamorists, or even cohabiting relatives and friends. And once everyone's relationship is recognized, marriage is gone, and only a system of flexible relationships is left? (Kurtz cited in Ashbee 2007: 102)

If state recognition were to transfigure marriage into a system of flexible arrangements 'linking two or three, or more individuals (however weakly and temporarily) in every conceivable combination of male and female' (Kurtz cited in Ashbee 2007: 102) then, perversely, might it not be the state itself that delivers (rather than hinders) the universalisation of 'legitimating effects' that Butler yearns for and the state that articulates a more encompassing universal?

The rub is, of course, that in the world of radical democracy there are no guaranteed outcomes or certainties of any kind. We thus cannot say for sure that same-sex marriage will contribute to a more radically democratic formulation of sex and sexual difference (cf. Butler 2000b: 147). But equally we cannot say that it will *not* contribute in this way. The best that can be deduced is that subversion of any kind only produces 'the kind of effect that resists calculation' (Butler 1993: 29; see also Lloyd 2005a: 143–6; Chambers 2007b). What is important, however, and what Butler underestimates, is the political context within which such allegedly subversive activity takes place.

Conclusion

We have seen in this chapter that Butler associates the project of radical democracy with the production of a more inclusive universal-to-come. When there is a prospect that this universal will be articulated through the state, when, that is, it appears that recognition is to be universalised through a framework of legal rights, Butler baulks at it. This is nowhere more apparent than in her evaluation of same-sex marriage as a political strategy. The problem, for her, concerns what it means to be legitimated by the state. It is not just that one is, as a consequence, subject to selective legitimation (to borrow Warner's phrase). It is not even that it makes marriage into the mechanism *par excellence* through which legitimacy will be conferred. It is simply the fact that the state does the legitimating. Here Butler assumes, in my view, that the state always already has an investment in practices of 'social abjection' (2004a: 112) whereby it instates hierarchies that divide the licit from the illicit; the legitimate from the illegitimate; where, in short, it establishes and maintains the conditions of cultural possibility and impossibility for gendered subjects. Some subjects become 'intelligible' within its terms; others remain – or are constituted as – unintelligible. I do not doubt that the state does this – on occasion, even on many occasions. What I question is whether this is all that it does and whether, as a consequence, daily social relations can *only* be radically reconfigured in a more democratic (universalising) direction in civil society as Butler surmises. After all, what is it about civil society that better guarantees – for surely, given that too is striated by power relations, it cannot fully guarantee – that the universals produced there will operate in a less regulatory, less normalising fashion than those articulated through the state?

If the goal of radical democracy is to struggle with norms that abject, discipline and regulate particular populations in order to recompose those norms in less violent ways, then surely that struggle should take place *wherever* those norms operate, including in and through the state. To maintain *a priori* and in advance that one site ought to be disavowed as a site of political intervention or democratisation seems to me to be highly problematic. The implication that '*eliminating state-sanctioned marriage altogether*' (Chambers 2007b: 675) is more subversive of heteronormativity at the level of public policy than seeking same-sex marriage, as Butler implies, is fine *if* we see marriage as intrinsically and irrevocably heteronormative whatever the context. If, however, we allow that marriage itself can be resignified (and as extensively as Kurtz implies), as I suggest Butler must, given her own theoretical assumptions, then the case against the current state-oriented political campaign for same-sex marriage carries less weight.[16]

The fact is that both options – refusing marriage and contending for its legal resignification – represent competing ways of intervening in the political social and cultural practices through which humans are constituted. They are both modes of radical democratic struggle with norms. Determining which is the more appropriate strategy depends on the (contingent) political conditions of the day. Opposing same-sex marriage in order to re-radicalise gay and lesbian politics when there exists a broad consensus in its favour is very different from opposing it where the state and other institutions, including the church, have acted in concerted fashion to retrench the heteronormativity of marriage and where same-sex marriage is officially disallowed. The radicalism of same-sex marriage as a policy depends on the context in which it is articulated. That Butler appears not to concede this in her comments on the state reveals a blind-spot in her theory in terms of the state's possible role in restaging the universal-to-come; a blind-spot that leads her, moreover, to neglect the (shifting) circumstances in which democratic politics actually occurs.

Notes

Thanks are due to both Adrian Little and Sam Chambers for their excellent comments on earlier versions of this chapter. You will both see where you have influenced me and where not!

1. By all of her books I mean all her single-authored books from *Subjects of Desire* through to *Giving an Account of Oneself*. This excludes *Contingency, Hegemony, Universality*, the text Butler co-authored with Ernesto Laclau and Slavoj Žižek. The fact that it does not contain an index, of even the most economical kind, will serve as no defence here. *Contingency* is important to the development of Butler's theory of radical democracy, not least since it is here that she sets out one of her more elaborated discussions of universality. It should not be read, however, as marking a break in her work – evidence perhaps of her conversion to radical democracy. The politics of everyday life has already been explored extensively in her earlier works.

2. There is one reference to *Hegemony and Socialist Strategy* in *Excitable Speech* (Butler 1997a: 177 n. 3), with a further seventeen references to Laclau and Mouffe in *Bodies that Matter*, though in this latter case there are duplicate entries for Laclau and for Mouffe (since the text in question tends to be their jointly authored book, *Hegemony and Socialist Strategy*). In this case, the number of references might justifiably be halved.

3. Claudia Card who is, like Butler, fervently in favour of the deregulation of marriage notes, by contrast, that changes in the political scene since 2004 'may call for some modification in, or qualification or clarification of [her] . . . stance' (2007: 32).

4. In 'Left Conservatism' (1998) Butler gives some indication of her reasons for turning to the universal.

5. In addition to Zerilli, Butler also draws on Hegel and his idea of competing conceptions of universality. I have already explored Butler's debt to Hegel at length elsewhere (Lloyd 2007a) so will not reprise those arguments here.

6. We might, of course, regard heteronormative sex and sexual difference as intrinsic to the liberal agenda; that, however, is part of another story for another time and place.

7. The first two generations are 'basic rights' and 'sex rights' (Wintemute 2005).

8. Much has been written about these topics. My account draws on the following: Warner 1999; Card 1996, 2007; Chambers 2003, 2007b; Baird and Rosenbaum 2004; Sullivan 2004; Ashbee 2007; Ferguson 2007; Robson 2007.

9. I am indebted to Samuel Chambers for this point. The key section of the proposed amendment (section 2) reads: 'Marriage in the United States shall consist only of the union of a man and a woman. Neither this Constitution, nor the constitution of any State, shall be construed to require that marriage or the legal incidents thereof be conferred upon any union other than the union of a man and a woman.' In the most recent attempt in 2006 to pass it the amendment failed to secure the necessary two-thirds majority in Congress.

10. The right to marry is enshrined in the Universal Declaration of Human Rights in article 16, section 1, where it states: 'Men and women of full age, without any limitation due to race, nationality, or religion, have the right to marry and to found a family.' On same-sex marriage as a human right see Wintemute 2005 and Card 2007.

11. Further discussion of the menu of rights that attach to marriage can be found in Warner 1999: 118–19. See also Card 2007.

12. Florida is a case in point where moves are afoot to include a constitutional amendment banning same-sex marriage on the ballot in November 2008.

13. It is important, of course, not to overstate the parallels. For a brief consideration of the class dimensions of the campaign for gay marriage see Goldstein ('Foreword' to Graff 2004) and Warner 1999.

14. Resignification itself is neither inherently radical nor democratic. Rather it facilitates the development of a more radical democracy by unsettling existing norms and allowing for their recomposition.

15. This is explicitly not to say, however, that were same-sex marriage to be made legal that it would remain, by definition, a radical practice. Arguably, it is the demand for the right to marry that is radical (in particular contexts).

16. For an account of how marriage has been resignified historically see Graff 2004.

3

Aboriginal Sovereignty and the Democratic Paradox

Andrew Schaap

Against Jürgen Habermas, Chantal Mouffe insists that there is no necessary conceptual relation between democracy and human rights but only a contingent historical relation. Moreover, these principles are fundamentally irreconcilable: while democracy presupposes an historical act of *exclusion* in the political constitution of a *demos*, human rights presupposes a universally *inclusive* moral community. Yet, Mouffe argues, the accommodation of these conflicting legitimating principles within a liberal democratic regime is productive. Although irreconcilable, their paradoxical articulation keeps the limits that enable democratic deliberation and decision-making in view for being political and, therefore, contestable. Radical democracy, she argues, is premised on the recognition and affirmation of this 'democratic paradox'.[1]

In this chapter I examine whether a commitment to radical democracy requires that we affirm Mouffe's account of the democratic paradox. Might one be a radical democrat and yet understand human rights and popular sovereignty to be co-original as Habermas does? Specifically, I want to consider what is at stake *politically* in conceptualising the relation between these two legitimating principles of modern regimes. I will suggest that what is at stake is the representation of political claims. To understand human rights and democracy as 'co-original' in the way that Habermas proposes is to peremptorily exclude radical political speech and action that would fundamentally contest the terms of political association. For it diminishes the representational space in which a claim could be articulated that would contest the particular determination of the 'we' that authorises that order in the first place.

Mouffe's Schmittian thematisation of the political brings this ideological aspect of the co-originality thesis into view. First, because it draws attention to the way in which Habermas posits the *contingent* and particular determination of political unity as a necessary condition for the universalising operation of law so that the demos, as socially determined, becomes a *given* within the field of instituted politics. Second, because it reveals how Habermas's characterisation of law as an enabling condition for politics means that social conflict is represented as already *internal* to the political unity that it necessarily presupposes. In other words, positing human rights and popular sovereignty as co-original removes the question of the determination of the 'self' of the demos from politics. This leads to a certain policing of the *agon* since only communal conflict can be recognised as legitimate.

I agree with Mouffe, then, that radical democrats ought to recognise the relation between human rights and popular sovereignty as paradoxically articulated. However, I also want to suggest that a fuller account of the democratic paradox is required than is afforded by a Schmittian conception of the political. Indeed, to identify democracy with an exclusive political identification and human rights with an inclusive moral cosmopolitanism, as Mouffe (following Schmitt) does, is to remain caught within the terms of liberal ideology. With Habermas, then, I concur that both popular sovereignty and human rights are 'janus-faced' since each principle has both a determinate institutional dimension (that *orders* ordinary politics) and a symbolic, quasi-transcendent dimension (that potentially *politicises* a social order). A radical conception of democracy requires that we affirm this symbolic (and, indeed, 'quasi-transcendent') aspect of the political rather than privileging its institutional determination.

Unpopular sovereignty[2] and political paradox

Rousseau is usually credited as the first political theorist to identify the democratic paradox in drawing a distinction between the general will and the will of all. Rousseau's point is that, while popular sovereignty means that what the people wills is right, it does not follow from this that the people has a right to will what is wrong. Rather, a people, by definition, always wills 'generally'. Whereas the 'will of all' refers to a simple aggregation of subjective wills, the formation of a general will involves the universalisation of these particular wills in relation to what is good for all (Rousseau 1997: II.3). The general will is good because it is public in the twofold sense of both appearing to all and being shared in common. In other words, the general will is good not just because a set of particular interests happens to coalesce around it but part of its being good is that it is publicly constituted by free and equal citizens. In Charles Taylor's (1995) terms, it is an 'irreducibly social good'.

As such, the social contract is not merely an agreement among private persons to collectively secure the conditions that best secure their mutual interests. Rather, it purports to describe how a set of determinate individuals come to recognise the general will and thus to think of themselves politically, as collectively intending the universal law that binds them together. Although, in fact, society is divided according to conflicting interests, wills, opinions, beliefs and identities, the representation of this conflict as internal to society presupposes an original (counter-factual) consensus on the founding law that unifies the polity. The political paradox emerges in Rousseau's attempt to conceptualise this original consensus, which would explain how those subject to the law might also view themselves as its co-authors (1997: II.6). If, as Rousseau supposes, law is a pre-condition for civil society and, hence, for political co-operation, how could an original consensus about the foundation of the law be possible in a state of nature? Rousseau famously describes the paradox as follows:

> For a nascent people to be capable of appreciating sound maxims of politics and of following the fundamental rules of reason of State, the effect would have to become the cause, the social spirit which is to be the work of the institution would have to preside over the institution itself, and men would have to be prior to the laws what they ought to become by means of them. (1997: II.7)

Prior to the law there is only a multitude; only with the institution of a law that would regulate their life in common, identifying each natural person in the abstract as a free and equal member of the legal association, does a people appear on the political scene. But how could a 'blind multitude' be capable of founding the law that brings the people into being (Rousseau 1997: II.6; see Keenan 2003; Honig 2007)?

Of course, Rousseau's philosophical paradox need not be debilitating for political action. Indeed, it is vividly revealed in the revolutionary Declaration of Independence: 'We hold these truths to be self-evident'. As Arendt observes, this declaration combines the necessary truth of (self-evident) human rights with a contingent agreement (the fact of their being declared and the imputation of this declaration to a collective author, the people). Moreover, it reveals that 'those who would get together to constitute a new government are themselves unconstitutional, that is, they have no authority to do what they set out to achieve' (Arendt 1991: 183–4). In the revolutionary moment, the will of the people lacks an institutional framework in terms of which it may be represented as such. As Bert van Roermund puts it, 'the people' who are supposed to be sovereign in a democratic polity are both inside and outside the legal order that is constituted; political power both institutes a new legal order while the newly instituted legal order is supposed to enable and restrain that very 'political power' (2003: 38). The democratic paradox here emerges in the circular relation between the constituent power and the constituted power, between the sovereign subject that founds the law and the law that delimits a space for politics within which the sovereign will can be expressed.

In his later work, Habermas has sought to resolve the democratic paradox by appealing to discourse ethics. Far from being potentially contradictory, he argues, the principles of popular sovereignty and rule of law necessarily presuppose each other in the self-understanding of a democratic society. Any apparent contradiction between these two principles of legitimacy could be resolved by recourse to the meta-political presupposition of the democratic enterprise: namely, that since self-determination is an act of co-legislation those engaged in this task must already implicitly recognise each other as legal persons (hence individual rights-holders).

To think through what is at stake politically in the conceptualisation of the democratic paradox, I want to keep before us the situation of indigenous people, their unpopular assertion of sovereignty and the representational space afforded to this claim within the actually existing democracy of Australia. In a national referendum in 1967, 90 per cent of Australians voted in favour of amending the constitution to include Aborigines in the census count and to allow the Federal Government the power over Aboriginal affairs, which had previously been reserved for State government. This has been commemorated in Australia as the moment in which Aborigines achieved citizenship rights. Yet, indigenous activist Kevin Gilbert objects that Aborigines 'never voted to be incorporated with non-Aboriginals. Australian citizenship was imposed on us unilaterally'(1993: 41). At stake in the political conflict between the settler society and indigenous people is precisely the sovereignty of the people, the terms of inclusion in the demos.

In this context, the (counter-factual) presupposition that indigenous people should be able to view themselves as co-authors of the law with non-indigenous people risks perpetuating the logic of internal colonisation. As James Tully explains, with internal colonisation the land, resources and jurisdiction of indigenous people are appropriated not only for the sake of exploitation but for the 'territorial foundation of the dominant society itself' (2000: 39). While liberation from external colonisation is possible by forcing the withdrawal of the occupying imperial power, such tactics of direct confrontation are ineffective in the context of internal colonisation in which 'the dominant society coexists on and exercises exclusive jurisdiction over the territories and jurisdictions that the indigenous peoples refuse to surrender'. Both the colonisers and colonised, therefore, view the system of internal colonisation as a temporary means to an end. Indigenous people would resolve this irresolution by 'regaining their freedom as self-governing peoples'. In contrast, the settler society would resolve the irresolution by the 'complete disappearance of the indigenous problem, that is, the disappearance of indigenous people as free peoples with the right to their territories and governments' (Tully 2000: 40; cf. Ivanitz 2002).

On 26 January 1972, four young Aboriginal men (Billie Craig, Bert Williams, Michael Anderson and Tony Correy) planted a beach umbrella on the lawn of Parliament House in Canberra. In doing so, they claimed to establish an embassy to the Australian state on behalf of the Aboriginal people(s) within its territory. The delegation insisted that, since they were effectively aliens in their own land, indigenous people needed an embassy like other aliens in this country. Since its foundation, the Aboriginal Tent Embassy has been a focal point of political struggle by indigenous people in Australia (see Waterford 1992; Robinson 1994; Dow 2000; Foley 2002). In Arendt's terms (above), the tent ambassadors were unconstitutional: they had no authority to do what they set out to achieve. They were authorised neither by the Australian constitution (which positions them as co-authors of the law together with members of the settler society) nor by the sovereign Aboriginal nation that they claimed to represent. In both instances, such authorisation would only be possible retrospectively.[3]

The tent embassy invokes Aboriginal sovereignty as a right while testifying to the lack of sovereignty in fact. On the one hand, the embassy has the symbolic trappings of sovereignty: it flies its own flag and it claims the right to negotiate with the Australian state as the representative of a sovereign people. It is this assertion of Aboriginal sovereignty that representatives of the Australian state have found troubling. The Minister for Aboriginal Affairs in 1972 said that the notion of an Aboriginal 'embassy' had a disturbing undertone since 'the term implied a sovereign state and cut across the Government's expressed objection to separate development'. This attitude has prevailed in the present government in relation to calls for a treaty between settlers and indigenous people. While in opposition, for instance, the former Prime Minister John Howard remarked that 'it is an absurd proposition that a nation should make a treaty with some of its own citizens' (cited in Patton 2001: 37).

On the other hand, the embassy is a tent rather than a permanent building. Resembling the fringe dweller camps of rural Australian towns, the tent embassy also symbolises the dispossession of indigenous people, their lack of sovereignty over their lands. This aspect of the embassy has equally troubled politicians who have frequently described it as an 'eyesore'. There have been several attempts by governments over the years to clean up the lawns of Parliament by offering to provide permanent meeting rooms, memorial plaques or reconciliation paths in exchange for the removal of the tent embassy. Following a review undertaken by the consulting firm Mutual Mediations in 2005, the Federal Government announced that the tent embassy will be replaced with a more permanent structure. A sign declaring 'No Camping' has been erected at the embassy, although the Minister gave an assurance that no residents will be removed against their will.

I want to consider what critical work Habermas's co-originality thesis and Mouffe's democratic paradox do for conceptualising indigenous people's unpopular claim to sovereignty *on its own terms*. To what extent are these frameworks adequate to understanding Aboriginal sovereignty as anything more than an 'absurd proposition'? Although recognised as citizens by the Australian state, it would be plainly difficult for indigenous people in Australia to regard themselves as authors of the law of this country. On the face of it, however, this would not invalidate Habermas's conceptualisation of the relation between democracy and rights. The question is whether indigenous peoples' struggle against colonisation can be adequately represented within the terms of Habermas's conceptual framework. Can indigenous peoples' objection to colonisation be accommodated in a demand to be recognised as free and equal participants in the legislative process? Or does the normative representation of indigenous and settler peoples as co-authors of the law lead to a certain co-optation of the insurrectionary political act of 'establishing' an Aboriginal embassy?

Mouffe's characterisation of the democratic paradox

Against Habermas, Chantal Mouffe asserts that there is 'no necessary relation' between human rights and popular sovereignty but 'only a contingent historical articulation' (2000: 3). In fact, these principles have distinct logics, which often come into conflict at the conceptual as well as the practical level. As is well known, Mouffe draws on Carl Schmitt to describe the opposing logics of human rights and popular sovereignty. Schmitt's work is attractive to radical democrats, such as Chantal Mouffe and Andreas Kalyvas (2005), because he insists on the primacy of politics over the rule of law, arguing against Hans Kelsen that 'the concrete existence of the politically unified people is prior to every norm' (cited in Lindahl 2007: 9). In a constitutional democracy there is a fundamental antagonism between its political aspect (at bottom a decision about the form the political unity will take) and its legal aspect (which imposes restrictions on political activity).

Appropriating Schmitt's interpretation of constitutional democracy, Mouffe (1993, 2000) argues that the democratic paradox arises from the fact that the exercise of popular sovereignty requires the delimitation of a demos, which necessarily excludes non-members in the act of including its members. This brings popular sovereignty into conflict with the universalism of human rights discourse. Stated in this way, the democratic paradox comes about because of the different constituencies to which popular sovereignty and human rights refer. Popular sovereignty refers to a political community: a concrete historical community that is necessarily *bounded*. In contrast, human rights refer to the moral community: an *unlimited* community that includes all humanity. Popular sovereignty is predicated on the substantive equality of citizens because it concerns, in Rawlsian terms, the distribution of the benefits and burdens of social co-operation. Human rights, in contrast, are predicated on the formal equality of moral persons because they rely on the ideal of human dignity and the categorical imperative (Mouffe 2000: 40–4).

Mouffe argues that in order to sustain robust liberal democratic institutions we need to acknowledge and affirm the democratic paradox (2000: 4). The tension between the principles of popular sovereignty and human rights cannot be philosophically resolved. They can only be negotiated politically – 'temporarily stabilised' in a way that establishes the hegemony of one principle over the other (Mouffe 2000: 5, 45). In other words, in certain periods liberal rights will take priority over popular sovereignty. At other times popular sovereignty will take priority over liberal rights according to the contingencies of social and political power, the outcome of the struggle between left and right.

But far from being a weakness, Mouffe insists, the paradoxical articulation of human rights and popular sovereignty is the strength of the liberal democratic regime:

> By constantly challenging the relations of inclusion-exclusion implied by the political constitution of 'the people' – required by the exercise of democracy – the liberal discourse of universal human rights plays an important role in maintaining the democratic contestation alive. On the other side, it is only thanks to the democratic logics of equivalence that frontiers can be created and a demos established without which no real exercise of rights could be possible. (Mouffe 2000: 10)

Mouffe is here in agreement with Schmitt in according a certain priority to the political (understood as the determination of the commonality of political community in terms of a relation of inclusion/exclusion) over the instantiation of a universalising normative order that it makes possible. In the absence of their declaration or enactment within political community, human rights are without value since, in Habermas's terms, they lack 'facticity' in being socially recognised and enforceable. Against Schmitt, however, instead of viewing human rights as an 'unpolitical' *limit* to politics, Mouffe understands human rights as having a *politicising* role within the democratic polity. For Schmitt, liberal human rights could only ever amount to an inauthentic politics: a polemical discourse that disavows its own politics in the sense of favouring one form of political community over another. In contrast, Mouffe sees human rights as potentially enabling a legitimate contest within the political association over the terms of belonging. Although the distinction between citizen and non-citizen is the fundamental political distinction (which would contain all other political conflicts), the appeal to human rights enables an 'agonistic' politics within the democratic polity by bringing into view the contingency of that founding distinction and hence the possibility that it might be drawn otherwise.

Mouffe argues that Habermas's search for a conceptual resolution of this paradoxical articulation of popular sovereignty and human rights is misguided because it puts 'undue constraints on the political debate' (Mouffe 2000: 93; see also Mouffe 2005a: 83–9). Why? Because Habermas seeks to resolve the relation between these two legitimating principles meta-politically rather than recognising this as an issue that can only be settled politically in a particular institutional setting. Mouffe accepts that some limits must be placed on democratic politics in order to make possible the kind of agonistic engagement that she favours. However, she insists, 'the political nature of the limits should be acknowledged instead of being presented as requirements of morality or rationality' (Mouffe 2000: 93). Mouffe's objection to determining the limits of democratic politics according to moral or rational standards is the same as Schmitt's critique of liberalism. Namely, that the appeal to supposedly meta-political criteria to set the boundaries of institutional politics is always disingenuous; it leads to an 'anti-political' politics, a denial of the political nature of one's own discourse, which is, in fact, a particularly intensive way of pursuing politics.

As Emilios Christodoulidis notes, the significance of the Schmittian conception of the political for radical politics is that it 'imports a reflexivity into politics, in the sense that the origin of political action is already political: it resides in the contingency of the recognition of what constitutes a political unity in the first place' (2007: 192). Radical politics thrives on the recognition of contingency since that is the basis of politicisation, opening the possibility that this unity might be constituted otherwise.

In this context, however, Christodoulidis draws an important distinction between the 'abstract conceptualisation' of the political and its 'concrete manifestations'. If, in its abstract conceptualisation, the political is the 'dimension of antagonism which [is] constitutive of human societies' (Mouffe 2005a: 9), its concrete manifestation would be the particular distinction that delimits the terms of belonging in *this* political association. The importance of differentiating these two levels of the political (i.e. between its abstract conceptualisation and concrete manifestations) is to show that the concrete manifestation could always be otherwise. Moreover, the abstract conceptualisation of the political is itself, to some extent, also contingent: what is integral to the concept of the political is that it refers to the institution of society. Whether this is brought about through antagonism or otherwise is also a matter of politics.

Habermas's co-originality thesis

In arguing that popular sovereignty and human rights are 'co-original' or 'equiprimordial', Habermas means that neither principle takes priority in the philosophical order of justification. As such, he wants to show that the basic idea of human rights – that everyone has a fundamental right to equal individual liberties – should not be understood as a pre-political moral constraint on the sovereign legislator, as in liberalism. Nor should it be understood only instrumentally as an enabling condition for democratic expression, as in republicanism. Rather, the twin principles of popular sovereignty and human rights, on which the legitimacy of law depends, presuppose each other. The co-originality of popular sovereignty and the rule of law (as guaranteed by human rights) is expressed in the ideal of self-legislation: 'that those subject to law as its addressees can at the same time understand themselves as authors of the law' (Habermas 1996: 104). We are the *addressees* of the law in our role as private persons or rights-bearers whereas we are *authors* of the law in our role as citizens or 'co-legislators' (see Baynes 1995; Scheurman 1999; Maus 2002).

The first step in Habermas's argument is to insist, against Marx, on the inter-subjective basis of human rights. Habermas acknowledges that these subjective rights delimit the legitimate scope within which individuals may exercise free choice, regardless of their moral motivation. In the well-established liberal parlance, rights aim to maximise the liberty of each individual compatible with the same enjoyment of liberty by others. As such, rights free individuals to strategically pursue their private interests without regard for the common good. Or, in Habermas's terms, rights entitle individuals to 'drop out of communicative action' insofar as the 'legal subject does not have to give . . . publicly acceptable reasons for her action plans' (1996: 120). But rather than viewing rights as thereby institutionalising an amoral possessive individualism, Habermas describes the 'moral unburdening' of individuals as a functional achievement of legal rights, which complements morality (1996: 114–18). In their relation to the law as addressees, he argues, law unburdens individuals from the unprecedented cognitive, motivational and organisational demands of moral judgement and action in a complex society.

While freeing individuals for competitive and self-interested behaviour, however, human rights do not necessarily presuppose an atomistic conception of society, as the radical tradition has often charged. On the contrary, they are a form of social co-operation: 'as elements of the legal order they presuppose collaboration among subjects who recognise one another, in their reciprocally related rights and duties, as free and equal citizens' (Habermas 1996: 89). The inter-subjective foundation of rights – their status as norms shared by members of a

legal community – points the way to the principle of popular sovereignty in terms of which they are enacted as law.

The second step in Habermas's argument is to claim that the 'legal
medium as such presupposes rights that define the status of legal
persons as bearers of rights' (Habermas 1996: 119). The primordial
human right of each individual to equal subjective liberties is a foundational principle of law such that a legitimate legal code cannot exist
without a system of rights: the subject of law is, by definition, a rights-
holder. Importantly, Habermas understands human rights only in
juridical terms (1996: 105). He rejects the natural law tradition,
according to which individuals possess pre-political moral rights in
the state of nature, which are recognised in positive law when they
enter into a social contract together. Rights do not exist in a determinate form in the state of nature but are mutually conferred when
individuals undertake to regulate their life in common through the
medium of law.

This brings us to Habermas's third step. Stated bluntly, popular
sovereignty can only be exercised through the medium of law and,
since the general right to liberties is constitutive of the legal form as
such, the recognition of human rights is a necessary presupposition of
democratic praxis. Insofar as the exercise of popular sovereignty
requires individuals to reach an understanding on the basic principles
according to which they should regulate their collective life, they view
each other as co-legislators. Yet, in employing the medium of law,
they must already recognise each other as legal subjects and therefore
entitled to equal subjective liberties. In a striking formulation,
Habermas insists:

> . . . the medium through which citizens exercise their autonomy is not a
> matter of choice. Citizens participate in legislation only as legal subjects;
> it is no longer in their power to decide which language they will make use
> of. (2002: 201)

Importantly, the medium of law does not presuppose any substantive
human rights. Rather rights are present in the form of law only as
'unsaturated placeholders' for the specification of particular rights
that are to be given substance through the exercise of political autonomy (Habermas 1996: 125).

In reconstructing the logical genesis of rights in this way, Habermas
claims to have established a *necessary conceptual* relation between
popular sovereignty and human rights in contrast to Mouffe's insistence on a *contingent historical* relation. This necessary connection

works in both directions to establish that the private autonomy of legal persons and the public autonomy of citizens mutually presuppose each other. On the one hand, human rights necessarily presuppose popular sovereignty to the extent that individuals can 'realise equality in the enjoyment of their *private autonomy* only if they make appropriate use of their political autonomy as citizens' (Habermas 2002: 202). Although rights are constitutive of the legal form, legality as such cannot ground any specific right. Rather, a system of rights can only be developed when the legal form is used to exercise popular sovereignty, i.e. when citizens exercise their right to submit only to those norms they could agree to in discourse. On the other hand, popular sovereignty presupposes human rights since individuals are only free to engage in democratic praxis to the extent that their independence from each other is guaranteed through the equal protection of their private freedoms, i.e. those rights that protect private goods (such as property, freedom of religious worship) thereby assuring the independence of civil society from the state.

It is no coincidence that Habermas's argument in support of the co-originality thesis bears a striking resemblance to the argument he makes to arrive at his discourse principle. As is well known, Habermas argues that certain validity-claims – to truth, sincerity and rightness – are *necessarily presupposed* in all communicative acts. As ideal conditions necessarily presupposed in factual communication these principles require no justification. Moreover, the fact that they are presupposed by language gives universal morality an immanent purchase within particular forms of life.

The structure of this argument is mirrored in Habermas's claim that human rights are a *necessary presupposition* of the legal medium through which democratic self-determination is enacted (Habermas 1996: 127). As a necessary condition of the legal form as such, the basic human right to equal liberty similarly requires no justification (Habermas 1996: 112). Moreover, like the presuppositions of the ideal speech situation, the presupposition of the basic human right in the legal form gives universal morality an immanent purchase within the historical project of democratic self-determination by a particular legal community.

As such, Habermas acknowledges the tension Mouffe identifies between the necessarily limited political community in which rights are articulated and enforced on the one hand and the unlimited moral community to which universal rights refer on the other. However, rather than presenting this tension as an external one between the contending traditions of liberal constitutionalism and democratic politics as Mouffe does, he recasts this tension as internal to the law and located in the system of rights itself.

This tension between what Habermas calls 'facticity' and 'validity' is manifest in positively enacted human rights insofar as their legitimacy depends on their guarantee of liberty through coercion: 'legal norms are at the same time but in different respects enforceable laws based on coercion and laws of freedom' (Habermas 1996: 29). By facticity, Habermas refers to the decisionistic aspect of the law, its origination in the will of the sovereign and the fact that compliance with the law is externally motivated by the threat of sanctions. By validity Habermas means that the law's legitimacy does not depend only on the fact of social acceptance but also on the presupposition that the law is the outcome of democratic deliberation and decision-making. When confronted by the law's facticity we experience it as a constraint on our free choice; we obey it out of our self-interest in avoiding legal sanctions. When confronted by its validity, in contrast, we comply with the law out of respect for it since we presume that it expresses a rational democratic will-formation among free and equal citizens.

The tension between facticity and validity inherent in law enables Habermas to deal with Marx's (1987) critique that human rights alienate men and women from their species being – that in a liberal democracy they live a 'double life' between their heavenly existence as communal beings in the state and their earthly existence as egoistic individuals in civil society. According to Habermas, although those rights institutionalised by the law unburden individuals from the requirement of communicative rationality, it leaves them free to take 'either an objectivating or performative attitude' to legal norms (1996: 30). As addressees, they can view the law strategically as establishing constraints on their freedom of choice or they can obey the law out of respect for it on the presumption that it is rationally acceptable.

Against Marx's early account of political alienation in terms of the bifurcation of the subject as concrete particular 'man' and abstract universal 'citizen', Habermas insists that the 'citizens who mutually grant one another equal rights are one and the same individuals as the private persons who use rights strategically and encounter one another as potential opponents' (1996: 89). The idea of popular sovereignty is thus indispensable for modern law since it provides the basis on which the law's claim to validity might be redeemed. While individuals are free to pursue their self-interest unburdened by the demands of communicative rationality within the constraints set by human rights, they are simultaneously free to recognise or contest the inter-subjective agreement on which human rights ultimately rest. By virtue of their public freedom to contest the validity of the law citizens are able to overcome their potential alienation from it.

According to Habermas, this tension between facticity and validity is originally present in everyday communicative practice. This is so because every speech act involves a validity-claim on which the hearer is free to take a yes/no position. In every speech act there is an implied promise to redeem our claim if challenged to do so by offering reasons that our addressee might accept as valid. Because validity claims implicitly refer to the 'ideally expanded audience of the unlimited interpretation community' in relation to which they might be redeemed, there is an 'ideal moment of unconditionality . . . ingrained in factual processes of communication' (Habermas 1996: 21). Consequently, every political claim contains both a universal aspect which transcends the spatial and temporal context in which it is raised and a particular aspect specific to the political-historical situation that is at stake in whether it is accepted or rejected. As such validity claims are 'janus-faced'. As claims they 'overshoot every context'. Yet they 'must be both raised and accepted here and now if they are to support an agreement effective for co-ordination – for this there is no acontextual standpoint' (Habermas 1996: 21). In the context of a constitutional politics, Habermas's point seems to be very close to Mouffe's when she argues that 'no real exercise of rights could be possible' in the absence of a bounded political community (2000: 10). The tension between facticity and validity is present in law to the extent that its validity depends both on the fact of its social acceptance and the presumption that it is rationally acceptable.

While Habermas barely remarks on it, this tension is particularly apparent in his reconstruction of the logical genesis of the system of rights when he refers to the interpenetration of the legal form which 'stabilises behavioural expectations' and the discourse principle according to which the 'legitimacy of legal norms can be tested' (Habermas 1996: 122). The discourse principle (D) states that 'just those action norms are valid to which *all possibly affected persons* could agree as participants in rational discourses' (Habermas 1996: 107). By 'those affected' Habermas means 'anyone whose interests are touched by the foreseeable consequences of a general practice regulated by the norms at issue' (1996: 107). While the norms of a legal order are necessarily expressed as rights, Habermas argues that the discourse principle is required to establish the liberal legal principle that 'each person is owed a right to the greatest possible measure of equal liberties that are mutually compatible' (1996: 123).

However, in order to institutionalise these rights it is necessary to 'demarcate the bounds of membership and provide legal remedies for cases of right violations' (Habermas 1996: 124). In other words, when the discourse principle interpenetrates with the legal form, we shift from the universal/cosmopolitan principle of *affectedness* to the historical/republican principle of *membership* in order to determine the relevant constituency in relation to which the validity-claims of the law must be redeemed. This limitation of the discourse principle 'follows simply . . . from the facticity of making and enforcing the law' (Habermas 1996: 124).

But while the limitation of the discourse principle certainly follows from the facticity of making and enforcing law, Habermas elides too much in passing this concession off as a simple matter. First, because in losing their reference to natural law, human rights appear to lose their context-transcending aspect, their 'ideal moment of unconditionality', which was for Mouffe precisely what accorded them their potentially politicising aspect. In understanding human rights only in terms of their institutional determination, Habermas risks relegating them to a wholly regulatory function within the democratic polity. Second, because Habermas's insistence that democratic self-determination can only be exercised through the medium of law tends to reify the 'self' that is to be determining as already constituted through law. If self-determination can only ever be exercised within the law then this rules out in advance the possibility of any kind of radical action, understood in terms of an act of constituent power.

The problem emerges of how the violence that founds the facticity of the law in delimiting a finite political community could ever be redressed by the infinite validity that the same legal order is supposed to carry in its very form – without, that is, this becoming an ideological moment (see, for example, Motha 2002). In the context with which we are concerned, of course, this returns us to the problem of how indigenous people might come to view themselves as co-authors of the law to which they were originally subject as colonised.

The 'absurd proposition' of Aboriginal sovereignty

We have seen that Habermas does not ignore the tension between political exclusion and moral inclusion that Mouffe draws our attention to. Rather than representing this tension as an external one between the principles of popular sovereignty and human rights, however, he casts it as one internal to law, between its facticity and its validity. The strength of Habermas's analysis is that it shows both human rights and popular sovereignty to be 'janus-faced' to the extent that we seek to realise them within particular contexts. This suggests that each principle has both an exclusive determinate aspect and an inclusive symbolic aspect. Yet, we have also seen that Habermas eludes the political since he passes too lightly over the exclusive foundation of law as following simply from the need to make and enforce it.

In other words, Habermas acknowledges but does not adequately address the 'boundary problem' in democratic theory (Whelan 1983). According to his discourse principle: 'Just those action norms are valid to which all possibly affected persons could agree as participants in rational discourses' (Habermas 1996: 107). But, as Habermas is aware, the principle of 'all possibly affected persons' will not do as a principle for identifying the relevant constituency for political decisions. This is because there is no democratic way of determining who all possibly affected persons are in the case of disagreement over whether particular persons are affected or not. Habermas readily admits that:

> From a normative point of view, the social boundaries of an association of free and equal consociates under law are perfectly contingent. Since the voluntariness of the decision to engage in a law-giving praxis is a fiction of the contractualist tradition, in the real world who gains the power to define the boundaries of a political community is settled by historical chance and the actual course of events, normally, by the arbitrary outcomes of wars or civil wars. (2001: 116; see also 2001: 144)

But there is a deeper conceptual problem with the cosmopolitan principle of affectedness which Habermas does not properly address. As Bert van Roermund observes, in determining those norms according to which the relevant constituency of the affected is to be decided we are left with three unsatisfactory options:

> Either the answer is simply decided upon (so that the phrase refers to the normative force of the factual), or it leads to infinite regression (who is to decide who is to decide . . . etc.), or it is based on *petitio principii* (who is involved is decided by who is involved in the first place). (1997: 150)

Habermas seems to opt for the first option, simply presupposing community as a legal fact.

Since Habermas understands human rights in terms of positive law, the relevant constituency must be defined in territorial terms if his discourse principle is to be translated into law. As Habermas acknowledges, as moral norms human rights 'refer to every creature "that bears a human face," but as legal norms they protect individual persons only insofar as the latter belong to a particular legal community – normally citizens of a nation-state' (2001a: 118). Thus, according to Habermas, the democratic principle, which is derived from his discourse principle, states that 'only those statutes may claim legitimacy that can meet *with the assent of all citizens* in a discursive process of legislation that in turn has been legally constituted' (1996: 110). But this is question-begging since it takes the demos as given rather accounting for how the 'we' that authorises the law is generated.

Following from this, Habermas's view of law as a medium for democratic expression places undue constraints on political deliberation because it represents social conflict as already internal to the political community. This is evident, for instance, in the following formulation:

> Political power is not externally juxtaposed to law but is rather presupposed by law and itself established in the form of law. Political power can develop only through a legal code, and it is, in the legal sense of the word, constituted in the form of basic rights. (Habermas 1996: 134)

It is certainly true that expressing political claims in terms of rights often provides a mechanism for translating one's private preferences into a publicly justifiable claim. Thus Habermas refers to democratic procedures as a 'filter that sorts out issues and contributions, information and reasons in such a way that only the relevant and valid inputs "count"' (1996: 462). The worry for radical democrats is whether law filters too much.

Sheldon Wolin, for instance, questions the identification of democracy with constitutionalism, arguing instead for an 'aconstitutional conception of democracy', which he defines as 'the idea and practice of rational disorganisation'. On this view democracy is 'inherently unstable, inclined toward anarchy, and identified with revolution' (1994a: 37). The value of Wolin's work is that it emphasises that democratic action fundamentally turns around the contestation of the 'we' that authorises the law. But whereas politics always refers to this 'we' as in the process of becoming, law represents the 'we' as always already (Christodoulidis 2007). To what extent, then, is the medium of law able to faithfully represent a claim that contests the 'we' on which its legitimacy depends? Or, to put it another way, to what extent are radical claims co-opted in being represented as rights-claims to be adjudicated by reference to the authorising 'we' that is contested in the first place?

In response to this kind of probing, Habermas is forced to fall back on the principle of implicit consent to hold the place of the counter-factual consensus: 'The right to emigrate implies that membership must rest on an (at least tacit) act of agreement on the member's part' (1996: 124–5). But the tacitness of this act of agreement is precisely what is at stake in fundamental political conflict, which contests the terms of political association. Having recourse to the principle of tacit consent in the situation of indigenous people in Australia is clearly problematic, if not perverse. In cases such as this, the principle of tacit agreement – which amounts to 'if you don't like it you can always leave' – appears to rest entirely on the facticity of sovereignty rather than its validity.

Indeed, to exercise one's rights as a citizen of Australia, in this context, might simultaneously be to legitimate the monopoly over the means of violence assumed by the colonisers. This is why abstention from voting is a common form of political protest. Similarly, the recourse to legal remedies that rights make available may contribute to the further dispossession of a group within a nation-state. This was spectacularly witnessed, for instance, by the claims brought by indigenous peoples to native title in Australia following the Mabo judgement, which effectively provided a legal means of extinguishing indigenous peoples' political claims to reparative justice by recourse to the facticity of sovereignty (see Motha 2002). As Kerruish and Purdy discuss, in making available the legal identity of 'native title claimant/holder' to indigenous people, Australian property law at the same time reinscribes the particular determination of the political unity that is at stake in the conflict between coloniser and colonised, namely that sovereignty was acquired through settlement rather than conquest (1998: 152f.). Indeed, it is precisely this presupposition that the tent ambassadors sought to contest by asserting the right that was not available to them in Australian law to demand a treaty with the invaders.

In certain circumstances, then, what Habermas calls the 'rational-ising character of the legal form as such' (1996: 126) can amount to just that: not an expression of an all-inclusive public reason but a rationalisation of political exclusion. Habermas acknowledges that the 'juridification of communicative freedom also means that the law must draw on sources of legitimation that are not at its disposal' (1996: 131). The question is how this is possible given his insistence on the co-originality of sovereignty and rights and, hence, of the constituent power as always already framed by the law. When understood as such, how could law account for what is not at its disposal except on its own terms? How might the extra-legal assertion of Aboriginal sovereignty register as anything other than an 'absurd proposition'?

Would indigenous peoples' unpopular claim to sovereignty fare any better when understood in terms of the democratic paradox? Mouffe's thematisation of agonistic politics certainly provides a promising starting point from which to understand the political conflict between settler and indigenous peoples in Australia. The advantage of understanding democracy, in this context, in terms of transforming an antagonistic relation into an agonistic one is that it resists co-opting the political claims of indigenous peoples by representing these as already reconcilable with the claims of the settler society.

As Mouffe puts it, 'agonism is a we/they relation where the competing parties, although acknowledging that there is no rational solution to their conflict, nevertheless recognise the legitimacy of their opponents' (1995: 20). The point of agonistic politics, as I understand it, is that it recognises that politics ultimately concerns the terms within which social conflict is represented; politics is the struggle to determine the public good in terms of which one's interest might be represented. As already noted, for Mouffe (contra Schmitt), it is the appeal to human rights that enables this politicisation of the terms of belonging within the political association. For, as a legitimating principle of the regime, human rights provide the 'shared symbolic space' that enables the casting of their conflict as 'social'. And, indeed, indigenous people have often appealed to indigenous (human) rights in their struggle for decolonisation.

Yet, as Paul Muldoon (forthcoming) has argued, the conflictual consensus that Mouffe advocates ends up being limited to a struggle *within* the (democratic) political association and consequently according to the terms of inclusion that it already affords in appealing to its shared symbolic space. The political limits of democracy come into view when conflict threatens the existence of the political association. As Mouffe puts it, 'in order to be accepted as legitimate [conflict] needs to take a form that does not destroy the political association' (Mouffe 2005a: 20). Passages such as this indicate the

70

limitations of the Schmittian conception of the political for a radical politics. In my view, a radical politics would precisely be one that would call into question the concrete manifestation of the political that delimits the terms of belonging within a particular political association. Indeed, it is precisely this (symbolic) threat that makes the assertion of Aboriginal sovereignty so unsettling to the settler society in Australia. Disturbingly, it seems that Aboriginal sovereignty might also amount to 'an absurd proposition' within Mouffe's framing of the democratic paradox because she understands the demos (with Schmitt) in terms of the determinate, concrete manifestation of the political while neglecting its symbolic, socially indeterminate aspect.

Conclusion

For indigenous people to effectively challenge the terms of their belonging within Australian society, they would need to be able to appeal not only to their human rights but to a notion of demos that would transcend its particular instantiation in the founding of the settler society. In other words, a radical politics must be able to contest a democratic regime in the name of democracy: to invoke the principle of equality in order to contest the exclusions of the demos's particular instantiation within a certain social order.[4] This, arguably, was precisely what the tent ambassadors sought to do in claiming a right (to sovereignty) that was not afforded to them by the liberal democratic order that they sought to contest. In Jacques Rancière's terms, it involved putting two worlds into one (2001: 21). On the one hand, they enacted their political equality by claiming to speak on behalf of a sovereign people. On the other hand, they demonstrated their social inequality as aliens in their own land. In this way, the tent ambassadors staged a dissensus by showing the world in which indigenous people are entitled to be addressed as a sovereign people and the world in which this sovereignty is in fact denied to be one and the same democracy that they share with their former colonisers.

Notes

1. Thanks to Keith Breen, Adrian Little and Moya Lloyd for their comments on an earlier draft of this chapter as well as to participants in workshops held in Melbourne and Florence in 2006.
2. I borrow this term from Bert van Roermund (2003) who uses it in a different but related context.

3. Indeed, this retrospective authorisation was arguably granted to the tent ambassadors by indigenous people. Despite the Minister for Aboriginal Affairs' claim that the 'campers' were unrepresentative militants, they were accorded full speaking and voting rights at a conference he convened of government-selected representatives of Aboriginal communities in October 1972. The conference passed a motion in support of the embassy, calling for it to be reinstated following its removal by police earlier that year.
4. In this regard, the recent work of Jacques Rancière (2004) is promising. See Schaap (forthcoming).

Judith Butler, Radical Democracy and Micro-politics[1]

Birgit Schippers

Introduction

If power, as Judith Butler argues, pervades the conceptual apparatus that constitutes us as subjects (see Butler 1992), determining 'what we are, what we can be' (2004a: 57), then this surely has implications for the way we live our everyday lives. This regulatory power that turns us into subjects also configures our political practices and the terrain where the struggle for hegemony takes place. How, though, does our political engagement connect with and transform daily social relations? Attempting to utilise Butler's ideas for such a political project proves to be an intriguing undertaking. Indeed, efforts aimed at constructing a politics which follows from Butler's influential interventions into the theory debates of the last two decades have occupied many commentators. Appropriating Butler for the project of radical democracy is an equally enthralling exercise, especially since she is not commonly associated with democratic theory or the exploration of democratic practices.[2] Her recent work, though, articulates an explicit interest in the project of radical democracy which is now beginning to be explored in the critical literature (see Lloyd 2007a; 2007b). This essay aims to contribute to this exploration, focusing on the implications of Butler's account of radical democracy for the terrain of micro-politics. With the term micro-politics, I refer to those political practices, beyond state and civil society, which engage everyday social relations for the purpose of social transformation.[3]

As I shall suggest in this chapter, the importance accorded to micro-political practices is central to Butler's account of radical democracy, articulated in her desire for 'a more radically restructured world' (2000c: 277). I consider this aspect to be a core element of Butler's account of politics which contributes to a potentially expansive understanding of the political and an enlarged realm of politics. It also situates Butler within the wider 'ethos' of radical democracy (Glynos 2003), with its emphasis on the transformation of relations of subordination, on the proliferation of sites of politics beyond the institutions of formal democracy and its focus on political practices beyond those of electoral politics. Butler's aspiration for the transformation[4] and rearticulation of everyday social relations, underpinned by her critique of state-centred politics, is informed by her Foucauldian-inflected analysis of the operation of the micro-physics of power,[5] and by the feminist concern with social transformation and the insistence on the political nature of the intimate sphere (see Pateman 1989; Phillips 1993). It follows that the terrain of daily social relations is neither pre- nor non-political; rather, it is where relations of power are lived, reproduced and challenged on a daily basis.

My interest in this chapter lies in exploring the possibilities for such a rearticulation and transformation of daily social relations. More specifically, I want to query how a micro-political radical democratic practice can be pursued through strategies of resignification. A critical examination of the practice of resignification, and its radical democratic potential, is thus of central concern to my discussion. To illustrate my argument, I shall explore two examples which figure prominently in Butler's work and which are said to stress the transformative character of micro-political practices: her discussion of linguistic resignification, and her work on transformative bodily practices.

Whilst my reading of Butler presented in this chapter is broadly sympathetic towards her ideas, several reservations remain. These relate, in the main, to the democratic promise of her version of radical democracy, and specifically to the democratic nature of the practice of resignification and to the democratic potential of the terrain of micro-politics as a site for political transformation. Through the examples discussed in this chapter I am hoping to highlight what I consider to be the radical nature of Butler's ideas on the one hand, and her shortcomings as a theorist of democracy, whether radical or otherwise. My second reservation builds upon Butler's critique of state-centred politics: I wish to contend that, despite intentions to the contrary, Butler's abandonment of the state as a possible terrain for political transformation results in a restriction, not an enlargement and expansion, of the possible sites for politics. I begin my discussion by locating Butler's focus on micro-politics within the debates on radical democracy; I then examine Butler's strategy of resignification, considering its relevance for a micro-political practice of radical democracy, followed by the exploration of two examples, language and the body. I conclude with some questions about Butler's status as a democrat, radical or otherwise.

Locating political transformation: micro-politics and/as radical democracy

As I indicated above, Butler's writings, which are probably best known for their focus on the performative constitution of gender, are not immediately associated with democracy, democratic theory or the project of radical democracy, and her references to democracy, radical or otherwise, are sparse and scattered (see Lloyd 2007a).[6] However, in her recent work she expresses an explicit interest in the project of radical democracy (see Butler 2004a), and she declares an intellectual and political affinity with the ideas of Laclau and Mouffe, including a commitment to a broad left political project (Butler 2000a: 11). Thus, despite the absence of a sustained discussion of democracy, it is, as I have already suggested, her adherence to a 'democratic ethos', and her consistent exploration of the possibilities for transformative politics, articulated throughout her writings and aimed in particular at subverting subjugating hegemonic norms, which foreground her understanding of democracy and provide the link to her more recent explicit interest in the project of radical democracy. Three elements, which I shall sketch in this section, are key to this project: her critique of state-centred politics, her endorsement of the politics of civil society and her insistence on the political nature of everyday social relations.

Throughout her work, Butler questions the efficacy and validity of those political projects, such as feminism or lesbi-gay politics, which seek recourse to the state in order to remedy existing injustices (see Lloyd 2005b).[7] Unlike other advocates of radical democracy, such as Laclau and Mouffe, Butler locates the terrain for transformative politics firmly outside the state, and she privileges subversive challenges associated with civil society and directed against the alleged subjugating institutions of the state. AIDS activism, such as kiss-ins and die-ins, as well as feminist campaigns and, more recently, peace activism against the 'war on terror' constitute such examples.[8] From a democratic perspective, this endorsement of associational politics is attractive and compelling, and it connects Butler's ideas with the wider project of radical democracy: the focus on civil society opens up new sites for political transformation, suggesting an expansive understanding of politics, above and beyond the state; the repertoire of associational political practices (see Young 2001) provides a strong participatory dimension, which exceeds the limited participatory possibilities of electoral politics; moreover, it facilitates the articulation of topics which may not normally pass through the filters of the formal institutions of representative democracy.[9]

As Passavant and Dean have argued (2001), Butler's pluralisation of the available sites of politics provides new and alternative opportunities for political practices, in particular those aimed at opposition and contestation. Her celebration of a seemingly enlarged realm of politics is indeed central to the project of radical democracy. Chantal Mouffe, for example, argues for such an enlarged understanding of the political, and for an extension of political practices beyond the state (1993: 20), whilst Ernesto Laclau advocates the expansion of the logic of equality from 'the public sphere of citizenship' (1999: 16) 'to increasingly wider spheres of social relations – social and economic equality, racial equality, gender equality, etc.' (2001: 4). Hence, democratic citizenship, including the contestatory and oppositional practices associated with dissident acts of citizenship (see Sparks 1997), are not confined to the realm of the state and the institutions of formal democracy; in fact, they even exceed those of civil society.

Building upon her assertion of the workings of regulatory power in everyday life, Butler opens the terrain of micro-politics as a further site for subversive practices. If, as I intimated above, the everyday is implicated in the operation of power which constitutes us as subjects, then it also provides the terrain in which 'everyday resistances' (see Disch 1999) come to pass. Butler suggests as much when she argues that 'social transformation occurs not merely by rallying mass numbers in favour of a cause, but precisely through the ways in which daily social relations are rearticulated, and new conceptual horizons opened up by anomalous or subversive practices' (2000a: 14); moreover, these micro-political transformative practices are firmly implicated in the struggle for hegemony. As Butler asserts:

> Distinct from a view that casts the operation of power in the political field exclusively in terms of discrete blocs which vie with one another for control of policy questions, hegemony emphasizes the ways in which power operates to form our everyday understanding of social relations, and to orchestrate the ways in which we consent to (and reproduce) those tacit and covert relations of power. Power is not stable or static, but is remade at various junctures within everyday life; it constitutes our tenuous sense of common sense. (2000a: 13–14)

Thus, building upon her claim that everyday life, including its most intimate aspects, such as sexuality, is formed by power and that we reproduce this power, Butler concludes that power should be challenged in its everyday manifestation.

There is clearly much value in Butler's emphasis on micro-political transformation, especially in her opening up of opportunities to challenge regulatory power and norms at the very level at which they operate. However, contrary to her intentions, Butler's problematic account of the state[10] undermines the prospects to expand the realm of politics. Her aspiration for social transformation beyond the realm of the state, in fact even in opposition to the state, constitutes a mere shift in terrain, away from the state and towards civil society and micro-politics. This *de facto* curtailment of the sites available for transformative political practices also limits the prospects for radical democratic politics, as these rely exclusively on the democratic potential of associational and micro-political practices.[11]

Yet, notwithstanding Butler's, admittedly problematic, account of the state, I want to take seriously her assertion of the democratic potential of the realm of micro-politics. Central to my analysis is the question of how her endorsement of micro-political transformation can be mapped upon the project of radical democracy. As I shall discuss in the next section, Butler proposes the deployment of resignification as a privileged mode of political transformation and as a crucial practice in her account of radical democracy.

'Dissonant tunes': resignification, transformation, democracy

Butler develops her notion of resignification in an intertextual space which borrows from Derrida and Derridean accounts, including the works of Laclau and Mouffe, but also from Paul Gilroy (1993) whose writings on the resignification of the terms of modernity figure prominently in Butler's ideas.[12] Central to her appropriation of Derrida is her assertion of the elasticity, malleability and openness of the signifiers of political discourse to contestation and resignification, and an insistence on the subversive citationality and iterability of these signifiers; it also entails the claim of the permanently deferred and futural dimension of democracy. From Gilroy she borrows the idea of the hybridity of ideas as well as the assertion of the instability and incompleteness of identity. This emphasis on the subversive iterability of signifiers, as I shall show throughout the remainder of this essay, is central to her understanding of radical democracy, and it accounts for the strongly linguistic dimension of Butler's politics. Yet, it is important to stress that the resignification of linguistic categories is essentially corporeal, a point already argued in *Gender Trouble*, where Butler demonstrates how a subversive body politics, for example via drag, challenges hegemonic, that is, heterosexist, gender norms governing femininity and masculinity.

Building upon the premise that signifiers are elastic, that they can be resignified, Butler avers that a speaker is never fully in control over his/her utterances. Hence, linguistic agency does not presuppose a form of controlling or original authorship over language (see Butler 1993: 219). In fact, the meaning of an utterance always exceeds the intentions of this 'post-sovereign' speaker, leading to a re-distribution of political agency towards the interpellated subject. In *Excitable Speech* (1997a), where Butler focuses on the question of how to deal with hate speech, she concludes that a speaker of injurious words is not the originator of this speech and thus not fully in control of the meaning of the words uttered; rather, the speaker is tied into an existing discourse. *Excitable Speech* is populated with examples which highlight the workings of injurious language, especially racist slurs uttered in everyday contexts, and which illustrate our vulnerability to hate speech. Yet, central to Butler's argument is the possibility that the speech of the addressee, the injured subject, may counteract hate speech through a resignification of the injurious term. 'Talking back' and the misappropriation of the injurious term constitute the principal elements of this strategy. By using the injurious term which constitutes the addressee and turning it around, resignifying it and giving it a new meaning, the injured subject can challenge the injurious interpellation he or she is subjected to.

This endorsement of resignification as a transformative political practice is a key aspect of Butler's political project in general, and of her understanding of radical democracy in particular. This aspect is further developed in her critique of Pierre Bourdieu, whom she faults for his claim that the power of language, including the power to subject, originates in the social power of the speaker. Butler contends that according to Bourdieu, the authority and social position of the speaker, including manner as much as substance, determine the efficacy of the speech act (see Bourdieu 2002: 109; see also McNay 2000: 59–61). She concludes that for Bourdieu, an absence of social power goes hand in hand with a lack of (linguistic) agency. Butler takes issue with this thesis, critiquing in particular Bourdieu's assertion that the social power of the speaker determines the efficacy of the speech act:

> [O]ne must understand language not as a static and closed system whose utterances are functionally secured in advance by the 'social position' to which they are mimetically related. The force and meaning of an utterance are not exclusively determined by prior contexts or 'positions'; an utterance may gain its force precisely by virtue of the break with context that it performs. (1997a: 145)

Against Bourdieu, who according to Butler forecloses options for political agency for marginal subjects (1997a: 156), she invokes instead the Derridean break with context: in her view, it is there that the possibility for a radical democratic transformation emerges, and where critical agency arises from the possibility of resignification and active misappropriation of subjugating signifiers.[13]

Butler's arguments are further developed in *Undoing Gender* (2004a), where she establishes an explicit link between resignification and a radical democratic practice. She contends that the contested nature of the meaning of the terms of political discourse should not preclude their deployment. Developing Gilroy's argument, that the political discourse of modernity, whilst intrinsically linked with the project of slavery, has nevertheless been taken up by those excluded from its terms, specifically by the slaves themselves, she envisages the prospects of 'a more radically democratic modernity' (Butler 2004a: 249; see also 223). Already in *Excitable Speech*, she engages this point, conceding that '[modernity's] basic terms are all tainted, and that to use such terms is to reinvoke the contexts of oppression in which they were previously used' (Butler 1997a: 160). This, however, should not preclude the use of these terms altogether, as it is precisely the assertion of (already existing) rights and entitlements prior to their authorisation which exemplify those acts that define radical democracy. As Butler contends:

> [S]uch terms are not property; they assume a life and a purpose for which they were never intended. They are not to be seen as merely tainted goods, too bound up with the history of oppression, but neither are they to be regarded as having a pure meaning that might be distilled from their various usages in political contexts. The task, it seems, is to compel the terms of modernity to embrace those they have traditionally excluded, and to know that such an embrace cannot be easy; it would wrack and unsettle the polity that makes such an embrace. This is not a simple assimilation and accommodation of what has been excluded into existing terms, but, rather, the admission of a sense of difference and futurity into modernity that establishes for that time an unknown future . . . (1997a: 161)

However, despite resignification's promise of inclusiveness and expansiveness, it remains an inherently ambiguous political practice. For one, resignification produces new realms of exclusion and marginality, a point illustrated in Butler's recent discussion of gay marriage (see 2004a). The struggle for the legalisation of gay marriage, according to Butler, seeks recognition in a context where marriage remains the hegemonic norm for relationships; as a form of regulating power, it may interpellate gays into a right and an institution from which they were previously excluded, but it also creates new realms of exclusion, as those unwilling to marry, or in relationships which do not qualify for marital recognition, fall outside the newly expanded norm of recognised relationships. (See Lloyd, this volume.)

It is therefore crucial to emphasise that for Butler, not any resignification will do. Besides, resignification is not unambiguously subversive or critical.[14] As I discussed earlier, resignification, according to Butler, works independently of the social position of the speaker, facilitating forms of transformative political agency arising from the margins. However, this ability to resignify is not restricted to those groups who seek to obtain inclusion into norms or gain access to rights or recognition. As Butler illustrates, appropriation can be used by a wide range of groups and movements, such as the Nazi appropriation of 'socialism' (and indeed democracy), or the various left-wing and right-wing appropriations of 'multiculturalism' and 'globalisation' (2004a: 223). It is thus important to recognise the ambiguity of the practice of resignification, and Butler concedes as much when she argues for a contextualisation of resignification: in order to qualify as a radically democratic practice, resignification must be expansive and inclusive, extending norms to those who are disenfranchised, and working towards a less violent future (2004a: 223–5).

Whilst Butler is acutely aware of the ambiguous effects which the practice of resignification may produce, I wish to suggest that her utilisation of subversive or expansive resignification as a radical democratic practice is equally ambiguous. On the one hand, it is fair to say that the potential implications of Butler's assertion, in particular their significance for the development of a radical political practice, are far-reaching. In a sense, anyone, anywhere can resignify and thus challenge and subvert. Thus, Butler's account of resignification contains a strong participatory dimension which also facilitates subversive political practices, especially for those marginal subjects lacking in social power. Besides, by severing the link between democratic politics and engagement in the formal institutions of the state, Butler shifts the site for political transformation onto new terrains. Yet at the same time, Butler gives little consideration to the egalitarian dimension of demo- cratic politics. Her emphasis on the openness of language to resig- nification, independent of the social position of the speaker, is highly ambiguous in the context of democratic practices, as it remains unspecified whose resignification and misappropriation counts. I shall return to some of these issues in the next section, where I consider how resignification, despite its ambiguity, may operate as a privileged practice of radical democracy in the context of micro-politics.

'Talking back': linguistic resignification and micro-politics

We have seen above that the practice of resignification suggests the deployment of terms in previously unauthorised contexts or by unauthorised speakers. According to Butler, this expansive use of resignification becomes inherently democratic because it opens up signifiers to challenge and contestation. Expansive resignification may manifest itself in a variety of forms; here I wish to focus on Butler's discussion of language, taking a closer look at the kind of linguistic resignification and its micro-political application that she envisages.

In a recent interview (2000d), Butler tells the story of a linguistic interpellation that she encounters whilst walking down a street. Asked by a child leaning out of a window whether she is a lesbian, she replies affirmatively, an affirmation which Butler interprets as a subversive appropriation of a potentially injurious linguistic interpel- lation (see also Lloyd 2007a: 121). As Butler concedes, we may not know the intentions of the speaker and thus cannot establish for certain whether an injury was intended or not. Nevertheless, the term 'lesbian' carries injurious connotations within a heterosexual hege- mony: it disputes its bearer's legibility and indeed intelligibility within a hegemonic heterosexual gender order which requires women to accede to heteronormative forms of femininity; it associates women with masculinity and thus with the wrong gender, an abject and potentially punishable state of being.

The example demonstrates how gender norms govern our daily lives; in fact, it could be argued that it is in the realm of daily rela- tions where gender is at its most pervasive, where we produce, repro- duce and, possibly, contest the existing gender order. With her affirmation, acceptance and misappropriation of the potentially hurtful term, Butler challenges this potential injury, exemplifying the subversive and transformative possibilities of such daily encounters; her 'talking back' is not contingent upon state-based politics, and it displays an agency without prior authorisation. Moreover, as Alison Stone suggests, it is not confined to individualistic acts, but, rather, depends upon the possibility of collective subversion (2004: 15). Subversive resignification, like the utterance of injurious language, cannot be understood outside an historical and social context which puts the speaker in a linguistic chain with other speakers engaged in the same communicative setting. So, to return to the example, neither the kid leaning out of the window nor Butler authored the term 'lesbian' or its potential meanings, be they injurious or transformative, but they both put themselves, although possibly differently, into a wider collective of language users. Butler's anecdote connects with wider feminist discussions about gender norms, specifically with the use of the category 'woman' within feminist discourses. Because 'woman' is a category in language, it is open to contest and to the strategies of resignification which I discussed in the previous section.[15] It is crucial to emphasise this, as Butler does not advocate the abolition of gender categories. Rather, she insists on the necessity to 'call into question, and, perhaps most importantly, to open up a term . . . to a reusage or redeployment that previously has not been authorized' (Butler 1992: 15), as it is there that democratic possibilities emerge. As she suggests, the term 'woman' does not describe a pre-existing constituency; rather, 'that constituency is perpetually renegotiated and rearticulated in relation to other signifiers in that field' (Butler 1993: 195). I return to this discussion in the next section, where I explore the link between a resignification of gender norms and its implications for a radical body politics. At this point, I shall explore whether there are any limitations to contestation, resignification and misappropriation.

Here I wish to draw on two further examples of linguistic resignification which Butler presents and which, in my view, illustrate the limits of the strategy of resignification. In *Bodies that Matter*, she refers to the resignification of the term 'queer'. Having overcome its homophobic connotations, the term is now appropriated by the gay community where it is used as a form of self-description (Butler 1993: 223), possibly even as an acceptable term used by heterosexuals to refer to homosexuals (see also Lloyd 2007a: 121). This suggests that the strategy of resignification has provided gays with the ability to engage in positive forms of name-calling, but also with the ability to 'talk back' and to counter a previously injurious term, through appropriation and repetition, giving it a different, non-injurious connotation (Butler 1997a: 163).

And yet, attempts at appropriating injurious language in ethnic vernacular, especially the 'misappropriation' of terms of racial abuse by Black rap artists,[16] indicate the limitations of the strategy of resignification (see also Lloyd 2007a: 122–3). Are there parallels to the appropriation of the term 'queer' by the gay community, where injurious words, through appropriation, repetition and resignification, can lose their injurious connotations and provide the injured subject with agency? Butler seems to suggest otherwise, and she claims that some terms may be too injurious to qualify for resignification (1993: 223–4; 2000d: 759): they are not generally accepted, even as a form of self-description or mimetical parody, within ethnic minority communities. Thus, linguistic resignification may work in some instances, but only partially, or not at all, in others. Crucially, as bell hooks has pointed out, the terminology and visual representation of violence and sex in some forms of rap, specifically gangsta rap, is a reflection of the prevailing values created by a hegemonic, that is, white supremacist culture which comprises a profit-driven, capitalist economy as much as the state (1994: 116). This insight, in my view, suggests the need for a more careful reflection on the interrelationship between the different sites of politics than can be found in Butler's writings. Besides, while Butler, rightly in my view, emphasises the possibilities for resignification which opens up channels for 'insurrectionary speech' (1997a: 163), it should be stressed that the resignification and misappropriation of a previously injurious term may sit alongside the continuation of injury, subordination and abjection. For example, the successful resignification of the term 'queer' does not prevent continued homophobia, and thus continued injury. Indeed, there may, after all, be some value in Bourdieu's emphasis on social power: it is, in fact, the context-bound nature of the use of these terms which may determine the injurious quality.

Notwithstanding the subversive or transformative quality of resignification, why should it be considered democratic? As Butler suggests, democracy should be defined via the contestation and renegotiation of linguistic categories (1993: 221). Arguing for the need to 'learn how to live the contingency of the political signifier in a culture of democratic contestation' (1993: 222), Butler affirms the connection between the critique and contestation of linguistic categories and the practice of democracy:

Paradoxically, the failure of [political] signifiers . . . fully to describe the constituency they name is precisely what constitutes these signifiers as sites of phantasmatic investment and discursive rearticulation. It is what opens the signifier to new meanings and new possibilities for political resignification. It is this open-ended and performative function of the signifier that seems to me to be crucial to a radical democratic notion of futurity. (1993: 191)

Clearly, there is much to be gained from a radical resignificatory challenge to subjugating norms: as I suggested above, by stressing resignification's potential to 'talk back' and 'misappropriate' injurious language, it provides those subjected to such language with forms of critical agency which can be exercised outside the terrain of the formal institutions of democracy. Thus, resignification challenges and contests linguistic norms in an everyday setting, opening up a new terrain for transformative struggles and participatory democratic practices. And yet, as I already intimated, Butler's focus on resignification fails to consider the egalitarian dimension of resignification, of whose misappropriation counts. Besides, the privileging of critique and contestation, which is implicitly contained in resignification's radical challenge to subjugating norms, is not sufficiently connected to the egalitarian dimension of democratic politics; in fact, Butler's implicit assumption of challenge and contestation as inherently radical democratic practices fails to interrogate their egalitarian credentials. As I shall argue in the next section, this democratic deficit, which sits alongside her radical challenge of subjugating norms, is also symptomatic of Butler's discussion of body politics.

Towards a radical democratic body politics?

As we have seen in the previous section, linguistic norms, according to Butler, constitute us as subjects, and they act and impact upon bodies. To claim that she privileges forms of linguisticism, at the expense of non-linguistic political practices (see Mills 2003: 261), thus misses the point, as for her, linguistic agency, including linguistic resignification, does not operate exclusively linguistically. As Alison Stone argues, 'linguistic norms concerning gender organize and constrain our corporeal life – which means, moreover, that the resignification of gender norms invariably occurs corporeally. Each act of re-using a normative term . . . is a *bodily* enactment of the norm (Butler 1999: xxv), so that all redefinition takes place corporeally' (Stone 2004: 12, emphasis in original). What interests me in this final

84

section is this: how can corporeal resignification challenge and transform those (linguistic) norms? What is the role of the body in radical democracy? Can we formulate a radical democratic body politics? And how does it operate on a micro-political terrain?

That the question of the body has vexed much of feminist theorising is well-known. Building upon the critique of the somatophobia of Western philosophy (see Spelman 1982), recent feminist scholarship has highlighted in particular the absence of a sustained discussion of the role of the body in relation to democratic citizenship practices. Beasley and Bacchi, for example, argue for the need to make the literature on citizenship and the literature on the body speak to each other (2000). Bodies, they contend, should not be conceived instrumentally or strategically, as embodied agency goes beyond demands for bodily autonomy, such as reproductive or sexual freedom. Rather, they contend that we always already act embodied, and that the body generates and configures our citizenship practices. Focusing on the role of the body in the process of democratic deliberation, Diana Coole criticises political studies, and specifically democratic theory, for its lack of a sustained discussion of the body (2007). Rectifying this gap in contemporary theorising, Coole stresses the central role of the body in processes of democratic deliberation, and she explores various strategies aimed at making deliberation more inclusive and more accessible to those 'space invaders' (see Puwar 2004), in the main sexed bodies which fall outside the norm of embodiment in democratic institutions dominated by male bodies. Coole argues that 'studies of democratic processes need to pay attention to the corporeal levels in which communicative interaction praised in democratic encounters occur' (2007: 430). This is clearly an overdue theoretical and political project, but the focus of my concern lies elsewhere: rather than exploring the, admittedly important, role of embodiment for democratic deliberation, I am interested in pursuing the prospects for what Coole refers to as 'somatic agency', that is, the prospects for a corporeal agency which takes the body as a central category in the pursuit of transformation and radical democratic politics.[17] Examples of embodied practices in non-institutional contexts abound: from the chaining to railway tracks of the suffragettes to the uses of hunger strikes in anti-colonial struggles, from the kiss-ins and die-ins associated with AIDS campaigns to, more controversially, suicide bombers. When, however, do these practices qualify as radical democratic?

As is well known, embodied politics constitute a leitmotif of Butler's work. Her body politics is probably most famous for her discussion of drag, which, she asserts, disrupts and undermines the heterosexist gender binary and may generate a proliferation of genders beyond the male/female binary. Arguing that gender is a form of drag, an assertion which emphasises the constituted nature of (gendered) identities and which refutes any naturalising or primordial assumptions, Butler stresses that gender norms are central to the functioning of a hegemonic heterosexual regime and, in turn, performatively reinforce this regime whilst marginalising and abjecting those who do not conform to these hegemonic gender standards. Neither femininity nor masculinity, nor the bodies styled in accordance with hegemonic norms of femininity and masculinity display an 'inner truth of gender'. Underlying this claim is her famous assertion that gender is an imitation without origin, and that it is drag which reveals the imitative structure of gender; it follows that 'the gendered body . . . has no ontological status apart from the various acts which constitute its reality' (Butler 1990: 136).

Given Butler's caution with respect to the subversive deployment of drag, what other options exist? In *Bodies that Matter* and elsewhere, Butler locates the subversive possibilities of body performances, such as die-ins and kiss-ins, firmly on the terrain of civil society. These bodily practices, according to Butler, constitute forms of resignified body acts against a hegemonic heterosexual regime which associates marginalised homosexuality with death and abjection. Like Beasley and Bacchi, Butler recognises the importance of claims to bodily autonomy and integrity, as it is on the basis of these claims that demands for reproductive and sexual freedom, for surgical body projects, for protection from violence and so on can be made. However, her main concern, especially in her recent work, lies elsewhere. It is guided by the aspiration for a 'normative reorientation for politics' (Butler 2004c: 28) which is premised on the assertion of a primary bodily vulnerability of humans. How, though, can this claim be developed in the direction of radical democratic politics? In other words: what kinds of bodily acts advance the project of radical democracy?

An examination of Butler's discussion of norms may help to illuminate this question. Throughout her work, Butler insists on the normative configuration of human life, in fact, on the way norms make (intelligible) human life possible in the first place. Norms, according to Butler, configure human life and they disguise the naturalising discourses which operate in the service of subjugating hegemonic projects. Already in *Gender Trouble*, she contends that

norms function violently, specifically the norms of compulsory heterosexuality which posit which genders are considered intelligible,
and which become abject (see also Chambers 2007a). This claim is
further fleshed out in her recent work, where she explores the workings of normative violence in the context of two developments: the
emergence of a 'New Gender Politics', a loose coalition of sexual
minorities, transsex and intersex movements, as well as feminist and
queer perspectives (2004a), and the political fall-out of US foreign
policy in the wake of 9/11 (2004c). She asserts that the regulatory
function of normative violence is enacted corporeally, making
bodies vulnerable to physical forms of violence. Butler avers that
this susceptibility towards corporeal vulnerability is a fundamental
aspect of human life, given the body's public exposure to others; crucially, though, she contends that the vulnerability to physical violence is grounded in 'normative human morphologies' (2004c: 33)
which mark out those bodies who do not comply with normative
notions of human embodiment. Thus, Butler concludes that vulnerability to violence, as indeed the public recognition for one's subjection to violence, is unevenly distributed, structured along sexed and
racial lines: some bodies, specifically those which fall outside regulatory norms of human embodiment, are more prone towards corporeal vulnerability than others (2004c).

This assertion of the operation of normative violence figures
prominently in *Undoing Gender*, where Butler demonstrates the
workings of normative violence against those 'gender outlaws'
(Bornstein 1994) who do not embody gender norms in compliance
with the hegemonic gender order. Her account of the normative violence which regulates bodies, and which makes those 'incoherently
gendered' susceptible to further violence, is very moving, and it illustrates starkly how the very conception of the human is tied into bodily
compliance with hegemonic norms.[18] Importantly, though, she contends that the failure to comply with bodily norms, as indeed the
exposure and vulnerability to violence, provides opportunities for
corporeal resignification which challenge the norms and the violence
exercised in their name. Here I wish to reiterate a point I made above:
that Butler does not envisage an abolition of the norms that do violence; rather, she suggests a 'departure from the norm' (2004a: 53),
as it is there that a radical challenge to the hegemonic regime of
gender regulation can be found, leading to the expansion and extension of norms. Butler thus suggests that we need to develop 'a new
legitimating lexicon for the gender complexity that we have been

living for a long time' (2004a: 31), as it is via a critical embodiment of the norm, or even an embodied opposition to the norm, that the conceptual apparatus of gender regulation is contested, becoming more expansive and more inclusive.

The transsexual and intersexual movements pose this kind of challenge to hegemonic gender norms and to the naturalising discourses which foreground our assumptions about binary and natural gender. Like drag, they expose the artificial and performative way in which coherently gendered bodies are constituted. Trans practices in particular suggest forms of bodily opposition which radically question norms about gender (Butler 2004a: 217; see also 52). As Butler argues:

> The embodied relation to the norm exercises a transformative potential. To posit possibilities beyond the norm or, indeed, a different future for the norm itself, is part of the work of fantasy when we understand fantasy as taking the body as a point of departure for an articulation that is not always constrained by the body as it is. (2004a: 28)

The embodied challenge to those dominant gender norms which rely on naturalistic accounts of bodies contributes to an expansive understanding of gender beyond the male/female binary, developing a 'new conceptual horizon' (Butler 2000a: 14) in our gender discourses. In this respect, both the transsex and the intersex movements engage in transformative body projects: in the first case, through a radical disruption of the sex/gender analogy, by severing the link between body morphology and gender identity, and in the second case, by questioning the overall framework of binary gender.[19] It would be misleading to suggest that either drag or transgender practices, or any other bodily practices for that matter, serve as a paradigm for radical politics. Rather, they illustrate how norms, according to Butler, can be embodied in ways which challenge hegemonic gender regimes.

Before I conclude, I wish briefly to attend to a further aspect which figures prominently in Butler's recent work: the role of an ethics of non-violence (see 2004c).[20] Above, I demonstrated how Butler posits the susceptibility to corporeal vulnerability as a formative feature of human life. As I intimated there, this corporeal vulnerability, according to Butler, provides the opportunity for a resignificatory body politics which contests and expands norms regulating and governing bodies. It also, as suggested by Butler, constitutes the basis for the development of ethical relationships with others, based upon the recognition of a shared corporeal vulnerability as a shared feature of human life. Arising out of this shared corporeal vulnerability, Butler envisages the building and development of communities and coalitions, especially on the international stage, leading to the development of 'more radically egalitarian international ties' (2004c: 40). These ties, according to Butler, can build upon the new gender politics, but they must also consider those whose racial morphology, in the current climate of the 'war on terror', lies outside the realm of the normatively human. This focus on the development of community and coalitional politics, grounded in shared bodily experience, constitutes an important development in Butler's work which goes beyond her previous emphasis on the exploration of gendered bodily practices and which grounds transformative body politics in an ethics of vulnerability. It also adds to her discussion of radical democracy, furnishing it with an enriched sense of citizenship which, in turn, could be utilised to address some of the deficiencies regarding the egalitarian nature of her work.

In conclusion, as I argued throughout this essay, Butler's persistent critique of the operation of regulatory power, and her contestation of the exclusionary workings of the norms which govern human life, constitute an important contribution to any radical political project. Moreover, by opening the terrain of micro-politics as a site for political transformation, Butler generates important opportunities for a wide array of political practices. Whilst I remain broadly sympathetic towards her ideas, my reservations concerning the democratic promise of her work remain. Her claim that expansive resignification is an inherently democratic practice is not fully convincing. For one thing, it pays little attention to the numerical dimension of democratic politics.[21] Moreover, by shifting the terrain for political transformation away from the state, and towards civil society and micro-politics, Butler does not just curtail the sites for transformative politics. She also leaves herself open to the vicissitudes of associational and micro-politics, and their potential disregard for the egalitarian dimension of democratic politics. This problem could be addressed by engaging the state more carefully, specifically by invoking the state's capacity to redress forms of subordination which operate in the realm of daily social relations. Taking into account this last reservation, I contend that Butler's account of a transformative micro-politics constitutes an important pillar of any radical practice which seeks to extend and enlarge the terrain for political transformation.

Notes

1. I wish to thank the participants of the 'Radical Democracy' workshop at the Second Manchester Workshops in Political Theory for their helpful comments on an earlier version of this paper.
2. See for example, Nancy Fraser's claim (1995b: 163) that Butler's commitment to democracy is an empty rhetorical gesture, not conceptually developed.
3. For a Deleuzian account of a radical democratic micro-politics see Widder (2004; 2005).
4. On the link between transformation and radical democracy see also Mouffe (2000: 52–3).
5. This power, as she argues, operates both socially and psychically. See Butler (1997b).
6. However, early explicit references to radical democracy, and to the writings of Laclau and Mouffe, can be found in *Bodies that Matter* (1993) and in the essay 'Contingent Foundations' (1992). Moreover, already in *Gender Trouble* (1990) she explores the possibilities for democratic politics.
7. *Excitable Speech* (1997a) is emblematic for this concern. The representative of this kind of state-centred feminism who is at the receiving end of much of Butler's critique is the feminist legal scholar Catharine A. MacKinnon.
8. See, for example, Butler (1993; 2004c). See also Michael P. Brown (1997) for an account of AIDS activism as a radical democratic practice.
9. The ecological movement in Germany provides a good example of the way ideas, demands and practices articulated in civil society become established in the wider political arena. The subsequent establishment of green issues and their institutionalisation in the Green party also illustrates the interwoven character of state and civil society, an aspect of associational politics which receives little attention in Butler's writings.
10. For a critique of Butler's treatment of the state see, for example, Passavant and Dean (2001) and Lloyd (2005b).
11. It is also in contrast to Laclau's and Mouffe's emphasis on the undecidability of the terrain for political transformation, and to their caution with respect to the potentially oppressive dimension of non-state politics, specifically in civil society. See Laclau and Mouffe (1985: 176, 180).
12. For recent assessments of Butler's notion of resignification see, for example, Jenkins (2001), Lloyd (2007a; 2007b), Mills (2000) and Smith (2001).
13. I shall return briefly to Butler's assessment of Bourdieu in the next section, where I shall argue for a more considered appropriation of Bourdieu's critical insight into the discussion of resignification.

14. Butler does not instigate, as Mills suggests, an '*a priori* designation of resignification as an insurrectionary strategy' (2003: 254; emphasis in original). For a critique similar to that of Mills see also Fraser (1995a: 67–8).
15. In the same interview, Butler refers to being asked whether she is a woman, a question she answers affirmatively (2000d: 743).
16. The rap artists NWA ('Niggaz with Attitude') have been embroiled in much controversy, over their choice of name as much as over the sexually explicit use of language in their lyrics. For an analysis similar to Butler's see also Bhabha's suggestion that the seemingly degrading and injurious self-description might be a form of subversive mimicking of the colonial master (Bhabha 1992).
17. I do not wish to imply here that corporeal agency or embodied politics should or can replace linguistic exchange, whether in the form of deliberation or in a more agonistic shape. Rather, I am interested in an aspect of democratic political agency which tends to be neglected in much of the critical literature.
18. For her discussion of the racialised operation of body norms, specifically in the context of the 'war on terror', see her *Precarious Life* (2004c).
19. Besides, they also call into question those feminist discourses which fail to critically interrogate the coherence of the category 'woman'.
20. To explore this aspect in detail would lead me beyond the scope of this essay.
21. I am not suggesting that democracy equals majority rule, but it deserves some consideration in the assessment of the democratic nature of Butler's account.

5

Post-structuralism, Civil Society and Radical Democracy

James Martin

What is the space of a radical democratic politics? Does 'civil society' constitute the domain most appropriate to radical democrats' concerns? In this chapter, I consider the value of the notion of civil society for conceptualising radical democracy from a post-structuralist perspective. Whilst in recent years a number of political theorists have seized upon civil society as a realm of relative freedom, pluralism and self-organisation ideally suited to reviving and deepening democratic politics, this chapter sounds a more sceptical note. Against the idealisation of civil society as an almost ready-made 'public sphere' in which citizens deliberate independently of power relations, I draw upon Ernesto Laclau's notion of 'dislocation' to underline the intrinsic contingency, unevenness and power-infused character of civil relations. Post-structuralism's concerns, I continue, are primarily with the limits of social identity and the impossibility of fully constituting 'society' as a stable order. Whilst contemporary ideas of and practices in civil society certainly capture some of this contingency, nevertheless it remains a complex and 'undecidable' domain, the site of efforts to hegemonise the field of dislocated identities.

A post-structuralist-inspired, radical democratic perspective on civil society, I argue, needs to take into account the linkage between social identities and the experience of dislocation. This is not simply to note the empirical particularity of civic associations and the limited nature of their demands, out of which forging some collective purpose might be practically difficult. Rather, emphasising dislocation raises the point that *any* constituted public sphere is necessarily incomplete and partially exclusive, an unstable and temporary 'spatialisation' that cannot succeed in constituting 'the public' as a unified entity. By expanding on this spatial orientation, I defend the view that civil society's value for radical democracy lies not in its capacity fully to represent the democratic community but the extent – often variable and restricted – to which it reminds us of the *impossibility* of such a representation. This argument gives a novel accent to the reception of the radical democratic possibilities of civil society as a domain of political intervention, one which seeks not to embed politics in that realm but which persistently works through its limits and unevenness, facing up to the conflictual potential therein. Civil society must remain a vital source for radical politics as the location for the promotion of a democratic ethics. But it cannot secure this ethics without exposing its own, necessary, limits. In keeping with this view, I end by underlining the significance for radical democracy of Étienne Balibar's notion of a 'politics of civility', that is, a politics directed at broadening the horizons of civil discourse whilst minimising the violence generated as social identities inevitably clash and conflict.

Civil society, democracy and the public sphere

For many on the left today, 'civil society' invokes the potential for a revived 'public sphere', a space that is relatively independent of instrumental economic or political interests in which multiple, collective aspirations can be freely deliberated and formed into a powerful resource for influencing political decisions (see Baker 2002; Cohen and Rogers 1995; Barber 1984). Whilst outside the formal apparatus of the state proper, the civil domain purportedly possesses distinctive qualities that (if suitably reorganised) permit a genuinely democratic order to emerge alongside the formal, administrative institutions of politics. Consisting of independent, self-organised groups and associations, clubs and voluntary organisations, civil society represents a sphere of semi-public activity uniquely suited to the free flow of ethical values based on authentic participation and intimacy between individuals. In short, because civil society mediates the division between public and private it has the potential to democratically conjoin ethics and politics in an age when the two seem increasingly divided.

The 'civil society argument', as it has come to be called, emerged as a powerful response to the shortcomings of traditional socialist, 'communitarian' and reformulated liberal conceptions of political community (see Walzer 1992). Put briefly, conceptualising politics through the frame of civil society emphasises value-pluralism as opposed to a uniform conception of the Good. Civil society's manifest diversity, relative informality and unregulated character give rise to the possibility of a non-oppressive sphere of social interaction inside which opinion can be freely exchanged, criticised and revised (see Young 2000: 157–67). The kind of public that emerges from this realm is one that cannot be reduced to 'interests' for aggregation or to a homogenous identity since such identities are fluid, multiple and overlapping. In such a domain, a variety of social differences can be expressed and mobilised to influence the whole but none can proclaim itself the superior perspective without violating the constitutive principles of civil society itself (see Keane 1998).

It is easy to see why civil society – understood generally as the non-institutionalised networks of associative activity outside the state – is welcomed by many radical democrats as the site of a new 'post-liberal' democratic politics: here 'difference' need not be limited to those of rational individual preferences but, rather, expands to include a diverse range of issues and identities which may express alternative forms of rationality. Equally, forms of community and association that do not fit with dominant models of 'national', religious or economic interest group identification can be envisaged as equal and legitimate agents in the self-constitution of the public. Having renounced class struggle as the exclusive route to total social transformation, radical democrats sometimes look to new social movements and other such self-organised groups to spearhead a revival of active citizens in a participatory politics. Instead of focusing politics narrowly on the state or within the institutions of economic production alone – sites that were often presupposed to symbolise the ultimate *unity* of social and political identity – civil society purportedly embraces the ongoing self-construction of democracy and the diversity of identities and struggles within it. Indeed, the sites of economic production and political administration are ultimately *depoliticising* institutions since they work to a hierarchical logic in which instrumental calculation, fixed goals and outcomes are dominant (Young 2000: 157–9). Civil society, on the contrary, invites an expansion of the political and the displacement of instrumental reason by notions of active participation and deliberation.

Of course, few radical democrats think that presently constituted civil societies can, in and of themselves, bring out about the kind of pluralism and participation that is suggested here. Too often, civil relations are dominated by institutional orders that limit and disperse whatever critical power exists within them. State bureaucracies, capitalist markets, illiberal cultures, economic interests and so forth often function to close down the democratic potential of civil space. Democratic theories of civil society, then, often qualify their idealisation of that sphere with an appeal to some kind of normative framework that, if sufficiently established, would enable the critical aspects of civil society to thrive and to dislodge the institutional orders and logics that presently subdue them.

One such argument emerged in the 1990s from the stable of 'critical theory' and took Habermas's 'communicative' model of rationality as its basis. As is well-known, Habermas has long been concerned to elaborate a normative political theory of the 'public sphere'. Since the 1980s he has developed an ethics of 'discursive will-formation' that he believes can ground rational-critical dialogue. Discourse ethics are procedural rules of argumentation that assist the production of an uncoerced 'rational consensus' on moral norms (see Habermas 1990: 57–76). 'The goal', he argues, is to 'erect a democratic dam against the encroachment of system imperatives on areas of the life world' (Habermas 1996: 444). This requires maintaining a functional separation of state and society and the institutionalisation of a 'political public sphere' in the 'life world' that is autonomous from the organisation of political and economic power. That way, rational discourse is not confined to any particular organisational space but is open to a diversity of practices of public debate. Habermas openly admits that this argument converges with those concerning the revitalisation of civil society as an arena of democratic self-organisation (see Habermas 1996: 452–7).

In their mammoth, jointly authored *Civil Society and Political Theory* (1992), Jean Cohen and Andrew Arato argue explicitly that discourse ethics 'translate' to a theory of political institutions that centre around the practices of civil society (1992: xvii). For them, discourse ethics contain quite clear, if general, political implications. The imperative to engage in open dialogue over matters of common concern in itself implies a notion of 'democratic legitimacy' and 'basic rights'. To assert that agreement on common moral norms must be based on uncoerced agreement between all those affected by a decision, that good reasons must be mobilised to defend a position, is simultaneously to promote a distinctive 'political ethics'. Discourse ethics reconstructs the procedural conditions for democratically justifying legal prescriptions. Thus law and morality are redefined as separate but mutually supportive conditions. What counts as 'private' (and therefore outside the realm of public discussion) and what can be included in the public realm is a matter for democratic debate.

Thus discourse ethics dictate some 'minimum conditions' for organising political institutions in the form of procedures of democratic validation and basic rights (Cohen and Arato: 389–410). The kind of rights they have in mind are not 'bourgeois' rights to property but civil rights to enable democratic legitimacy. These rights support a 'symmetric reciprocity' amongst different kinds of subjects with a variety of different types of demands. They help institute public spaces through which legitimacy can be generated (Cohen and Arato: 400–1). The concept of civil society best suited to these arrangements is therefore one that differentiates the civil sphere of democratic dialogue from functional spheres such as the economy and state and is itself differentiated into private and public spaces. The public sphere of civil society can be continually replenished by the associations, groups, clubs and movements etc. of the 'life world' whose private, particularistic claims are protected by law and are open to discussion as the potential basis of public policy. The public sphere – comprising numerous different kinds of dialogue and debate – can then organise opinion into a form of 'influence' over the political system (see Habermas 1996: ch. 8, esp. 359–87).

In a more recent discussion, however, Darrow Schecter (2000) rejects Cohen and Arato's 'functionalist' argument because, he claims, it assumes that civil society can rest harmoniously alongside other institutions such as economic or state apparatuses, without radically altering them (Schecter 2000: 81). By contrast, he proposes civil society as the basis for a renewed public sphere that can radically transform society by opening up other institutional orders to political contestation. Drawing on the work of Hannah Arendt, Schecter counter-poses the open-ended, non-hierarchical character of civil society's public sphere to the sovereign, hierarchical order of the state. Only the former, he argues, can adequately stage 'political action' in the sense of 'self-disclosure which takes place in a space of political visibility, the outcome of which can never be predicted, and whose course can take many different, unforeseeable turns depending on how others in that space act' (Schecter 2000: 99). Schecter's vision builds on Arendt's 'classical' notion of the political as a distinct space of collective self-determination. Whilst state and parliamentary politics reduce the degree to which the political can assert itself, civil society represents a public sphere 'for the voice and visibility of incommensurably different ways of "standing" in the modern world' (Schecter 2000: 106). Moreover, this sphere needs to be enlarged to prevent civil society remaining narrowly focused on established interests or entrenched 'identity politics'.

Schecter's emphasis on plurality and the incommensurability of different perspectives bring a refreshing sense of the unpredictable and unstable nature of politics to the idea of the public sphere that Cohen and Arato's theory lacks. Indeed, his effort to define civil society in terms of political relations rather than formalised moral deliberations is by far an advance. However, his notion of the public sphere retains a number of significant shortcomings that he shares with the other radical democratic proponents of civil society; in particular, the idea that the political domain engendered by civil society can constitute a realm of human action free from power and antagonism (see Schecter 2000: 50–1). But this is still to idealise the democratic moment of the political and to play down the extent to which antagonism and conflict structure that realm. Whilst Schecter avoids the fetishisation of consensus common to Habermasian accounts of communicative rationality, his view of civil society as a site of democratic politics follows a common tendency on the left to spirit away the moment of antagonism as if it were marginal to the experience of the public sphere. As a consequence, the political is imagined as an arena purified of dangerous and destabilising tendencies. Its parameters are foreclosed (hence they employ such metaphors as 'democratic dam' or the 'space of appearances') and remain, if not outside the political contest itself, then at a safe distance from its disruptive effects. Indeed, in both these approaches, the politics of civil society comes pre-spatialised, conceived either as the 'immanent' boundaries of 'deliberative discourse' or as transparent 'performances' on a public stage immunised from conflict and division.

This tendency to treat public action as 'immune' from conflict and danger has been noted in other contexts by thinkers such as Roberto Esposito (2006) and Jean-Luc Nancy (1991). Communal bonds, they argue, are often misconstrued as positive properties internal to subjects that, if properly acknowledged, are somehow expected to render those subjects relatively impervious to external threats. Likewise, civil society has been understood as effecting a certain kind of closed space, a loose kind of self-renewing community. But perhaps this is not surprising. The civil condition is indeed a spatial conception, one figured around the *proximity* (physical and symbolic) of subjects to each other. To talk of 'civil relations' or to engage in 'civil discourse' is to invoke reciprocal responsibilities drawn from a distinctive sense of proximity, one that differs from the 'thick' intimacy of the familial relations, where what we share with others are not the close bonds of blood but common laws and customs (see, for example, Oakeshott 1975).

Yet, as both Esposito and Nancy claim, rather than premised on a positive essence, community extends originally from a shared openness of Being, a common exposure to the world and hence to the vulnerability of existence. For Esposito, the *munus* of *communitas* first signified a shared debt or loss, not a sense of belonging (see Esposito 2006: xiii–xv). This perspective offers a notion of commonality disclosed precisely through the *absence* of essential properties, firm borders or protection from conflict. How, then, can such a common exposure be imagined in relation to civil society if not through a sense of an enclosed space?

Below I set out an alternative, post-structuralist-inspired approach to conceptualising civil society that draws on Laclau's idea of dislocation. In this approach, the exposed, spatially open character of social identity underlines the political constitution of public space, that is, its dependence upon hegemonic practices that delineate frontiers around which civil relations are only ever temporarily settled.

Post-structuralism, dislocation and civil society

Post-structuralism is a complex and diverse strand of theoretical positions, none of which necessarily aligns unproblematically with the other (see Williams 2005). But central to its various proponents' claims are the following: an understanding of human identity as a fundamentally unstable construct, produced through the interaction of various material and cultural forces which displace the idea of an autonomous, rational and self-willed subjectivity; the absence of some 'ultimate' foundation, centre or 'essence' to social reality – Divine, rational or otherwise – accessible and open to universal agreement; and an analytical and normative openness to the failure of human reason to grasp the world without some remainder or 'excess'. As Michael Dillon puts it, post-structuralists underscore the awkward persistence of what he calls a 'radical non-relationality' – that is, a destabilising excess of meaning in all identity – whose intractable nature 'continuously prevents the full realization or final closure of relationality, and thus the misfire that continuously precipitates new life and new meaning' (Dillon 2000: 5).

It is this radical, anti-essentialist orientation to social and political practices and its focus on the contingency (or incalculability) of structural logics that gives a critical vitality to post-structuralist theories. This opens them to a sense of politics not as a process of bargaining between preconstituted agents but as the constitution and transgression of certain kinds of *limits* to identity itself (see Williams 2005: ch. 1; Connolly 1991). Furthermore, it elicits a theoretical approach with a distinctively spatial mode of reasoning; that is, an awareness of the disorderly and marginal as intrinsically implicated in any sense of social or intellectual field. As Marcus Doel argues, 'poststructuralism is always already spatial' (Doel 1999: 10). But this is not a sense of space as the static horizon of temporal unfolding but space as it is penetrated by time, constantly disrupting fixity, as the currents of a river perpetually dislodge the sedimented ground beneath it. Thus post-structuralists typically understand space as an 'event', a radical and passing creation, rather than a static background, and place as a process, a 'becoming', rather than a fixed co-ordinate. The spatiality of post-structuralism is therefore one of 'perverse duplicity', a reading of the self-same as itself different. Stability and order are produced through difference, an otherness that lies within order itself but which distorts it (Doel 1999: 34).

Different thinkers underscore different moments in this combined sense of 'space-time' (see May and Thrift 2001). Here, however, I want to concentrate on one theory in this post-structuralist mould. In his *New Reflections on the Revolution of Our Time*, Ernesto Laclau (1990) draws attention to the centrality of 'dislocation' in the formation of social and political identity. For Laclau, all identities are dislocated insofar as they can never be fully constituted or 'self-identical' spaces of subjectivity. Rather, they are discursively constructed through relations of difference that never tally positively with positions in 'objective' social structures. For instance, workers do not passively fulfil their structural function as employees but agitate for better conditions, a situation that is not strictly given within production relations. Indeed such structures themselves are 'radically undecidable' in Laclau's view, for they never exhibit the autonomous, determining power that some (often Marxists) attribute to them. Structural roles are always *relatively* structuring – or contingent – because their effect is never one of total determination. Relations of production co-exist alongside other structures such as those of political authority, kinship, religion, etc. with which they overlap and, often, clash. In this situation, there is no 'pure' structural principle that neatly organises all social relations. Instead, subjects are formed as agents through the *failure* of structures to fully determine their identities. Thus it is because workers cannot work if in poor health or paid at subsistence level that they identify with the trade union and the socialist movement. Here workers' political identities do not emerge purely by virtue of their structural position but, rather, because their position is dislocated by experiences outside the wage relation.

This is what is meant by the 'discursive' construction of identity: the perpetual reinscription of the experience of structural failure into a language of potential fulfilment. According to Laclau, it is through specific discourses that dislocated subjects make identifications with principles, persons, ways of life, etc. that often make sense of the experience of dislocation by identifying its 'cause', namely a blocking force that supposedly, once removed, will return the subject to its 'proper' identity. Yet dislocation is constitutive of the subject: it is what blocks identity that gives rise to the subject in the first place. Nevertheless, these contingent origins of identity – its dependence on whatever blocks it to furnish it with distinguishing characteristics – are typically obscured by emancipatory discourses, invoking as they often do the promise of social harmony, consensus and the achievement of self-identity (see Laclau 1996a).

What is the significance of Laclau's discussion of dislocation for our understanding of civil society? In short, the concept of dislocation gives a novel complexion to the idea of civil society as a space of freedom and social self-organisation. There are two approaches to civil society to be elaborated here. First, the idea of civil society as an accumulation of various, dispersed dislocatory experiences and second, civil society as an undecidable terrain upon which there occurs a struggle to hegemonise these experiences.

Civil society, dislocation and undecidability

Laclau's argument concerning dislocation has remarkable parallels with the way civil society is commonly conceived, that is, as a domain of relative freedom in which subjects avoid being fully defined by formal institutional structures and strive to carve out their own projects. However, unlike most discourses on civil society, the idea of dislocation brings to the fore the 'perverse duplicity' – the simultaneous spatial order and disorder – and hence irreducibly political character of this experience.

Let us consider Laclau's remarks further. He goes on to underline three mutually related 'dimensions' of dislocation: 'temporality'; 'possibility'; and 'freedom' (see Laclau 1990: 41–5). These, as we shall see, are directly relevant to aspects of civil society. Dislocation, he begins, is the form of temporality as opposed to fixed spatiality.

That is, dislocation constitutes an experience of change, difference as opposed to sameness, movement rather than stasis. Indeed, the sense of overcoming fixity, hierarchy and tradition are primary experiences of political and cultural modernity and central aspects of civil societies as they emerged from feudal orders. As Lefort argues: 'Modern, democratic society seems . . . like a society in which power, law and knowledge are exposed to a radical indetermination, a society that has become the theatre of an uncontrollable adventure . . . This society is *historical* society *par excellence*' (Lefort 1986: 305, emphasis in original). Modern, western society forms around an accumulation of dislocations – political, intellectual, economic – that are widely experienced as a dynamic, temporal movement relegating established identities to the past. Sometimes this is an exhilarating experience, but it is also a profoundly disorienting one. Western civil societies, insofar as they bear the imprint of temporality, replace the hierarchical, 'natural' reciprocities of kinship and Cosmos with those more fleeting, egalitarian connections of commercial exchange, social contract and, later, democracy (see Berman 1983; Tester 1992).

Equally, Laclau continues, dislocation 'is the very form of possibility'. The absence of a structural point of reference is what permits identities to be formed in the first place: 'the dislocated structure thus opens possibilities of multiple and indeterminate rearticulations for those freed from its coercive force and who are consequently outside it' (1990: 42–3). Of course, Laclau adds, not all possibilities can be enacted at once. Different types of identification occur within the context of *relative* structuration. Thus the promise of liberal civil society is often that of finding multiple opportunities to be and do differently. Precisely because civil societies are relatively unstructured, they offer up a sense of possibility that the structured realms of family, work or state do not allow. Indeed, it is this externality to structured practices and institutions that, to varying degrees, permits *those other structures* to be conceived as contingent, artificial, potentially accountable and open to redesign. For Keith Tester, it is this sense of indeterminacy creating the conditions for the 'ceaseless reflexivity' and sense of 'moral symmetry' between subjects that is commonly expressed in modern civil societies (see Tester 1992: 44, 35).

Finally, Laclau relates dislocation to 'freedom' in the sense of partial self-determination. That is, the failure of a structure to fully determine social identity is what produces subjects able to make identifications. This kind of freedom stems not from certain positive features of the human essence (e.g. its intrinsic ability to rationally calculate utility) but instead flows from the radical absence of such an essence: 'freedom exists because society does not achieve constitution as a structural objective order' (Laclau 1990: 44). Paradoxically, then, subjects are 'condemned to be free' insofar as they are compelled to identify, to insert themselves within discursive formations that furnish them with a stable identity. As Laclau points out elsewhere, the mutual link between dislocation and freedom makes the experience of freedom somewhat ambiguous: 'Freedom is both liberating and enslaving, exhilarating and traumatic, enabling and destructive' (Laclau 1996a: 19). For Nikolas Rose, this precarious sense of freedom in modern societies is simultaneously the experience of 'being left without a clear source of guidance, left to one's own motivation and choice' (Rose 1999: 66). As a result, 'individuals are forced into a profound inwardness, and cling for comfort to a belief in their own uniqueness, in the process elaborating a complex inner world of self' (Rose 1999: 66). In contrast to the common depiction of civil society as a settled realm of relatively ordered differences in which subjects pursue their own freely chosen projects, this image of freedom (through dislocation) suggests a more unstable and potentially disruptive scenario. Associative life, we might say, is born from the often traumatic threats to identity brought by modernity and not from an intrinsic 'sociality'.

Laclau's three dimensions of dislocation underscore the wider, ontological claim he is keen to make, namely that we cannot comprehend political events in terms of a 'positive' or preconstituted conception of the social. That is, events do not represent the expression of some independent societal essence (such as economic laws, human sociality or Divine purpose). Social and political identities emerge through a radically creative process of mutual dislocation that throws up new possibilities for the articulation of identity through discursive struggles. These possibilities cannot be contained within a schema that settles in advance the relations between the identities, be it a 'rationally' agreed 'normative consensus' *à la* Habermas or even a theory of material 'interests'. Such approaches, as I have indicated, already 'spatialise' dislocations, that is, they *relocate* them as internal moments *within* a (potentially) stable, rational order immanent to them (Laclau 1990: 42). In this respect, they close down politics to movements within preconceived parameters. For Laclau, however, dislocation marks the constitutive indeterminacy of social identities as such, that is, the disruption (but not eradication) of all structured space by temporality.

Whilst Laclau's conception overlaps with some common images of civil society, it also departs from them significantly. Rather than the expression of a structural principle such as economic exchange or human sociability – that is, fully intelligible within a purely spatialised logic, discernible in advance – we might more usefully understand civil society as a site of multiple, dispersed social dislocations. Civil societies are therefore characterised in part by the presence of subjects 'freed' from structural relations that fail fully to absorb them – but which nevertheless remain bound up with those structures – whilst at the same time being compelled to reconstitute their failing identities through social practices that restore the promise of order. Depending on which dislocations are most felt and what resources social groups have available to them, civil societies have formed in various, diverse ways. It is no surprise, then, to find that the historical emergence of national civil societies has rarely conformed to the 'bourgeois' model of the western liberal imagination (see Hann and Dunn 1996).

Thus we find in civil societies diversely stratified organisations of class, race, gender, nationality, religion and so forth (e.g. working men's clubs, women's institutes, religious organisations and charities, etc.), each a specific instance of the diverse ways dislocation is experienced and responded to. This complex mixture of relative structuration and indeterminacy makes civil society an 'undecidable' terrain. That is, its intrinsic diversity and partial structuration make contingent the possible kinds of relation amongst the various spaces of civil society and between these and the (economic, political, cultural) structures against which they define themselves.

Hegemonising civil society

A common, liberal image of civil society is of self-limiting, voluntaristic activities: all containable within the rule of the parliamentary state. Indeed, liberal political thought has made a virtue of the idea of a well-ordered civil society built upon a society of individuals of moral character, tolerant and independent. However, when conceived as a site of multiple, dispersed dislocations, civil society seems less the spontaneous and benign order of self-limiting subjects and more a fragmented, uneven field of overlapping and mutually limiting social identities. This dispersed terrain of dislocated subjects achieves degrees of order not 'spontaneously' but through the mobilisation of competing discourses that supply subjects with a temporary means of identification. This is precisely the situation that Laclau and Mouffe, adapting Gramsci, call 'hegemony' (Laclau and Mouffe 1985). That is, the ongoing efforts to unify a field of particular, differentiated identities through their representation by what Laclau terms a 'mythical space' (Laclau 1990: 61–7). This mythical space functions as a global representation of the totality of differentiated identities, articulating them around a vision of future fulfilment.

The historical emergence and development of civil societies, then, is both a history of the liberation of social groups from hierarchical and prescriptive identities *and* simultaneously a history of efforts to contain and regulate freedom, making it compatible with certain 'universal' visions of order, and the struggles this regulation then produces. Various discursive representations and practices of 'civility' have been deployed in liberal societies aimed at hegemonising emergent dislocations to maintain their orderly dispersal. As Foucault and later sociologists of 'governmentality' have shown, liberal conceptions and practices of freedom are often highly regulated and disciplinarian, not in order to advance a totally ordered society but so as to cultivate subjects capable of 'self'-regulation at a distance from immediate control (see Barry et al. 1996; Foucault 2007; Rose 1999). According to Rose, liberal freedom was 'inextricably linked to a norm of civility' through social reforms and forms of state intervention in housing, schools, health and education, public streets and gardens and so forth, in the service of what he calls 'a well-regulated liberty' (Rose 1999: 69, 73). The spaces of the modern city, for example, were designed with this desire for orderly freedom in mind (see Joyce 2003). Thus it is precisely because dislocated subjects do *not* spontaneously choose to identify with liberal values nor limit themselves to exclusively particularistic ends that such subjects must be disciplined in order to be free.

The notion of civil society as a mythical spatialisation in the context of multiple dislocation also gives us a rather different perspective on the character of the groups and organisations that make up its contemporary content. Social movements, leisure clubs, churches, neighbourhood groups, voluntary organisations and so forth rarely exhibit purely self-regarding and limited intentions. Rather, they are often organised around images of social fulfilment that expand beyond their own immediate particularity. They mobilise intensely held fantasies of social order invested with a profound, libidinal energy that project contrasting visions of civil life. Even if understood as 'self-limiting', insofar as they organise around specified experiences and goals, they are equally *other-limiting*, too.

Environmentalist groups, church organisations, charities or sporting associations typically present themselves through discourses that react to dislocation by identifying 'enemies' (corporate businesses, homophobia, meat-eaters, foreigners, men, alcohol, Muslims, racism, pop music and so on) as the cause of their dislocation. Such groups provide localised sites of identification for subjects to invest their energies and order their identities. To preconceive these varied demands as contained, or containable, within an already unified civil space is rather to miss the way they are constituted through dislocations that open them to new, potentially subversive, sometimes even violent, efforts to redefine the boundaries of social space.

My suggestion here, then, is that we think of the domain of civil society as one that is intrinsically uneven, limited, contingently articulated around certain dominant discourses that cannot possibly embrace all the dislocations of modern social orders. Rather than being a transparent domain in which certain subjects interact in a spontaneously ordered way, civil society involves an ongoing spatialisation of identities, selectively and temporarily articulating its different components, centring some, excluding and marginalising others. To follow Gramsci, civil society is the site of 'hegemony', a series of dislocated spaces subject to ordering projects of civility. We must, therefore, seek out not only the positive characteristics that structure its dominant relations (e.g. its class structures) but also its limits, its excesses (often pushed to its margins), the dislocations and structural failures that are the conditions of existence of the myths that structure the civil domain (see Laclau 1990: 38).

Democracy and conflict: towards a politics of civility

The discussion above lays the basis for a post-structuralist reading of the significance of civil society for radical democratic theory. Indeed, it suggests an alternative understanding of radical democracy to that promoted by the proponents of civil society noted earlier. Instead of seeking to relocate democracy in a distinctive domain of its own, a civil or communitarian space immunised from conflict, Laclau's concept of dislocation implies an awareness of the limits of spatial containment, the impossibility of fully domesticating difference within a domain that, on our reading, constantly exceeds itself. Such a view supports what Sheldon Wolin once called a 'fugitive' conception of democracy, that is, what he defined as a 'mode of being' rather than a form of government, one open to the transgression of established boundaries, and not a self-regulating, internally ordered domain (see Wolin 1994b).

In this respect, the notion of radical democracy suggested below is not a 'model' of democratic life, an institutional architecture that maps out the external boundaries and internal procedures of democratic decision-making. Arguably, post-structuralism is not much use for political theorising of that variety. Instead, its value lies in its attention to the constitutively incomplete character of democratic identity, the inevitable partiality and contingency of social identity even as it engages demands for universality. From this perspective, a radical democratic project should avoid seeking to root democracy in idealised social relations or purely spontaneous struggles (see Day 2005) and, instead, develop a spatially aware politics sensitive to the possibilities for contest typically displaced to the margins of social life (see Newman 2007: esp. ch. 5). This involves a two-way manoeuvre of engaging the conflictual nature of democracy, drawing such conflicts back into the democratic game (however constituted), but also minimising the violence that such conflict might entail. In this latter respect, a post-structuralist approach to radical democracy supports a version of what, rather tellingly, Balibar calls a 'politics of civility', an effort to bring the margins back into public life by extending civil discourse to those who live beyond its frontiers.

The politicisation of conflict

The view of civil society sketched above tallies to some extent with a suspicion held by some democratic theorists that the civil domain has limited capacity for expanding democratic life. As Warren (2001) indicates, not all civil groups and associations relate to democracy in the same way. The late Iris Marion Young (2000), too, made a strong case for the importance of civil society in promoting forms of self-determination, but not of what she refers to as 'self-development'. Certainly, she argues, the relatively indeterminate nature of civil society permits associations of various kinds to articulate new experiences and generate forms of social solidarity and resistance against domination and oppression. In so doing, aspects of civil society can contribute to the formation of a democratic public sphere to hold states to account and raise the critical concerns of citizenry (Young 2000: 164–80).

However, Young continues, the fragmentation and plurality of civil society work against the promotion of public goods that permit the self-development of citizens. Such goods include material resources like food, shelter, health care and a supportive legal framework that promotes rights. States, rather than civil society, are much better suited to this kind of activity, and radical democrats who promote social justice cannot do without the superior forms of organisation and control that states provide (Young 2000: 180–8). Rather than look exclusively to civil society, argues Young, radical democrats need to envisage a 'balance' between state and civil society in which the strategic organisation and resourcefulness of the one can be 'coupled' with 'the flexibility and critical accountability' of the other (Young 2000: 187; see also Fraser 1997).

Young's sense of civil society's limits, however, is itself limited to concerns about the co-ordination of resources in the cultivation of democratic life. She alerts us to a creative tension between civil society and the state, but fails to note the constitutive tensions *within* civil society; tensions that, very often, direct themselves towards the state. As a domain of relatively dislocated subjects seeking places of identification, civil society is an uneven, conflictual and potentially violent realm as much as it is a realm of co-existing differences and civic activity. It is this potential for both associative and *dis-associative* activity that Chantal Mouffe explores in her work on democracy (see Mouffe 1993, 2000, esp. 131). For Mouffe, contemporary democratic theory has a persistent tendency to invoke models of democratic community in which differences are fundamentally harmonised, with conflict reduced to uncontentious matters of interpretation within a wider context of consensus. Such a view – expressed both in Rawlsian liberalism and, more recently, in 'deliberative' theories of democracy (see Dryzek 2002) – evacuates the political dimension of its conflictuality. That is, it tries to remove the ever-present possibility of antagonism and conflict from political debate. Instead, pluralism is conceived as a situation in which differences co-exist without antagonism. Rationally agreed procedures within a formal assembly or a public sphere are often presented in these arguments as the guarantee of a peaceful, inclusive democratic order free from power relations that might distort it.

Mouffe's critique of consensus politics is echoed powerfully by Jacques Rancière who argues that democracy has lost its original, Greek connotation with disagreement and the staging of grievances: 'Democracy is neither compromise between interests nor the formation of a common will. Its kind of dialogue is that of a divided community' (Rancière 1995: 103. See also Rancière 1999). For democracy to function, he argues, we must set aside the search for consensus and agreed parameters to allow existing spaces of agreement to be challenged from the outside. In this respect, the political community can be opened up to its own intrinsic heterogeneity and instability by endorsing principles such as disagreement (for Rancière) or dis-association (for Mouffe). For both Mouffe and Rancière, it is conflict rather than consensus that defines the political character of a democratic ethos. Without conflict, division, antagonism and so on – markers of difference and otherness – democracy loses its function as a practice of regulating difference and collapses into an oppressive homogeneity. This is a direction both authors perceive in contemporary trends in modern politics concerned with shaping public opinion and creating 'partnerships' throughout society so as to administer to a consensual population (see Rancière 2006). A radical democratic politics, on the other hand, one informed by a sense of the spatially uneven nature of civil relations, must suspend the idea of community as an ethical consensus and, in Rancière's words, 'repoliticize conflict' (Rancière 1995: 106).

Although they differ in emphasis, both Mouffe and Rancière share a sense of the spatial unevenness of democratic life, that is, its basis in what we have seen Laclau describe as the experience of dislocation. By smoothing over differential effects of dislocation by appealing to consensus, mainstream liberal democratic theory often narrows down citizenship to those who already agree its parameters. In underscoring the presence of disagreement and conflict, Mouffe and Rancière promote a democratic ethos which constantly looks to the margins of the public realm. Like Laclau, or Nancy and Esposito, they recognise the impossibility of spatial closure, or immunisation, of the democratic community from difference. Democracy, in their accounts, is a condition generated not from the protective enclosure of agreement but, rather, from the very possibilities of conflict brought by our common exposure.

Towards a politics of civility

At first glance, the exhortation to repoliticise conflict may sound like an invitation for chaos. But neither Mouffe nor Rancière wishes to promote widespread disorder. Rather, they seek to reconstitute democratic life as an engagement with alterity, rather than the fetishisation of sameness. And in this respect, post-structuralism might be said to have its own kind of unifying civil project, one that also traverses the boundaries between public and private life, but not to eliminate difference so much as to cultivate its ethical potential. Far from suggesting a desire for violence, their views overlap with the notion of a 'politics of civility' developed by Étienne Balibar (see Balibar 2002, 2004). By politics of civility, Balibar understands various efforts to regulate the violence brought by the disruptions to identity increasingly met in contemporary society. 'Civility' is not conceived here as a rigid codification of a social ethics, nor indeed as the eradication of all violence, but, rather, as strategies designed to make space for political engagement without the violent antagonisms that sometimes ensue from a desire for consensus (2002: 21–35). For Balibar, whose concerns of late have been with the democratic potential of an enlarged European Union, this involves engaging, for example, the 'radically excluded', such as immigrants whose lack of full 'national' citizenship condemns them to a marginal status in European states (see Balibar 2004).

Like Mouffe, Balibar accepts the ever-present possibility of violence in modern democracies, a violence caused not simply by malice but by the contradiction of defining a national community with 'universal' pretensions but exclusive parameters (Balibar 2004: ch. 7). In this sense, inclusion and exclusion, statehood and violence are intrinsically related. Balibar also accepts the need to suspend the idea of a singular community as the natural space of citizenship, raising the possibility of a 'citizenship without community', that is, a sense of belonging that exceeds settled borders of national communities. A politics of civility, then, is not simply a matter of extending legal status to excluded groups, but of democratising citizenship, transforming the political community in the process by a 'permanent reopening' of its own borders (Balibar 2004: 77).

As with Mouffe and Rancière, Balibar defends an idea of politics where the limits are placed at the centre of concern (what he calls 'the politics of politics'): the violence of clashing identities, the exclusions of institutional forms of citizenship, the racisms mobilised inside and outside the state; these all return us to a view of a democratic politics with various degrees of conflict at its core. The objective is not to imagine ways of reconciling difference but, instead, to promote an ethos that seeks the elimination of violent antagonisms so that alternative, more inclusive, encounters between conflicting identities may arise. Mouffe even calls this a 'conflictual consensus', an agonistic politics of 'adversaries' rather than outright antagonists (Mouffe 2000: 103). Democratic theory, she suggests, should attend not to the location of a privileged space of communication but to the infusion of various social practices (be they in the state or throughout civil society) with a 'grammar' or 'language of civil intercourse' that commits associations, civic organisations and so forth to democratic values (see Mouffe 1993: 65–73; 2000: ch. 3).

However we phrase it, a post-structuralist-inspired radical democratic ethos clearly refuses the idealisation of civil society as a site of moral consensus in which power and antagonism are eradicated. This applies also to the emerging concept of a 'global civil society', where ethical norms have been imagined outside the restrictive politics of – increasingly beleaguered – nation-states (see Baker and Chandler 2006; Keane 2003). Whatever potential for democratic criticism exists among independent networks and associations, either nationally or globally, civil society should not be the privileged space of the political community, for no such space can be fully delineated. On the contrary, the relative indeterminacy of civil relations is a crucial source for disrupting the closure of community around anything but temporary frontiers. As such, civil society may function not as the foundation of a political community but, instead, as one condition of its ultimate groundlessness.

Conclusion

Radical democrats will no doubt continue to focus their attention on social and political movements across the general domain termed civil society. For it is predominantly there that opportunities arise to question power and to imagine alternative ways of living and being. Yet, as I have tried to demonstrate, from a post-structuralist theoretical perspective, this domain is itself part of a hegemonic politics through which struggles for power are conducted. Civil society therefore can never be a neutral space of freely interacting subjects – the purified moral 'core' of a democratic community. Whilst the realm of civil association is undoubtedly the site of myriad forms of democratic activity, cultural experimentation and innovation, it is undoubtedly true that civil societies have been, and remain, highly variable in the degree to which they foster democratic values. Through Laclau's work I have argued that the reason for this ambiguous situation lies in the contradictory condition of dislocation which gives rise to a pervasive undecidability to the civil domain. As the site of both a range of experiences of freedom *and* projects for order, contemporary civil societies are, undoubtedly, crucial to radical democratic aims insofar as they exhibit a relative indeterminacy that permits a range of differences to co-exist; and yet they also limit and constrain civil association, giving rise to potential and real explosions of violence.

It would be wrong, then, to privilege civil society as the proper space of a radical democratic politics, if by 'privilege' we mean locating an autonomous democratic community uncontaminated by power struggles. Fantasies of committed citizens, action groups and people's assemblies deliberating their concerns in an environment of mutual respect and recognition often overstate the potential for solidarity, free communication and participation in civil society. Such activities can certainly form a vital part of any deepening of democracy, but we should avoid regarding these as transparent, power-free domains. Radical democracy, as post-structuralists define it, enjoins us to regard civil society – global or national – as a site for contestation and subversion of democratic values as much as their promotion. But it is precisely this potential for conflict and contest, I have claimed, that supplies the resource for a repoliticisation of difference and a politics of civility aimed at extending democratic encounters between those at the centre of democratic life and those pushed to its margins.

6

Hegemony and Globalist Strategy

Mark Wenman

Globalisation is an essentially contested concept which seeks to capture the contemporary shift in scale of social and economic processes, from the local and the national to the inter-continental and the planetary. The onset of globalisation has clear implications for conventional accounts of democracy, and this has been at the forefront of debates in political theory over the past decade. There is widespread recognition that globalisation undermines the capacity of national governments to exercise sovereign authority over their territory, especially in the developing world where newly emergent states have established their formal independence from former colonial powers. To the extent that national governments are understood in conventional democratic theory to be the legitimate representatives of the people, globalisation undermines democracy. Political theorists of different persuasions have re-examined the theory and practice of democracy under conditions of globalisation. Most prominent in this respect has been the emergence of liberal theories of cosmopolitanism and of 'global civil society'.[1] This paper seeks to make modest steps towards the development of a theory of 'radical democracy' appropriate to the era of globalisation.

The term 'radical democracy' can be used in a broad sense to refer to a range of contemporary thinkers associated with post-structuralism and left politics, including Ernesto Laclau, Chantal Mouffe, Judith Butler and William Connolly.[2] These theorists share important points of commonality – an emphasis on the primacy of the political, on the contingency of identity formation, and on the agonistic nature of democratic politics – that sets them apart from other contemporary approaches such as analytical liberalism and deliberative democracy. However, in this chapter I use 'radical democracy' to refer specifically to the work of Laclau and Mouffe. Their understanding of radical democratic politics was first fully elaborated in their co-authored *Hegemony and Socialist Strategy* (subtitled 'Towards a Radical Democratic Politics'). Because of the overwhelming success of this book Laclau and Mouffe's work is often treated as a single coherent 'project'.[3] Nevertheless, I have argued elsewhere that there are important differences that distinguish their respective understandings of radical democracy in domestic politics (Wenman 2003). Here we see that these differences are confirmed when we consider the possibility of radical democracy in world politics.

Hegemony and Socialist Strategy was originally published in 1985, before the collapse of Soviet Communism and the emergence of globalisation. To Mouffe's credit, she has subsequently explored the implications of the onset of globalisation for her particular conception of radical democracy (Mouffe 2005a: ch. 5). Mouffe's account of world politics rejects cosmopolitanism and emphasises the need for the renewal of democracy at the level of the nation-state. By way of contrast, Laclau has made no attempt to engage in a systematic way with the emergence and the challenges of globalisation.[4] Nevertheless, in this chapter I consider what global politics looks like when viewed from a Laclauian perspective: I extract a globalist strategy from Laclau's theory of hegemony, and I argue that his theory of radical democracy (*qua* necessary but impossible universalism) points in the direction of a militant form of cosmopolitanism. Although it is clear that Laclau himself has not explored this possibility, I argue that this militant cosmopolitanism is a crucial strategy for radical democrats in the era of globalisation and, in contrast to Mouffe, I maintain that this is a necessary supplement to the struggle for the renewal of democracy in domestic politics.[5]

In the first section I give an outline of four principal elements of globalisation. These are increasing interconnectedness, the emergence of global issues, the new modalities of power associated particularly with economic globalisation, and the new trans-national actors and forms of political protest that have emerged to counter economic globalisation. Following this, I give an overview of Laclau's understanding of radical democracy. I explain the emergence of his thought out of the Marxist tradition and consider his relationship to the work of Antonio Gramsci, and I argue that Laclau's innovation is best understood in terms of his persistent attempt to provide a non-topographical conception of the political. For Laclau, all social topographies – base/superstructure, state/civil-society, domestic/international politics – are precarious discursive constructions and cannot be treated *a priori* as the foundation or 'ground' of social and political relations. This creates the theoretical space for an understanding of social relations in terms of the primacy of the political, and of radical democracy in terms of the universalising effects that materialise from hegemonic practices understood as a distinct modality of political power. Curiously, however, I show that the nation-state remains the *implicit* locus of the political in Laclau's work, whereas what is needed today is an understanding of how to bring about universalising (or cosmopolitan) effects on a global scale.

In section three, I consider Michael Hardt and Antonio Negri's account of globalisation in their celebrated book *Empire* (2001). Hardt and Negri work within an entirely different paradigm from Laclau, and he has rightly criticised them for the inadequacy of their account of the political and for their reduction of strategic thought and practice to metaphysics (Laclau 2003; 2005b: 239, 244). The point here is not to establish some kind of synthesis of Hardt, Negri and Laclau, which would be neither possible nor desirable. However, there can be no doubt that their book offers a compelling description of the principal elements of globalisation, and identifies in stark relief the radical shift in power that this implies: away from national executives to the operations of large corporations and their representatives in organisations such as the World Bank and the IMF. Their work is introduced here to better express the challenges that radical democrats face in the era of globalisation, before I sketch the outline of a possible response.

In the final section, I first consider Gramsci's and Mouffe's reflections on the most effective sites and the appropriate scale of political mobilisation. They both emphasise the primary importance of building counter-hegemonic struggles at the national and the regional level, and Mouffe denies the very possibility of effective democratic politics at the global level. I reject this claim and insist on the importance of an effective globalist (or cosmopolitan) strategy in the struggle for radical democracy in the era of globalisation. This will take many different forms and include struggles in many different sites of power. Here, I single out the importance of the hegemonic struggle for the construction of a cosmopolitan consciousness in the terrain of global media politics, through the effective mobilisation of images of a 'common humanity' and a 'global solidarity' understood as (empty) signifiers of the necessary (but impossible) object humanity-as-a-whole. This is a vital strategic complement to the struggle for radical democracy in domestic politics.

Globalisation

According to some commentators the processes of globalisation are wildly exaggerated, others think there is nothing new about globalisation, while most agree that the late twentieth century saw the emergence of a series of transformations best captured by this term.[6] For some the onset of globalisation is an inherently progressive phenomenon ushering in conditions for new cosmopolitan forms of governance, while most perceive the uneven effects of globalisation to be at best ambiguous and at worst highly problematic, especially for those living in the global south. Here, I single out four salient aspects of globalisation, which point to the demise of the 'sovereign' nation-state as the exclusive – or perhaps even the principal – site of politics. Globalisation is often presented as a set of social and economic processes that have greatly accelerated the experience of 'interconnectedness'. Driven by technological developments in the communications industry (the internet and the commercial use of satellites), globalisation has drastically reduced the mediating effects of physical distance, as individuals and groups from diverse cultural backgrounds and from far-flung parts of the globe are brought together in media-projected broadcasts of daily events in 'real time'. Every day I am potentially drawn into the fray of a whole series of issues, as graphic images of physically distant events – such as 9/11, the Asian Tsunami and the conflict in the West Bank and Iraq – are beamed into my living room virtually instantaneously. It is no longer sufficient to assume that political public spheres and political opinion are formed principally within the locus of the nation-state. Contemporary citizens from different states and distinct national traditions are now immediately caught up in each other's circumstances, and any viable theoretical engagement with democratic politics must account for this changed context. The experience of intensified interconnectedness has engendered a growing public consciousness of a series of issues that can only be conceived as global, both in terms of the extent of their consequences and the effort that will be required to do something about them: most notably climate change and global poverty and inequality. By their very nature these issues point towards the inadequacies of the Westphalian image of the independent nation-state: as rising sea levels, catastrophic storms and the unequal flows of economic goods and opportunities pay scant attention to the 'sovereign' democratic authority of national governments and their capacity to determine the outcome of events and processes within their own territory, especially in the developing world.

The demise of the democratic 'sovereignty' of the nation-state is particularly accentuated by the processes of economic globalisation and the hegemonic consolidation of neo-liberalism across the globe. This is a highly complex development which I explore in more detail below. For now it will suffice to say that economic globalisation is manifest particularly in the escalating volume and velocity of the movement of capital across state borders (as a consequence of information technology and moves towards flexible exchange rates since the collapse of the Bretton Woods system in 1971), the increasing tendency of producers to relocate their operations to the developing world (where costs are low and where workers' rights are not adequately protected) and the growing power of large corporations and their representatives in the World Bank, the IMF and other powerful institutions. Together, these developments point not only to the transfer of power away from the people's 'representatives' in national parliaments and towards unelected capitalist elites, but also to the emergence of new forms of power, where power is characterised principally by its mobility and by the increasing multiplicity of its tactical agility and its effects.[7]

These developments in turn have given rise to the emergence of new political movements that not only seek to draw attention to global issues and to challenge the new forms of power and disciplinary control associated with globalisation, but who also make use of information and communications technology to operate above and beyond state borders. The growing importance of trans-national political actors can be seen in the continued prominence of conventional NGOs such as Oxfam, Amnesty International and Greenpeace; the widespread popularity of campaigns such as Make Poverty History; but more importantly – for theorists of radical democracy – in the insurgency of new militant forms of politics associated with the 'alternative globalisation' and the 'anti-capitalist' movements, with summit protests against the World Bank and the G8 in Seattle, Genoa and elsewhere, and with the politics of the World Social Forum.[8] The purpose of this chapter is to try to make sense of these developments, and to sketch a theory of militant globalist politics using concepts and categories taken from Laclau. In the following section I reconstruct the principal components of his theory of radical democracy, and show how this provides the necessary framework for a theory of militant cosmopolitanism, even though Laclau himself has not pursued this idea.

Radical democracy

The basic components of Laclau's theory were first elaborated fully in *Hegemony and Socialist Strategy*, and his subsequent work has refined but not fundamentally altered these central elements.[9] As I have said, this was published in 1985 at the height of the second Cold War and before the collapse of the Berlin Wall and the subsequent emergence of globalisation. However, in order to understand the impetus behind Laclau's theory we need to look further back to the events of the late 1960s (for example, the anti-war protests in North America and the student uprising in Paris in May 1968) and to the emergence of the New Social Movements, based around issues of the environment, second wave feminism, civil rights campaigns, student politics, and so on. This proliferation of political struggles created insurmountable difficulties for conventional Marxist accounts of militant politics, and especially for the pivotal notion of the ontologically privileged agency of the industrial working class understood as the historically defined subject of progressive social change. Indeed, Laclau's post-Marxist theory of radical democracy has been generated through a creative confluence of Marxism (in particular the work of Gramsci) with Derridean deconstruction and Lacanian psychoanalysis. Laclau turned to these theoretical traditions in order to rid Marxist theory of the 'last remnants of class essentialism'. One could pursue many different routes into Laclau's work; however the direction I take here focuses on his persistent critique of what he calls the misguided attempt to develop 'a general theory of politics on the basis of topographic categories' (Laclau and Mouffe 2001: 180). In this section, I identify the key components of Laclau's non-topographical conception of the political. This theory is radical both in terms of its ontology (where no political interests, identities or topographical categories are given a privileged status) and its conception of the political: where the notion of radical democracy is figured in terms of the universalising effects that materialise from the successful articulation of hegemony.

The primary topography that governs conventional Marxist thinking about politics – from Marx to Louis Althusser – is the base/superstructure distinction. In the 1859 Preface to the *Contribution to the Critique of Political Economy* Marx famously argued that:

> the sum total of the . . . relations of production constitutes the economic structure of society – the real foundation, on which rises a legal and political superstructure and to which correspond definite forms of social

consciousness. The mode of production of material life determines the social, political and intellectual life processes in general. (Marx 1983: 159–60)

This passage exhibits the economism that beats at the heart of Marxist theory, and that finds its most sophisticated elaboration in Althusser's notion of the economy as determinant only in the 'last instance' of a complex dialectic in which all social and cultural relations are 'overdetermined' (Althusser 1977: 111, 113). Gramsci's great innovation – *vis-à-vis* the highly deterministic accounts of the primary topography characteristic of the Marxism of the Second International – was to reassert an element of voluntarism into this model of the social. Taking his inspiration from Lenin and the success of the revolution in St Petersburg in October 1917, Gramsci emphasised that Marxism is a philosophy of action or praxis, and he pointed to the reciprocal relationship between the infrastructure and the superstructures, the latter being understood as the realm where – as Marx said – 'men become conscious of their history and fight it out' (1988: 197). Gramsci emphasised the need for the working class to strategically enlist the support of other 'subordinate classes' in order to construct an effective alternative to bourgeois hegemony (1988: 205). For example, in the context of Italy in the inter-war period, the Communists would need to win over the support of the peasants, the petite bourgeoisie and other subordinate groups to prevent these elements being won over by the Fascists. Taking this as his premise, Gramsci elaborated a 'science of the complex superstructures', i.e. of politics. Drawing upon Machiavelli, Hegel, Georges Sorel and others, he developed a sophisticated range of concepts and categories, including the reconfiguration of the political as the site of the construction of 'collective wills', the notion of 'hegemony' understood as a form of power characterised by a combination of 'force plus consent' and conceived also as a decisive moment in politics where a 'fundamental class' is able to present its 'own corporate interests' as the 'motor force of a universal expansion' by winning over the support of other subordinate groups (Gramsci 1988: 205, 240). In the exercise of hegemony, says Gramsci, the 'dominant group become[s] the interests of other subordinate groups', creating a genuinely Universal or 'Ethical State' (1988: 205, 234).

Laclau is deeply indebted to Gramsci's thought. However, he also recognised that Gramsci's work is insufficient to the new forms of politics that have emerged since the 1960s (Laclau and Mouffe 2001:

65–70). Gramsci's innovation was to rethink the efficacy and the scope of the political, conceived as the theatre of strategic action, but understood as an element of voluntarism *within* the base/superstructure topography and also *within* a general theory of history. In other words, for Gramsci political praxis enabled a degree of choreographical movement for those who find themselves on the stage of world history, but the casting – i.e. who gets to go on stage – is always ultimately decided by economic relations of production. The principal actors in Gramsci's account of the political are always ultimately 'fundamental classes' and their interests. From this perspective the emergence of the new forms of political struggle from the 1960s – environmentalist struggles, feminist struggles, civil rights struggles, students' struggles, the struggles of sexual and ethnic minorities and so on – could only be figured as somehow less fundamental to the struggles of the industrial working class, and socialist strategy could only be conceived in terms of building a collective project by winning over these 'peripheral struggles' to the world historical interest of the proletariat.[10] In order to break with this paradigm, and to put each of these forms of politics on a par (in terms of the ontological status of their claims), Laclau recognised he would need to break with the base/superstructure topography in its entirety, and the way to do this was to radicalise the Gramscian notion of the primacy of the political to the point where politics (understood as the strategic articulation of relations of force) becomes constitutive of all social, cultural and economic relations (Laclau and Mouffe 2001: 136–8).

In order to develop fully his account of the primacy of the political Laclau turned to resources outside the Marxist tradition, and most importantly to Derridean post-structuralism and Lacanian psychoanalysis. From Jacques Derrida, Laclau took the idea of the discursive construction of social relations. This has been misread as a form of idealism, but both Derrida and Laclau have insisted on the materiality of discourse (Laclau and Mouffe 2001: 108; Derrida 1976). For Laclau, the fundamental status of 'discourse' simply denotes a materialist ontology where (non-dialectical) relations are primary (Laclau 2005b: 68). Social symbolic relations can best be understood in terms of the kinds of relations that we find in linguistic practices and the formal structures of language (Laclau 2005b: 68). Just as Derrida has emphasised the excess of meaning that overflows every attempt to establish fixed synchronic structures, so too in politics there is an inherent 'subversion of each of the terms by a polysemy which prevents their stable articulation' (Laclau and Mouffe 2001: 121). From psychoanalysis Laclau has taken the idea of the libidinal or affective nature of the social bond, and the idea that the partial fixation of social relationships follows from the perennial struggle for the 'impossible object' society-as-a-whole (Laclau 2005b: 118–20). Gramsci recognised the political significance of myth understood as a 'concrete fantasy which acts on a dispersed and shattered people to arouse and organize its collective will' (Gramsci 1988: 239). Similarly, Laclau adopts the Freudian–Lacanian emphasis on the role of fantasy and on the subject's struggle for an imaginary wholeness which is retroactively posited as the original lost object of the drive (Laclau 2005b: 111–13). For Laclau, the struggle for hegemony is conceived as the necessary (but impossible) struggle for a moment of social plenitude or fullness. This struggle never instantiates the sought after plenitude – which is strictly impossible – but nonetheless results in the 'partial fixation' of social relationships around privileged 'nodal points' (Laclau and Mouffe 2001: 112).

According to Laclau, every political context is characterised by a series of demands or struggles, for example workers demands for higher wages, feminist demands for equality in the workplace, anti-racist struggles, gay struggles for public recognition of homosexual relationships and practices, and so on (Laclau 2005b: 73). These demands remain in a relationship of subordination, all the while that they remain blocked from forming a 'chain of equivalence' with one another (Laclau and Mouffe 2001: 153). However, to the extent that these struggles enter into a relationship of equivalence in their collective antagonism to the dominant power in society, relations of subordination are transformed into relations of oppression and a radical democratic subjectivity begins to emerge (Laclau 2000: 54–5; Laclau and Mouffe 2001: 153–4). Laclau describes 'hegemony' as a type of power relationship whereby 'a particularity assumes the representation of an (impossible) universality entirely incommensurate with it' (Laclau 2001: 5). This is 'politically constructed only through the equivalence of a plurality of demands', whereby one of those demands stands in strategically for all the rest, and in relation to the external force that is presumed to antagonise them all (Laclau 2000: 55). Unlike Gramsci's 'fundamental classes', in Laclau's theory none of the *contents* of the alternative struggles is destined *a priori* to universalise its demands (Laclau and Zac 1994: 16). As he sees it, the universal fullness of the social order 'has no necessary body and no necessary content; different groups, instead, compete between themselves to temporarily give to their particularisms a function of universal representation' (Laclau 2000: 35). Nevertheless, for Laclau the effective hegemonic contiguity of one set of 'demands' with the 'plenitude of a fully fledged communitarian order' brings about a temporary embodiment of a moment of universality. The hegemonic – or radical democratic – object (*objet a* in Lacan) is the object of libidinal investment which produces universalising (or cosmopolitan) effects that radiate throughout the entire social body (Laclau 2005b: 115).[11]

For Laclau, the establishment of every hegemonic formation is only ever temporary, in the sense that (unlike Gramsci's conception of the tasks of the proletariat) it will not bring us to the end of history. Nonetheless moments of hegemony are not transitory *events*. For Laclau, hegemonic formations become embedded in sedimented practices, in the relative stability of an 'historical bloc', and when the struggle for hegemony is won it tends to be settled for 'the entire historical period'. Furthermore, Laclau also theorises hegemony in terms of the struggle to articulate the 'empty signifiers' of universality. Signifiers like 'liberty', 'equality', 'justice' and so on, are – he says – strictly 'signifiers without a signified', because they designate the impossible object society-as-a-whole (Laclau 1996a: 36, 40). Hegemony is therefore understood in terms of the generalised struggle to establish the contiguity between particular sets of demands and the empty signifiers of universality.

Laclau acknowledges that national boundaries cannot be taken as given and that the frontiers that bind the imagined communities of the 'sovereign' nation-state are – like all frontiers – contingent and politically constructed nodal points (Laclau and Mouffe 2001: 144). Nevertheless, there is no *explicit* deconstruction of the domestic/ international topography in his work, in the same manner that he deconstructs the base/superstructure topography. Furthermore, there appears to be an *implicit* assumption in his writings that the nation-state is the principal locus of the struggle for hegemony. His examples of hegemonic formations are almost exclusively taken from domestic politics, and the majority of empirical studies that work with Laclau's discourse theoretical approach also tend to focus on domestic politics.[12] Apart from a few scattered references to globalisation and how it has intensified the contingency of social relations in the latter part of the twentieth century, there is scant theorisation of world politics or the onset of globalisation in Laclau's writings. However, as I see it, a theory and practice of militant cosmopolitanism is inherent in Laclau's understanding of hegemony in terms of (impossible) universalism, and there is certainly nothing in his theory which precludes the possibility of the struggle for hegemony on a global scale. I explore this possibility in more detail below.

First, however, it will be advantageous to introduce the key ideas that Hardt and Negri have put forward in *Empire*. As I have said, they work within a different theoretical framework from Laclau, and he and Mouffe and others have rightly criticised the Spinozan/Deleuzean ontological underpinnings of their work and their inadequate conception of the political (Laclau 2003; Mouffe 2005a: 107–15). Nevertheless, there is no question that *Empire* represents an impressive cartography of the main developments of globalisation, and an attempt to account for the new forms of power associated with these developments, and especially the increasing autonomy of large corporations *vis-à-vis* the 'democratic' authority of the nation-state and also *vis-à-vis* the traditional institutions of 'disciplinary society'. In the next section, I consider the main claims they make about the operations of 'Empire', before briefly saying something about the inadequacy of their conception of the kinds of agency required to counter the new forms of power associated with globalisation. This is to understand better the challenges of globalisation, so that we can then consider an alternative account of progressive globalist strategy in the final section of the paper.

Empire

Hardt and Negri present the 'globalisation of economic and cultural exchanges' and the nation-state's diminished capacity to 'regulate these flows and impose its power over the economy' as the defining feature of contemporary politics (Hardt and Negri 2001: xi). This has engendered a new form of power that they call 'Empire', and which – following in the footsteps of Michel Foucault – they contrast comprehensively to centralised forms of 'sovereignty' (Foucault 1991; Hardt and Negri 2001: xii). As Hardt and Negri have shown, the operations of Empire are unlike earlier manifestations of colonialism and:

> imperialism [which] was really an extension of the sovereignty of the European nation-states beyond their own boundaries . . . [whereas] Empire . . . is a decentred and deterritorialising apparatus of rule that progressively incorporates the entire global realm within its open, expanding frontiers. Empire manages hybrid identities, flexible hierarchies, and plural exchanges through modulating networks of command. (Hardt and Negri 2001: xii)

They are onto something when they claim that this should be understood as a 'fundamentally new' development, where the mobility and dynamism inherent in capitalist accumulation has *largely* set itself free from the 'sovereign' nation-state and its borderlines. This has resulted in a *relative* transfer of power away from national governments to the global agents of Empire (large corporations, the agencies of the United Nations, as well as the IMF, the World Bank, GATT and so on).

Under conditions of globalisation, capitalist processes of accumulation have also established their supremacy over the principal institutions of 'disciplinary society' – schools, factories, the family, hospitals, prisons and so on – that mediated social relations in the era of high modernity, and which were so carefully mapped by Foucault (Foucault 1977, 1989). Adapting Foucault's ideas and drawing also on Gilles Deleuze, Hardt and Negri emphasise how under conditions of globalisation economic, cultural and political exchanges 'increasingly overlap and invest one another' in a singular process of bio-political production (Deleuze 2001; Hardt and Negri 2001: xiii). Globalisation, in other words, has not only hollowed out the state, but also the family, the school and the workplace.

> Capital has indeed always been organised with a view toward the entire global sphere, but only in the second half of the twentieth century did multinational and trans-national industrial and financial corporations really begin to [directly] structure global territories bio-politically. (Hardt and Negri 2001: 31)

Hardt and Negri's claims about the singular operations of Empire – a singularity that supposedly manifests as rhizomatic multiplicity – are no doubt exaggerated, and unlike Laclau their theoretical framework lacks the resources to theorise the partial fixation of relations of power around temporarily privileged nodal points. However, in certain respects their account of Empire captures the principal aspects of economic globalisation which are characterised by the *relatively* unfettered power of capital and the constant mobility of its operations.

According to Hardt and Negri, the 'passage to Empire and its processes of globalisation [also] offer[s] new possibilities' to the manifold contemporary 'forces of liberation' (Hardt and Negri 2001: xv). In their view, the task of contemporary radical politics is not to 'resist' globalisation, but to 'reorganise' these 'processes' and to 'redirect them toward new ends' (Hardt and Negri 2001: xv). The objective is to 'accelerate the[se] process[es]' by pushing them 'past their present limitations' (Hardt and Negri 2001: 206, 209). These claims also have some validity in the sense that any viable 'alternative globalisation' movement needs to take heed of the generalised mobility of corporate power under conditions of globalisation, and find ways of engaging these processes on their own terms. However, where Hardt and Negri go dreadfully awry is in their assumption that these struggles can become effective without any need for tactical or strategic considerations (Hardt and Negri 2001: 58). From their perspective, the 'multitude . . . is capable of *autonomously* constructing . . . an alternative political organisation of global flows and exchanges' free from the imperatives of capital accumulation (Hardt and Negri 2001: xv). This assumption is rooted in their Spinozan/Deleuzean cosmology and their reduction of political action to a metaphysics of immanence. As they see it, the various social 'struggles' that make up the 'movement of the multitude, in its myriad faces', create 'powerful singularities' with no explicit 'mediation between them' (Hardt and Negri 2001: 61, 393). Their invocation of the (supposedly) *spontaneous* and *undirected* emergence of progressive social forces reproduces the Spinozan idea of the multiple *qua* the actualisation of immanent Substance, and resembles Deleuze's claim that the 'immanent . . . carr[ies] with it the events or singularities that are merely actualised in subjects and objects' (Deleuze 2001: 29). Indeed, the lesson of Hardt and Negri's theory of immanence is that progressive social forces need simply immerse themselves in the flow of becoming, where Nature (God) does the planning and delivers the results. On the contrary, what is required today is precisely the strategic considerations necessary to achieve cosmopolitan effects. It is to these considerations that we now turn.

Hegemony and globalist strategy

One consequence of the onset of globalisation – and the relative demise of the nation-state as the locus of democratic politics – has been a resurgence in arguments for liberal cosmopolitanism. For example, commentators like David Held have argued that global social and economic problems require global solutions and these can only ultimately be brought about through democratic reform of the United Nations and the use of trans-national institutions to strengthen global governance and to ensure the effective implementation of international human rights law (Held 1993, 1995).

Arguments for liberal cosmopolitanism can be traced to Kant (Kant 1991a, 1991b). However, at a time when these are in vogue it is important to remember that (although neither Marx nor Gramsci used the term) Marxism is also a form of cosmopolitanism. Unlike Hegel, who insisted that political universality could only be realised in the ethical-life (*Sittlichkeit*) of the nation (Hegel 1967: 208–16), Marx envisaged the end of history in terms of a universal proletarian solidarity that would transcend national and cultural differences. This would be a militant cosmopolitanism grounded not in individual rights (*à la* Kant), but in the 'world historical' (or universal) interests of the proletariat, in which the workers of the world would unite. The idea of an inherent proletarian solidarity was thrown into chaos by the events of the First World War when workers signed up in their hundreds of thousands to slaughter their fellow workers in the great fight for King and Country. This question emerged again in post-revolutionary Russia, when the Stalinist notion of 'socialism in one country' triumphed over Trotsky's desire to export the revolution on a global scale. In this section I consider the question of the appropriate link between *polis* and *cosmo-polis* in a post-Marxist theory of radical democracy, which no longer believes in the universal interests of the proletariat, but nonetheless recognises the importance of the hegemonic construction of universality. First, however, I look again at Gramsci's thought and consider how he addressed these questions, and I also discuss Mouffe's reflections on the appropriate sites of radical democratic struggle in the era of globalisation. As I have said, Mouffe has engaged with the challenges of globalisation and developed an account of how radical democrats should respond to the relative demise of the nation-state. Nevertheless, her account is inadequate to the task because she denies the possibility of constructing counter-hegemonic formations at the global level. By way of contrast, I argue for the importance of a militant form of cosmopolitanism understood as a necessary component of the struggle for radical democracy in the era of globalisation.

Writing in the Italian context (with its precarious national unity, strong regionalism, north–south divide, and as host to the institution of the Roman Church with its cosmopolitan aspirations), Gramsci was keenly aware of the importance of building proletarian hegemony at the national level. Indeed, it is a basic tenet of Gramsci's Marxism that the 'international situation should be considered in its national aspect' (1988: 230). He said, a 'class that is international [that is cosmopolitan] in character has to nationalize itself in a certain sense' (Gramsci 1988: 231). Indeed, whilst:

the line of development [in the proletarian struggle] is towards interna-
tionalism [by which he meant globalism or cosmopolitanism] . . . the
point of departure is 'national' – and it is from this point of departure that
one must begin. Yet the perspective is international and cannot be otherwise. Consequently, it is necessary to study accurately the combination of
national forces which the international class will have to lead and develop,
in accordance with the international [global] perspective and directives.
(Gramsci 1988: 231)

Mouffe's recent account of how best to struggle against neo-liberal
globalisation is clearly indebted to Gramsci. However, whereas
Gramsci's emphasis on the importance of the 'national-popular' was
tied to a vision of the ultimate cosmopolitanism of the Proletarian
struggle, Mouffe's account of radical democracy denies any element
of cosmopolitanism. She is highly critical of the bold objectives of
contemporary liberal cosmopolitans. Instead of resorting to 'false
universalisms', she says, we should acknowledge that the 'implementation of a cosmopolitan order would in fact result in the imposition
of one single model, the liberal democratic one, on the whole world'
(Mouffe 2005a: 103). Because of the 'deeply pluralistic nature of the
world', attempts to institute this ideal would aggravate the anti-
western sentiment that is already prevalent in many parts of the world
and add fuel to the fire of 'global terrorism' (Mouffe 2005a: 91). By
way of contrast, Mouffe calls for a revival of national and regional
politics. She says that nation-states are still 'important players' even
'if multi-national companies operate according to strategies largely
independent of them' and 'regional and local forums such as those
which have been organized in Europe and in many cities of the world
are the places where a variety of resistances can become intercon-
nected and where the 'war of position . . . [against neo-liberal glob-
alisation] . . . can be launched' (Mouffe 2005a: 114).

These arguments are important. Nevertheless, what is disconcert-
ing about Mouffe's approach is that her position is completely disso-
ciated from any globalist vision. Indeed, Mouffe says 'world order' in
the era of globalisation 'needs to be a multi-polar one' constructed
around the 'recognition of a multiplicity of regional powers', and she
envisions the possibility of 'a new global order based on the existence
of several autonomous regional blocs' (Mouffe 2005a: 116–17). In
order to find 'ways to pluralize' sites of national and regional hegemony, she says we must establish 'an equilibrium among regional
poles whose specific concerns and traditions will be seen as valuable,
and where different vernacular models of democracy will be accepted'

(Mouffe 2005a: 129). Again, Mouffe is right to express concern about respect for cultural differences in a world that is dominated by western imperatives and values. However, it does not follow from this that every form of cosmopolitanism is incompatible with the 'democratic rights of self-government for the citizens' of independent nation-states. Throughout the remainder of the chapter I sketch the outline of a radical democratic globalist strategy that should be seen as a necessary supplement to the struggle for the renewal of democracy at the national and the regional levels.

It is not necessary to retain a fixed topography to distinguish domestic from global politics. These differences can be figured in terms of alternate political strategies or logics. Radical democracy emerges domestically when a collective will of progressive social forces is established through its common opposition to a dominant force that tends to have libidinal affects predominantly at the level of the nation. These struggles weld together a 'national popular' identity through the counter-hegemonic construction of a chain of equivalence between distinct social interests that are (relatively) localised geographically and through the effective contiguity of some local particular initiative with empty signifiers that are tendentially associated with the cultural, social, economic, institutional and libidinal life (*Sittlichkeit*) of a particular domestic context. For example, in UK politics 'devolution', 'Thatcherism', 'the post-war consensus', 'the welfare state', 'Europe', and even the 'Norman Yoke' operate as floating signifiers which can potentially function as empty signifiers through their association with an effective hegemonic formation. Whereas in a different context (say a North American context), these signifiers have little or no potential to function in this way, because they tend not to be the object of libidinal investment by the various forces in play there.

Radical democracy emerges at the global level on the other hand when a collective will of progressive social forces is established through its common opposition to a dominant force that tends to have libidinal effects that bypass the nation-state and operate predominantly at the global level (such as 'corporate' or 'neo-liberal globalisation'). The purpose of globalist strategy is to weld together a cosmopolitan moment of consciousness through the counter-hegemonic construction of a chain of equivalence between distinct social interests that are geographically dispersed and through the effective contiguity of some local social initiatives with empty signifiers that are tendentially associated with globalism or with the cultural, social, economic, institutional and libidinal life of humanity-as-a-whole. For example, 'human rights', 'global justice', 'anti-capitalism', 'alternative globalisation' are floating signifiers which can potentially function as empty signifiers through their association with an effective hegemonic formation. We will of course never arrive at the *telos* of cosmopolitan community, which is an empty signifier and not – as the liberal cosmopolitans fail to understand – a determinable signified or a (possible) referent. Nevertheless different groups compete to temporarily embody this moment of necessary (but impossible) global fullness.

The struggle for global hegemony is being waged in a number of distinct theatres of operation. These include the summit protests against the World Bank and the IMF, the politics of the World Social Forum and struggles which make use of the internet, both as a means of constructing and mobilising social forces and as a site of struggle in its own right. Here I focus on the struggle to determine the images that are beamed across the planet by the mass media. As Hardt and Negri have suggested, the techno-media-communications conditions already exist for distinct local struggles to 'leap vertically' from the detail of their localised dissent and to 'touch . . . on the global level' (Hardt and Negri 2001: 55). However, there is nothing *immanent* about prospects for success in the struggle for global media hegemony. On the contrary, this requires recognition that global media politics represents a distinct theatre of operations which calls for consideration of the strategic moves necessary to articulate chains of equivalence between struggles which are spatially dispersed and against agile and transient targets. The struggle for hegemony in this terrain resembles the constant mobility of maritime or aerial combat, which precludes the possibility of a land-based defensive strategy, of a 'war of position'.[13]

One of the insights of Laclau's theory is that the chain of equivalence becomes weaker the more extensive the numbers of elements it includes (2005b: 231). Globalist strategies are therefore by their very nature precarious and short lived, as they attempt to establish chains of equivalence between geographically dispersed and culturally distinct struggles and demands. The links in these chains are perpetually being broken and reformulated, and this points towards the need for one crucial alteration to Laclau's theory in order to make sense of the specificity of globalist strategy. The principal difference between the struggle for domestic hegemony and hegemony in global politics is the recognition of the inappropriateness of the concept of 'historical bloc' at the global level. The temporary nodal points that are formed by moments of global hegemony should be understood in the manner of fragmentary or fleeting *events*. These events (of cosmopolitan consciousness) are brought about by the temporary effective contiguity of some localised demand with empty signifiers of a 'common humanity'. They radiate across the planet in the form of media projected images (increasingly in 'real time'), and these projectiles become floating signifiers in the relatively more stable struggles for hegemony at the national and the regional levels, but they do not themselves form something like an 'historical bloc'.[14]

The media is controlled by large corporations, but nonetheless requires powerful and evocative images in order to function. The kind of images (of cosmopolitan praxis) I have in mind are the images associated with the civil rights campaigns in the US in the 1960s, with the collapse of the Berlin Wall and of the single person standing up to the tanks in Tiananmen Square. These exemplary images (potentially) construct a moment of common humanity, that is, in their affirmation of a common vulnerability, or the human capacity for tremendous courage. This 'commonality' is a radical construction: it is an empty signifier that does not refer to any substantive entity. Nevertheless, the construction of this (impossible) object – humanity-as-a-whole – is the potential effect of the successful articulation of these powerful images: they generate momentary chains of equivalence across the planet as billions of people are forced to sit up and take notice.

Unfortunately, however, the most effective example of what I have in mind by the idea of the hegemonic media construction of a moment of global consciousness has been affected by the forces of reaction: everybody knows where they were when the images of 9/11 unfolded globally in real time. This event has subsequently shifted global consciousness in a fundamental way, but unfortunately in the direction of widespread fear and reaction. One task for the radical democrat in the era of globalisation is to generate images of positive non-violent global action and identity and to struggle to have these images cut and pasted on the screens of the global media. This will become increasingly imperative as we head towards the mid twenty-first century and the consequences of the climatic crisis and global poverty become more and more acute. However, it is also clear that this is a case of asymmetrical warfare where the dominant forces – large (media) corporations and their representatives – are far superior to the forces of opposition in terms of their technological and communications capacity and their access to resources and supply. These reactionary forces will struggle to retain the visual hegemony of images of passive and conspicuous consumption, and to cover up the negative images that represent the consequences of neo-liberalism. The forces that struggle against corporate globalisation will need plenty of tactical agility and resolve if they are to raise consciousness of global issues by changing the content of the dominant images, let alone defeat the neo-liberal Goliath.[15]

Conclusion

Globalisation represents the principal social and economic revolution of our times. This presents particular challenges for democratic theorists, as they struggle to conceptualise the political implications of globalisation and the relative demise of the nation-state as the principal locus of politics. A theory of radical democracy in the era of globalisation needs to be responsive not only to the new mobility of power associated with the supremacy of large corporations, but also to the new forms of political activism that are facilitated by the emergence of globalisation. Laclau's theory provides the necessary categories for the development of a radically democratic global praxis, but it is clear that he himself has not pursued this possibility. This paper has provided an initial sketch of a radical democratic theory of global politics. In particular, I have focused on the strategies that are required in the theatre of global media politics. I have argued that contemporary social movements must seek to establish hegemonic moments of cosmopolitan consciousness through the production of positive images of global action, and must struggle to establish the contiguity of these images with the particular demands of localised social actors. These fragmentary moments of hegemony do not form anything like an historical bloc. Nevertheless, they become floating signifiers to be contested in the conventional arena of the struggles for democracy in domestic politics. My sense is that a great deal will depend on how effectively radical democrats mobilise these strategies, in order to raise consciousness about global issues and the destructiveness of neo-liberal globalisation.

Notes

1. For prominent accounts of liberal cosmopolitan governance see Held (1993 and 1995), Linklater (1998) and the discussions in Archibugi, Held and Kohler (1998). For theories of global civil society, see Falk

(1999), Kaldor (2003) and the discussions in Baker and Chandler (2005).

2. See, for example, Laclau (2001), Mouffe (1995 and 2000), Butler (1990) and Connolly (1991 and 1995).

3. See, for example, Townshend (2004).

4. There are scattered references to 'globalised capitalism' and the politics of the 'anti-capitalist movement' in Laclau's writing. See, for example, Laclau (2005b: 231, 239).

5. Previously I expressed concerns about the notion of (impossible) monism that is at the core of Laclau's problematic, and expressed my preference for Mouffe's way of theorising hegemony in a manner that is sensitive to plurality and difference. Whilst the analysis of the differences between them is correct, I now find myself persuaded by Laclau's approach to these issues. What is needed more than ever in the era of globalisation is the hegemonic formation of a moment of (impossible) global solidarity in the face of the perpetual fragmentation of people's lives by the forces of neo-liberal globalisation.

6. For sceptical reflections on globalisation see Hirst and Thompson (1996) and for other prominent accounts see Giddens (1999) and Held and McGrew (2002).

7. Of course, many have argued – Marx, Weber and Michels for example – that the democratic credentials of the modern liberal democratic state have always been more of a myth than a reality. The onset of globalisation has exacerbated the elitist tendencies inherent in modern 'representative' institutions.

8. For analysis of the politics of the 'anti-capitalist' and the 'alternate globalisation' movements, see Starr (2000) and Tormey (2004). Starr flirts with Laclau's theory in her interpretation of these movements, but Laclau's categories are not elaborated in any detail in her book.

9. These ideas were initially sketched in a short paper entitled 'The Impossibility of Society', which was first published in 1983 and reproduced in *New Reflections on the Revolutions of Our Times* (Laclau 1990).

10. For a classic statement of this understanding of socialist strategy, see Mouffe's work before her conversion to post-structuralism: Mouffe (1979a) and (1979b).

11. In his recent book Laclau has refigured the moment of universalism that is generated from the construction of hegemony in terms of 'populism'. He says in order to have populism 'we need a *plebs* who claims to be the only legitimate *populus* – that is, a partiality which wants to function as the totality of the community' (Laclau 2005b: 81). The terminology may be different, but the basic elements of the theory remain the same.

12. See, for example, the essays collected in Howarth, Norval and Stavrakakis (2000).

13. Laclau rightly points out that strategic thought inevitably becomes more short term, once we have rejected the Marxist idea that long-term predictions are made possible by the study of the laws of history (2005b: 242). What needs to be added to this insight is that the onset of globalisation has generated an entirely new theatre of operations – the corporate- and media-driven terrain of global (as opposed to international) politics – which requires alternate strategic considerations to the terrain of domestic politics.

14. A thoroughgoing consideration of the application of Laclau's theory to global politics would examine similarities and differences between his approach and the various 'neo-Gramscian' perspectives in international relations. Unlike those who work with Laclau's discourse theoretical perspective, the neo-Gramscians have sought to explain the operations of hegemony at the international level. For the classic statement of this approach see Cox (1991) and, for other significant contributions, see Gill (2000) and the essays collected in Bieler, Bonefeld, Burnham and Morton (2006). These theorists retain the classical Gramscian conception of the base/superstructure distinction, and of the political as a moment of agency within this basic topography, and they have sought to explain the 'dialectical relationship' between changes in (economically determined) 'social forces' and in 'forms of state' and 'world orders' (Cox 1991: 452). It would be fruitful to think through these same questions using Laclau's post-Marxist categories, and to examine how the analysis differs from the neo-Gramscian perspective. There is not the scope to explore this here.

15. According to Paul Virilio, the 'instantaneous speed of transmission' of media images in the era of globalisation denies the addressee the necessary time to reflect upon their significance and to form an opinion, so that once active citizens have now been reduced to the status of passive 'tele-spectators . . . transfixed' on the images packaged by large media corporations (Virilio 1991: 1–16). Clearly the media and communications industry have a massive capacity for effect in the struggle for the construction of contemporary subjectivities. However, Virilio exaggerates the lack of opportunity for critical reflection – as families, friends, work colleagues and citizens discuss and debate the issues and the images that are circulated on the silver screen – and he does not explore the political opportunities to shape the global circulation of images.

7

Is 'Another World' Possible? Laclau, Mouffe and Social Movements

Andrew Robinson and Simon Tormey

The slogan 'another world is possible' is regularly seen on anti-capitalist protests and the publications of critics of the current system. For these critics, the ugly face of neo-liberalism – massive poverty and exclusion, exploitation, immiseration, ecological destruction, the perpetuation of a wide range of oppressive and destructive relations, permanent emergency and war – is a human construction that can be reversed or overcome.

As radicals, Laclau and Mouffe would no doubt embrace certain aspects of this movement. But do they believe in this core proposition? In certain ways, Laclau and Mouffe do allow for the possibility of social change through rearticulations and changes in which a group is hegemonic. But in other ways, the core structure of the current system is put beyond challenge in their approach. There is only one way to 'do politics', which is to seek to represent a multitude of floating signifiers under the umbrella of a despotic signifier; ultimately this means a statist politics, complete with exclusions, violence, alienation and the rest. This is Laclau and Mouffe's major contribution to the strategies of social movements, urging radical activists and single-issue campaigners to give up on goals of revolution, overthrow and fundamental transformation and instead pursue hegemonic rearticulations which play by the rules of liberal democracy and recognise their own particularity and resultant subordination to the state's regulatory function. This would be a dreadful pessimism were it not for the fact that they also celebrate the possibilities of this 'radical democratic' practice, constructing a quasi-teleological account of its progress into an ever-expanding democracy.

Our purpose in this chapter is to stand up for the view that 'another world is possible', against what for us appears an almost dystopian submission to the totalising logic of the dominant system. To seek this defence, we look to social movements themselves. We believe that the basic claims of Laclau and Mouffe's theory about matters of social ontology and the necessity of certain discursive logics are to a degree empirical, and that these claims can be falsified by counter-examples within the field of social movement activity. Therefore, our main purpose is to demonstrate the existence of a range of social movements that do not have characteristics Laclau and Mouffe take as necessary. We believe such a demonstration is decisive in showing that Laclau and Mouffe have unduly constrained the field of the possible, and that a more open conception of structural possibilities is needed to understand and engage with radical social movements.

Laclau and Mouffe on social unity

There are subtle differences between Laclau's theory and Mouffe's, but they share a position on the importance of the state. This section treats their theories as a single body of work because of their significance for the construction of 'radical democracy' in general, for which they remain part of a basically unified theoretical field. One of the things taken as necessary in their theories is what Deleuze and Guattari term the gesture of despotic signification – the gesture by means of which one signifier stands in for the entire social field, constructing itself as equivalent to order and meaning as such and its other as radically excluded (as a 'social symptom' in Žižek's terms). We use the Deleuzian term for theoretical reasons, but we recognise this phenomenon has had many names, each with different theoretical inflections – Laclau and his followers (and his critic Day 2005) call it 'hegemony', Lacan called it 'master-signification' or 'quilting' (*capitonnage*), the function of the 'empty signifier' being similar if not identical to the hegemonic signifier. Žižek and Badiou theorise the Act-Event in much the same way, and the term 'sovereignty' sometimes has similar meanings. The Deleuzian version of the concept is especially apposite as it differentiates the phenomenon from others. In particular, a movement which is based on despotic signification necessarily takes a vertical form, reproducing the logics Laclau takes as universal – the demonisation of an excluded Other, the subordination of particularities to a 'universal' moment, the identification of a particular actor or signifier with the social field 'as such', etc. But the vertical form is not the only form of social action; one (though not necessarily the only) other kind of articulation is horizontality, based on the interconnection of rhizomes in a smooth space.

The defence of despotic signification is put forward mainly by Laclau, but we have reason to believe it is also endorsed by Mouffe, as well as by many of their followers. According to Laclau, social unity is possible only if changes in meaning (the Lacanian 'slipping of the signified under the signifier') are halted. This requires ideology, because ideology performs this function of halting the slippage of signification (Laclau 1990: 92). The 'basic split', the constitutive lack which haunts every hegemonic agent, 'finds the form of its discursive presence through [the] production of empty signifiers representing the general form of fullness', which operate to signify 'the structural impossibility of signification as such' (Laclau 1996a: 95, 37). Precisely because of their emptiness, empty signifiers are interchangeable with any other signifiers in a series, and this makes them indispensable to ideology (Laclau 1996b: 208–9). 'The condition for the emergence of an imaginary is the metaphorization of the literal content of a particular social demand', through which it comes to stand for the absent fullness. If a particular element fails to perform such a metaphorisation, it returns to its literal meaning and ceases to be a hegemonic element (Laclau 1990: 62–5). Thus, 'the universal results from a constitutive split in which the negation of a particular identity transforms the identity in[to] the symbol of identity and fullness as such' (Laclau 1996a: 15).

Laclau's case for the 'necessity' of empty signifiers is deduced from a set of assumptions which portray everyday life as fundamentally lacking. Empty signifiers are necessary to construct ideologies, ideologies institute socio-symbolic orders and socio-symbolic orders are a pre-condition for individual and collective identity. The case for the necessity of empty signifiers, therefore, relies on an overarching commitment to social order, a commitment Laclau is enthusiastic to make. Above all, according to Laclau, people need and desire some form of socio-symbolic order, and this in turn renders legitimate anything that is necessary to institute such an order.[1] Further, since Laclau and Mouffe treat the 'social field' as a kind of limit on effective discourse and existing social logics as 'structural limits' (Laclau and Mouffe 1985: 168, 190), they are unable to consider changing beliefs or social relations below a superficial level. Actually, Laclau and Mouffe seem to deny the possibility of changing existing beliefs, since it is precisely by fitting with existing beliefs that Laclau and Mouffe see philosophies becoming organic (Laclau and Mouffe 1985: 175). Laclau's examples of political action involve accepting what he terms the 'unshakeable beliefs' of the 'masses' (Laclau 2000: 82–3), and he even uses such beliefs as the proofs of theories – as what he calls 'conditions of credibility' (Laclau 1990: 244).

One effect of such a position is an advocacy of radical social exclusion. In order for one particular element to stand in for social fullness, argues Laclau, another must be defined as the embodiment of negativity and disorder, and 'presented as anti-space, as anti-community' (Laclau 1990: 69). Not only are such people excluded, but they are identified with negativity as such, so that all threats to the in-group constructed around a particular nodal point are perceived as equivalent (Laclau 1996a: 14). Mouffe concurs that violence is to be accepted as part of human nature, and as part of something called the 'dimension of the political' which is treated in a manner akin to an essence (Mouffe 2000: 130–1; 1993: 2). Inequality, however 'unpleasant . . . to liberal ears', is necessary in all societies (Mouffe 2000: 42).

The included are also subordinated. In Laclau's theory, particularities are assumed to have no claims against universality in general, because the particular identities are themselves the product of social totality and are threatened if it is undermined (Laclau 1996a: 13). 'Totality is impossible and, at the same time, is required by the particular: in that sense, it is present in the particular as that which is absent, as a constitutive lack which constantly forces the particular to be more than itself, to assume a universal role which can only be precarious and unsutured' (Laclau 1996a: 15). It is necessary to give meaning to both subject and object. 'A society from which myth was radically excluded would be either an entirely "spatial" and "objective" society . . . or one in which dislocations lacked any space for representation and transcendence . . . either the cemetery or the lunatic asylum' (Laclau 1990: 66–8). Articulation is 'a political construction from different elements' in which 'organisation is . . . external to the elements themselves' and the role of articulation is to link subject-positions or antagonisms together discursively, establishing chains between otherwise separate concepts, coming after and integrating pre-existing dispersed elements (Laclau and Mouffe 1985: 85, 94, 168–9, 174; Laclau 1990: 196). Subordination to the despotic signifier and the law is thus demanded. 'Citizenship is not just one identity among others,' says Mouffe. It is an 'articulating principle' (Mouffe 1993: 84). 'To be a citizen is to recognize the authority of [political] principles and the rules in which they are embodied' (Mouffe 1993: 65). The state 'must have primacy' (Mouffe 1993: 99). To deny a role to the state as something 'different and decisive', over and above associations, is 'to deny' the 'essence of the political' (Mouffe 2000: 51–2).

Thus, the social is so meaningless and inadequate in itself that it will look to anyone and anything to provide the political content it needs. 'In a situation of radical disorganization there is a need for *an* order, and its actual contents become a secondary consideration' (Laclau 1994: 3; cf. Laclau 1996a: 44). Radical democracy is to fill this gap, since otherwise it is open to more authoritarian solutions. The basic demand for an 'order' is not to be questioned. Laclau and Zac quote and reconstruct Thomas Mann in such a way as to make the importance of an ordering discourse very clear. Freedom is only 'realized through its alienation' (Laclau and Zac 1994: 12), in the form of 'law, rule, coercion, system' and even dictatorship (Mann cited in Laclau and Zac 1994: 11). ' "Order and quiet are good, no matter what one owes them" ' (Mann cited in Laclau and Zac 1994: 15), and faced with anomie, 'what would be required would be the introduction of *an* order, the concrete contents of which would become quite secondary' (Laclau and Zac 1994: 15). 'We human beings are by nature submissive,' they continue, citing Thomas Mann (Mann cited in Laclau and Zac 1994: 16). Granted, the signifier 'order' does not have to perform this ordering role; the same role can be performed by signifiers such as 'revolution' or 'democracy'. But the basic ordering, striating function is the same in these cases.

Mouffe broadly concurs with Laclau's advocacy of despotic signification. She does not refer as often to hegemony, but does refer constantly to the supposed need for social exclusion as a means to construct identity and order through a logic of differentiation of 'us and them' (Mouffe 1993: 85, 114; 2000: 12–13, 40–2). Mouffe claims that Lacan has 'shown' the necessity of a master signifier to which individuals submit, 'founded only on itself' and 'introducing a non-founded violence', without which 'the [discursive] field would disintegrate' (Mouffe 2000: 138). So 'the most that a theory of justice can aspire to is to cement a hegemony, to establish a frontier, to provide a pole of identification . . . in a field necessarily criss-crossed by antagonisms' (Mouffe 1993: 57). The role of politics is to 'reduce the margin of undecidability' (Mouffe 1993: 141). In Mouffe's case, the function of despotic signifier guaranteeing exclusion is largely performed by rules and laws. 'Citizenship is not just one identity among others'; it is an 'articulating principle' (Mouffe 1993: 84), and it is constructed by principles enshrined in rules. 'To be a citizen is to recognize the authority of such principles and the rules in which they are embodied' (Mouffe 1993: 65).

This 'us and them' logic is associated with the figure of Carl Schmitt. The political should be 'the realm of "decision" not free discussion', a 'domain of conquering power and repression' (Schmitt) which does not evade 'state and politics' (Mouffe 1993: 111). A Schmittian decision is another version of the despotic signifier, a quilting gesture by which a state agent integrates the social field on a more-or-less arbitrary basis. According to Mouffe, Schmitt 'indicates the limits of any rational consensus and reveals that any consensus is based on acts of exclusion' (Mouffe 1993: 123). Schmitt's main role in Mouffe's work is in differentiating her from the ethics of openness associated with deconstructive and post-colonial discourses on undecidability by insisting that, while undecidability is constitutive, it is not the 'last word'; rather, it is to be closed down by a violent, ungrounded decision (Mouffe 1993: 151–2; 2000: 105). This power to 'decide', denied to particularities and social movements, is made the sole prerogative of the state.

In Mouffe's theory, acceptance of contingency is supposed to necessitate acceptance of one's own limitation and contingency, and this is supposed to establish the state's right to trample on or interfere with one's own concerns (Laclau 1990: 83, 125; Mouffe 2000: 21–2). Mouffe specifies that she does not want an 'endless conversation' with the 'Other', because such an approach is 'unable to come to terms with "the political" in its antagonistic dimension'. Rather, 'what is missing' in such an endless conversation is 'a proper reflection on the moment of "decision" which characterizes the field of politics' and which 'entail[s] an element of force and violence' (Mouffe 2000: 129–30).

Laclau and Mouffe thus pathologise the rise of radical activism. For instance, Mouffe denounces individualism for undermining the social fabric (Mouffe 2000: 96), and claims that the idea that people have rights separate from social institutions is 'at the origin of our problems' (Mouffe 1993: 95). Citizens are only to receive equal rights to the extent that they are members of the *demos* (Mouffe 2000: 40). 'Extreme forms of individualism have become widespread which threaten the very social fabric' and 'put in jeopardy the civic bond' (Mouffe 2000: 96). Similarly, for Laclau, there is to be no more 'childish and foolish rebellion' (Mann cited in Laclau and Zac 1994: 15): one is only to rebel in the name of a specific social order which manages the positivity of the social through the imposition of a nodal point (Laclau and Mouffe 1985: 189). People are to 'accept the particularity and limitation of their claims' (Mouffe 1993: 151), i.e. to accept their own repression by the state, and are to avoid 'non-negotiable moral values' which could limit state power (Mouffe 1993: 6). Although articulated more frequently by Mouffe, this kind of statism also typifies Laclau's work. In the early part of *Hegemony and Socialist Strategy* usually attributed to Laclau, hegemony is identified with the state, and the possibility of being exterior to the state is denied (Laclau and Mouffe 1985: 35, 69).

One effect of this is to exaggerate the role of politicians, both descriptively and normatively. Laclau's discussions of Hobbes imply that the possibility of social communication is established at the level of elite politics, as do some other passages – for instance, questioning the political order is seen as leading to identity crisis, and democracy has become 'the fundamental instrument of the production of the social' (Laclau and Zac 1994: 15; Laclau and Mouffe 1985: 96, 126, 155). They define the problems of the present, not in terms of the threat posed to actual people by global capitalism and an ever more violent state, but in terms of a supposedly growing problem of a chaotic mess of pluralisms which threaten the possibility of 'democratic' unity and identity. The threat posed by the 'loss of common premises' is 'certainly a danger' (Mouffe 2000: 55) and liberalism is menaced by an 'exacerbation of differences and disintegration', an 'explosion of nationalisms and the multiplication of particularisms' and a problem of 'growing ungovernability' (Mouffe 1993: 150, 147, 92). Mouffe also endorses the usual solution: that there is a need for a 'new form of bond' to 'infuse a little enthusiasm into our societies' (Mouffe 1993: 139, 132). Therefore, for Mouffe, the crucial issue nowadays is 'how to establish a new political frontier capable of giving a real impulse to democracy' (Mouffe 1993: 6).

This feeds into a vitalistic demand that politicians take up their designated function of assigning meaning – an assignation to politicians of an almost messianic function of renewing society. This zeal (and its corrosive effects on political constraints on the executive) is similar to that of the 'new right' and 'new Labour'. Not simply problem-solvers or representatives, these politicians view themselves as the creators of a new collective will, as carriers of an almost religious 'mission' which it is their duty and entitlement to realise. This leads to the elimination of modesty and 'realism' in politicians' sense of what they can achieve *vis-à-vis* society, and the elimination of any felt need to remain responsive to social forces that either are or should be beyond their control. It confuses surface with depth, assuming that those who hold political power really are representing and altering the depth structures of society. When they come up against everyday life as a resistant 'substance', the result is either impotence or arrogant outrage, with its correlate of an attempt to bludgeon through the 'necessary' changes by *creating* – through real relations of domination and violence – the 'real subsumption of society under the state' (Negri and Hardt 1994: 269) that politicians take as their entitlement. In concrete terms, it funnels into a creeping project of expanding state control.

The missing 'everyday'

What is elided in Laclauian theory is everyday life as a field in which social identities and activities are constructed immanently. Among the issues and possibilities which thus disappear are the direct, immanent role of the political economy on the formation of everyday relations, the emergence of everyday networks of survival and resistance, and the complex articulations of *substantially formed* (not simply floating) identities and beliefs which political 'hegemony' always in fact involves. Everyday meanings and identities are not simply floating, waiting for a political signifier to quilt them; they actively constitute forms of life that have their own internal perspectives and density.

We interpret Laclau and Mouffe's theory as having empirical implications, because the kind of claims they make include many which amount to truth-claims about the world, and which have restrictive and specifying effects for social movement studies. It is true that they are working at a higher level of abstraction, but they are prone to make general claims which apply restrictively to the world. Claims such as that liberal societies are menaced by disintegration, that people naturally need an order and that a society without inequality is impossible, are clearly of an empirical type. What is more, Laclau himself – in his work on populism (Laclau 2005) – and Laclau and Mouffe's followers, such as Norval and Stavrakakis,[2] apply their views in specifically empirical contexts. Lasse Thomassen (2007) has used their theories to attack our own references to Zapatismo as an actually-existing movement which tends to go beyond representation. We therefore feel confident in asserting that Laclau and Mouffe's theory provides an empirical view of social movements which reads general theoretical assumptions into specific movements in such a way as to make claims which both interpret empirical situations and restrict what is taken to be empirically possible. Of course this raises issues about the relationship between theory and empirical research, some of which we have addressed previously (Robinson 2005a). Such issues are largely outside the scope of this paper, however.

At the root of Laclau and Mouffe's approach is a misunderstanding of the phenomenological origins of social relations. Human action is the result of conscious or unconscious motives, so that there is no such thing as radical disorder, only different, and sometimes oppressive, 'orders'. As a result, there is no such thing as 'order as such' either. The concepts of generalised order and disorder are mythical and ideological ways of refusing to engage with the libidinal and motivational structure of opposing movements. They are an excuse for repression. As Daniel Singer rightly puts it, '[w]hat the powers that be term "anarchy" [or disorder] is in fact "dual power"' (Singer 1970: 232–4).

The cases discussed here – of indigenous peoples who organise entire societies without master signifiers, of everyday resistance that occurs without such signifiers and of political and social movements that operate in a horizontal way – are not intended solely as *theoretical* counterpoints. We are not here speculating about the utopian form of a future society which has not occurred or projecting into reality a set of fantasies about ideal arrangements. Rather, we are providing direct *empirical* examples of *actually-existing* societies and movements which are elided in Laclauian theory and which falsify important claims of this theory, particularly regarding the universality of a certain 'political logic'.

We are seeking to demonstrate the basic falsity of two central Laclauian claims – first, that 'the social' is integrated by 'the political' (in Laclau's sense), and second, that everyday life is open to superficial political articulation, rather than being a dense space of already-articulated meanings resistant to such articulation. The image is overwhelming in Laclau and Mouffe's work of everyday life as a transparent, insubstantial space which is given meaning and agency from 'outside' – from the political, or more precisely, from the gesture of despotic signification. It is something which would be nothing but a worthless mess without this outside valorisation.

'The political' – usually identified with the populist or statist ideologies of elite politics – is taken to actually have an overwhelming impact on the construction of individual identities and everyday social relations. Given the general contempt with which politicians

are viewed even in the west, not to mention the superficial implanta-
tion of the state form in the post-colonial world, this is implausible to
say the least. Although they expand their concept of the 'political'
beyond official politics, they also refuse this label to many everyday
resistances (Laclau and Mouffe 1985: 152–3).

Among the possibilities which this construction elides or denies are:

1) the possibility that meaning can be constructed immanently in
   everyday life (whether as immanent relations or as an interior
   transcendence);
2) the possibility of substantial conflicts and heterogeneous social
   forms arising from conflicts between everyday life and elite politics;
3) the operation of everyday life as a 'thick' substance which 'blocks'
   the intrusion of the political, as in the metaphor of *Resistenz* which
   is used in studies of everyday life in totalitarian societies.

Thus, everyday life operates without any inherent need for a structuring role of 'the political' in the Laclauian sense. This is not to say
that everyday life is 'apolitical'. Of course 'politics' in a more general
sense (contestation of meanings, conflict between different priorities
or perspectives, deliberation and dialogue) operates in everyday life.
We are not counter-posing to the idea of necessary lack an image of
social relations as a self-present fullness. Indeed, the assumption that
the denial of the former necessarily implies the latter is crucial to the
way 'radical democrats' foreclose the possible. The more modest, but
also more radical, point we are making is that the contestations,
conflicts and dialogues need not take the form of vertical, despotic-
significatory construction. They can also occur immanently and
horizontally, without any moment of 'the political' *in the special
Laclauian sense* ever emerging.

Societies without the despotic signifier: Laclau and Mouffe versus indigenous peoples

The claim that political representation is constitutive of the human
condition logically implies the empirical claim that it exists in all
human societies without exception – and the onus would seem to be
on the advocates of this claim to demonstrate the point. Not only do
Laclauians consistently fail to do so, but there is plenty of evidence
against this assertion. Political anthropologists of course dispute the
matter, but as seems clear all manner of societies have and do subsist

without recourse to political representation: Kropotkin, Barclay, Sahlins, Lee and Clastres famously document numerous such cases, and there are many indigenous communities today such as the Mbuti, the !Kung and other Bushmen groups, and the Andaman Islanders which are documented by anthropologists as able to function without political or intellectual leadership.[3] The !Kung for instance, 'have no formal authority figure or chief, but govern themselves by group consensus. Disputes are resolved through lengthy discussions where all involved have a chance to make their thoughts heard until some agreement is reached'.[4] Clastres goes as far as to argue that stateless societies are organised in such a way as to ward off the formation of the state, and of transcendental signification – a claim cited by Deleuze and Guattari in *Anti-Oedipus* and used as part of their account that these societies formed not states but war-machines (Deleuze and Guattari 1987: 357–9).

Indigenous perspectives are frequently immanent on a very radical level; the spheres of nature, humanity and the supernatural and the subject and object worlds are not separated ontologically,[5] and speech-acts are conceived in entirely situated terms (de Souza 2004, 2003, 2002). This leads many anthropologists, not to mention indigenous people exposed to western culture, to question western assumptions about what 'humanity' involves. Sahlins, for instance, analyses some indigenous societies as being without conceptions of scarcity and lack, constructing rather a condition of 'primitive affluence' where the smooth immediacy of existence is taken as a kind of existential fullness. He analyses the metropolitan fascination with lack as a psychological rather than material factor, derived from a particular frame of reference (for instance, using concepts such as time and resources to construct existence as finite and limited). Hence, 'the primitive analogue of social contract is not the State, but the gift' (Sahlins 1972: 169).

A similar tendency to resist the imposition of systems of scarcity can often be heard in the voices of indigenous resistance movements themselves. Take for instance comments made in an interview by an activist in the Organisasi Papua Merdeka (OPM), a group resisting Indonesian rule in West Papua. The Papuans resist the imposition of western and Indonesian regimes of knowledge and power, not on the basis of the need for a signifier to produce social integration, but rather on the basis of an immanent life world which is under attack from the despotic signifiers of state power. The OPM member says, 'I would say that we have our own way, which is better. We know how to balance the ecosystem'. The diversity of Papuan immanence is contrasted with the transcendental integration of Indonesia, which is experienced as violence and imposition. 'Indonesia have a policy of uniting the diversity; everybody's Indonesian and must speak the Indonesian language, behave like Indonesian people and don't say anything which distinguishes you from the others' . . . 'There is a certain way you must have your hair, how to put on your clothes. If this is not the way they want then you are rebelling'.[6] The interviewee's uncle was killed by Indonesian soldiers for being dressed untidily. In other words, it is the *elimination* of despotic order, not its construction, which is the movement's political goal.

In response to this control agenda, the OPM insist on their right to remain outside this oppressive system. An OPM communiqué makes this clear:

> [P]eople might ask, 'Do they want a nation state called West Papua?' The answer of course is 'Nein!' We instead want to be left alone as we have been and as we are. It does not matter if we are regarded as primitives. The struggle to free West Papua is not to take away one government and then replace it with a new government. We do not want to administer ourselves the capitalists 'profit-making'. It is a struggle between modern society and tribal people. It is a struggle between an ecologically harmonious life and an environmentally exploitative one.[7]

How could a Laclauian read this discourse? It would either have to be misread as a statist form of discourse, or dismissed as a messianic claim to social fullness. Yet its basis is not a claim to represent an absent fullness, as such a messianism would involve. It refers to immanent forms of life which are themselves experienced as a fullness. This expresses a possibility which cannot be theorised in Laclauian terms.

Thus, the perspectival 'conditions of possibility' identified by Laclau and Mouffe with the 'human condition' turn out to be parochially metropolitan, arising primarily in urbanised societies at the core of the world system. In a typically Eurocentric gesture, this European particularity is then 'globalised', identified with humanity as such. Indigenous perspectives are thus elided, declared in advance to be impossible and silenced within a discourse which treats metropolitan 'reason' as universal. To open discourse theory to the possibility of listening to indigenous discourse, it is necessary to move beyond the Laclauian paradigm and make space for thinking about immanence.

Indigenous peoples are not alone in having their experiences amputated from Laclauian theory. The emotional experience of an ecstasy or joy in immediacy of the kind expressed in Bakhtin's concept of carnivalesque is also something which occurs experientially, not simply a romantic reconstruction of a lost past. 'Participants in insurrection invariably note its festive aspects,' notes Hakim Bey, 'even in the midst of armed struggle, danger, and risk. The uprising is like a saturnalia which has slipped loose (or been forced to vanish) from its intercalary interval and is now at liberty to pop up anywhere or when'.[8] One reason for this is that carnival and festivity channel active intensities instead of reactive constructs. 'When I was a very young child,' claims Feral Faun, 'my life was filled with intense pleasure and a vital energy that caused me to feel what I experienced to the full'.[9] Is this simply a matter of 'myths of lost fullness' as Laclauians would have us believe? The problem is that, when it isn't doused in blood or tear gas, this type of experience is typical of social protest (and of some aspects of indigenous life worlds also). Laclauian theory can account for the *pursuit* of experiences of ecstasy conceived as stolen *jouissance* or impossible fullness, but the lived actuality of such experiences is rendered impossible.

There is also a repression of the real issue of psychological exclusion in Laclau's work. In Lacan's theory, refusal ('foreclosure') of the despotic signifier ('name of the father') is not impossible as such; rather, it has a cost – departure from normal neurotic subjectivity into psychosis – which is taken as unquestionably bad. Indeed, it is important to notice that Lacanian analysis derives a good deal of its motivational force from a half-disavowed hostility to psychosis. In this context, it is important to emphasise the significance of Deleuze and Guattari's critique of Lacanian psychoanalysis, in which they openly advocate 'psychosis' as a solution to the oppressive and authoritarian structures of contemporary societies. Interestingly, the 'moments of madness' of mass revolts, the immanentist spiritual practices of some indigenous peoples and the Dionysian carnivalesque practices of political resistance are all metaphorised in contemporary discourse as psychotic. On a broader level, it is once again the case that psychosis exists, and furthermore, that 'psychotic' people enter into social relations of various kinds, sometimes in the form of anti-psychiatric political movements.[10] By excluding psychosis from 'the human condition', and by insisting on the pursuit of 'neurotic' forms of political organisation based on despotic signification, Laclau and Mouffe implicitly oppose the emancipatory demands of movements for 'mad liberation' and 'neurodiversity', reinforcing an oppressive privileging of those labelled 'normal' in psychiatric discourse.

Immanence and social movements: the politics of everyday life

Following on from the above, there are all manner of horizontal movements in which identities are negotiated within the movement and without necessitating leadership in some overt or even tacit manner. A number of authors have carried out detailed ethnographic studies of the formation of meaning in everyday life, and have confirmed that such meaning-formation has little relationship to elite or state political forms. James Scott, for instance, has revealed the existence of a distinct 'little tradition' among the peasantry, constructed through everyday communication, primarily in the medium of 'hidden transcripts' which are concealed from political and intellectual 'leaders' in the wider society (Scott 1977a, 1977b, 1990).

Scholars have revealed through ethnographic and discursive enquiry the operation of horizontal, immanent movements under the very noses of constituted power, across settings ranging from African and Latin American shanty towns to Soviet and American factories.[11] Hecht and Simone (1994: 14–15) provide a series of examples from African societies of horizontal social forms that operate invisibly to inflect, undermine and sometimes overthrow states and formal institutions. The uncontrollability and unpredictability of these movements is the source of their strength. In Senegal for instance, 'diverse groups are doing more than developing a critical language. They are taking things into their own hands . . . attempting to reinvent their surroundings . . . asking for or demanding . . . taxes to finance their society independently of a larger authority . . . creating public protests and the occasional riot' (Hecht and Simone 1994: 104).

Larissa Lomnitz (1977) studies survival and mutual aid networks in Latin American shanty towns, revealing that kinship and neighbourhood relations form an entire informal economy enabling a layer of excluded people to survive on the periphery of major cities by means of horizontal relations. Partha Chatterjee (1993) shows how the formation of Indian national identity leaves a trail of 'fragments' – identities based on class, caste, ethnicity, region, religion and so on – which provide the basis for entire areas of social life organised beyond the reach of the state, in private associations and homes. The power of the state is thus very much partial, constrained by and always at risk from the subcultures and countercultures emerging from the space beyond its reach.

Even in mass societies, everyday relations are often networked and horizontal, and thus implicitly anarchist – a point made clearly by Colin Ward, who goes as far as to portray 'apolitical' kinds of social affiliation such as the local music scene in Milton Keynes as anarchist due to their structure, a network of overlapping voluntary associations existing for practical purposes rather than as part of a political principle of domination (Ward 1992: 116–31).

David Matza puts forward an empirically-based explanation for social deviance based on interviews with admitted 'juvenile delinquents'. Challenging the view that 'delinquents' hold a distinct value system – a view apparently falsified by his interviews – he argued instead that meanings derived from the dominant social and ethical system are reconfigured immanently. For instance, justifications for actions are extended or applied unconventionally. Furthermore, deviance is often associated with a type of psychological state, 'moods of fatalism', in which humanist assumptions are suspended. The result is a process of 'drift' between conformity and resistance, rather than a straightforward binary. Thus, deviant action emerges without the emergence of an alternative to the existing despotic signifier. Rather, the meanings arising from dominant discourses are modified to express a different libidinal and micro-social content (Matza 1964).

The process demonstrated by Matza is one instance of a broader process by means of which dominant significations are changed by subaltern people. Similar processes are documented in Mathiesen's study of the ways prisoners use dominant prison discourse to expand their rights (1965), Vaneigem's work on medieval Christian movements which reinterpreted orthodox doctrine in radical, 'heretical' ways (1994), Ang's work on readings of media texts (1985), Bhabha's discussion of 'sly civility' (Bhabha 1994: ch. 5) and Scott's discussion of the ways in which subaltern groups such as peasants reinterpret and alter the content of the 'public transcript' they ostensibly share with their rulers (Scott 1990). This suggests that, even in a society with a dominant despotic signifier, this signifier does not really 'quilt the field' but rather that the slippage of meaning continues without regard for it. Social power in systems with a despotic signifier is thus not a matter of hegemony – even where leading ideas are ostensibly 'shared', dominant meanings are imposed only by means of violent repression.

Piven and Cloward (1977) provide empirical evidence from four mass movements, including the 1930s American labour movement and the welfare rights movement, to argue for two theses contrary to

Laclau's – first, that political action by ordinary people typically occurs in the everyday settings familiar from their own lives, not in centralised movements seeking to take power, and second, that this preference for the everyday is politically useful because it involves fighting on a battlefield where the poor are comparatively strong. They document the ways in which movements were undermined by 'organisationalism' and their transmutation into pressure groups directed at electoral politics and lobbying.

Rick Fantasia's work (1988) on trade unionism similarly suggests that everyday worker action is not a result of the operation of despotic signification by the union hierarchy. Rather, 'rank and file' workers have their own significations that are constructed immanently, through interactions with other workers and conflicts with management. When strikes happen, workers act on their own conceptions and not on the official 'line', giving their own meanings to concepts such as solidarity and mutual protection. The overwhelming impression left by Fantasia's detailed empirical study is that worker identities are constructed immanently, not transcendentally. This is also the implication of E. P. Thompson's claim that class struggle precedes class, and of the early works of *operaismo/autonomia* scholars such as Sergio Bologna and Romano Alquati who studied everyday resistance in the workplace in developing concepts such as the 'refusal of work' (Thompson 1963: 10; Bologna 1980: 36–61; Alquati 1974).

This kind of everyday activity easily turns into resistance to despotic signification in particular instances, as in studies of *Resistenz* in Nazi Germany and elsewhere. The idea of *Resistenz* suggests the emergence of a fragmentary resistance to Nazi power. Developed by empirical researchers in the 'history of everyday life' (*Alltagsgeschichte*), such as Broszat, Peukert and Grunberger, the concept likens everyday life to a substance through which a technician is attempting to pass an electrical flow. While Nazi power explicitly conceived itself as *Gleichschaltung* – the co-ordination of society as an integral apparatus through which flows pass without opposition, *Resistenz* consists of a range of everyday practices that make this 'substance' of life resistant to the flows passing through it. The thesis of widespread *Resistenz* has been confirmed by historical studies in the Nazi context, and the model has been further applied to East German society and is echoed in studies of life in the Soviet Union.[12]

How is *Resistenz* a problem for Laclauian theory? One point about *Resistenz* is that it contains no despotic signifier. It is motivated by meanings that arise within everyday life and which are resistant to the

148

project of control pursued by the political elite. Indeed, it is in many ways a modality of action that resists the despotic signifier as such – it operates immanently in everyday practices. Thus, as a matter of fact ordinary people in fascist and Stalinist totalitarianisms engaged in micro-political acts of resistance, in the absence of political leadership or a hegemonic anti-regime signifier, and without going through the processes of transcendental meaning-construction which for Laclau are necessary for political action.

There are also specifically political aspects of horizontalism, expressed in anti-capitalist summit protests, the social forum movement and the affinity-group approach of many direct action groups. Graeme Chesters and Ian Walsh analyse the anti-capitalist movement as a new kind of social activity emerging in a context of social complexity, which responds in innovative ways to this complexity instead of falling back on simplifying political forms (Chesters 2006; Chesters and Walsh 2006). Richard Day similarly attacks 'hegemony' (inclusive of despotic signification and sovereignty) as politically repressive and unable to capture the empirical complexity of resistance. The 'dead Gramsci' of his title bears more than a passing resemblance to Laclau. He also singles out Laclau and Mouffe for particular critique, stating that they 'attempt to deconstruct marxist theories of hegemony only to land in firmly liberal – that is, still hegemonic – territory' (Day 2005: 159). Laclau and Mouffe, argues Day, are basically offering a variant of liberal politics, 'more of a return than an advance' (Day 2005: 133). He sees their theory as linked to the identity politics of new social movements, but unable to account for or theorise the 'newest' social movements which are based on affinity and which often reject capitalism and the state form. The social movement studies that arise from this theory fail to recognise the multiplicity of modes of struggle and hence advocate liberal, counter-hegemonic responses to oppression. It expresses 'a logic of representation of interests within a state-regulated system of hegemonic struggles'. Laclau's case for representation is not simply descriptive, but normative (Day 2005: 75). Hence, 'democratic' in Laclauian parlance means 'properly oriented to a postmarxist liberal politics of demand that does not challenge the state form' (Day 2005: 169). The politics of demand here refers to a kind of interest-group politics tied into the status quo, as opposed to a politics of the Act which breaks this frame (Day 2005: 89–90).

The point of Day's book is to explode the view that hegemony is necessary by counter-posing it to what it forecloses, the alternative logic of affinity (a manoeuvre which had been performed earlier by Kropotkin, Buber and Ward with regard to the 'social principle', and Deleuze and Guattari in their break with the Lacanian master or despotic signifier). In the process, he discusses a wide range of social movements – from activist initiatives such as the Billboard Liberation Front, Reclaim the Streets, Indymedia, Ontario Coalition Against Poverty and the Italian social centres movement, to majority-world movements such as the Argentine piqueteros, Brazil's Movimiento Sem Terra, Via Campesina, Mujeres Creando, Karnataka State Farmers' Association and the Chipko 'tree huggers', not to mention various indigenous movements such as the Kahnesatake Mohawk mobilisations.

Other political movements which can be said to operate in a similar way to the anti-capitalist movement, as networks of rhizomes, include the OPM, the social protest movement in Manipur, which was co-ordinated through a locally variant alliance of protest groups,[13] and the Zapatistas, who, although they practise a legislative modality of power through democratic mass assemblies, also emphasise localisation and diversity at the expense of centralised power (Tormey 2006). Indeed, the Zapatistas emerged as a politics of hybridity and immanence, in large part because the 'constructed identity' of the 'Indian' was already articulated in the dominant structure (Higgins 2005). 'The Story of the Sword, the Tree, the Stone and the Water' makes clear how the Zapatistas work (or play) within the immanence of everyday life, a substance which absorbs the sword which strikes it and makes it rust (Marcos 2001). Zapatista figurehead Subcomandante Marcos is very explicit about avoiding a constitutive exclusion even of neo-liberalism and avoiding imposing a Zapatista model in the same way that the government imposes its model as many of his speeches testify.[14]

There is thus a vast literature which documents ways in which the 'powerless', the 'deviant', peasants, indigenous peoples and so forth have elaborated mechanisms of mobilisation (or non-participation) that avoid leadership or representative structures and which retain control over collective objectives. Far from requiring leadership to formulate what it is that such societies or movements 'really are', they are characterised by the development of goals, objectives and meanings immanently or between members on a dialogical, reciprocal or horizontal basis.

It may seem strange to conflate three quite different approaches – Marxist analysis of the situatedness of everyday meanings in socio-historical and economic processes, anthropological and culturalist appreciations of the relativity of experiences and meanings to world-views and perspectives, and radical post-structuralist critiques of the supposed necessity of fixed meanings – but these approaches converge in rebutting the claims of Laclauian theory. Marxism in its purest or most 'orthodox' forms certainly has despotic and transcendental signifiers and claims representation, but the location of social meanings and relations in the context of existential constructions of exploitation and oppression through the regulation, incorporation and control of social and material spaces gives to everyday life a density which is lacking in the Laclauian approach. Similarly with perspectivist approaches, the emphasis on immanent meanings increases the depth of understanding of everyday life; as does the post-structuralist approach, applied to textualities of everyday life. In three supposedly different fields, or through three different lenses (historical/economic – perspectival/ethnographic – discursive/textual), these approaches all undermine Laclauian assumptions in much the same way.

What is 'hegemonic' politics?

So Laclau and Mouffe are not able to theorise forms of social movements beyond the state form. What about movements which use, or aspire to use, the state? Do these consistently follow a Laclauian model?

The exaggeration involved in Laclau and Mouffe's analysis of politics becomes clear when they slip across into conjunctural analysis. It is clearly a blatant overstatement to call Thatcherism – a surface-level political phenomenon which won the temporary and syncretic allegiance of at best 20 per cent of the population – an 'organic ideology' which 'construct[s] a new hegemonic articulation', can 'unify multiple subject positions' and cause a 'displacement of the frontier of the social' (Laclau and Mouffe 1985: 176). The change effected by Thatcherism is clearly in official, public discourse, not in everyday life (except, of course, for its disastrous social effects). This exaggeration leads to a use of the concept of 'common sense' which is equally superficial, referring mainly to the pseudo-consensus created by politicians' manipulation of official, 'public' political discourse – which Laclau and Mouffe accord the high-flung status of a 'social imaginary' (Laclau and Mouffe 1985: 160, 163). Doubtless there are phenomena of social imaginary operative in contemporary Britain, in the formation of everyday practices, the effects of the mass media and the complex emergence of in-groups and exclusionary relations within society. But the 'political' inscription of these effects is a secondary reinscription of a phenomenon more properly viewed as 'everyday'.

Laclau's reading of Gramsci elides a crucial aspect of the latter's theory. For Gramsci, hegemony is constructed not between a despotic signifier and floating signifiers but between a political movement and immanent existential forces in everyday life. People have conceptions of the world which form entire ways of seeing and acting; the point of transformative praxis is to alter or overcome conservative and 'common sense' conceptions by articulating beliefs and desires which exceed the existing system of inscription. Hence the importance that ideologies and intellectuals be 'organic', speaking to active and immanent forces, rather than simply 'arbitrary' or 'willed'. Indeed, hegemony is viewed as operating in civil society as well as the state, as an active force; the gesture of despotic signification is identified with the absence of hegemony, with *transformismo* and passive revolution. Thus, Gramsci's politics is not at all about elite manipulation or the appeals of signifiers on the elite political level; it is about the construction of an active politics in everyday life.[15] In this case, Laclau's elision is symptomatic – what he ignores in Gramsci is precisely what must be repressed for his own theory to operate, the 'density' of everyday life as a field of meanings and immanent activities rather than as a set of floating elements just waiting to be articulated by a despotic signifier. Laclau's version of hegemony involves showing oneself to be able to manage and control a political community (Laclau and Zac 1994: 16), so that, for instance, the main public forms of a totalitarian regime can be described as hegemonic (Laclau 1990: 238). This inverts Gramsci's usage, where hegemony as persuasion and cognitive and emotional appeal is distinct from domination, that is, rule by force (Gramsci 1971: 57–9).

As Gramsci rightly saw, where political elites are able to establish popular support, it is usually by channelling identities and concerns already arising in everyday life as a 'dense' social field. Hence one finds phenomena such as clientelism or patronage, and political systems integrated with the mass media. Political elites are always in fact faced with a need to *re*articulate elements operative in everyday systems of meaning, rather than to construct articulations from scratch.

Let us look, similarly, to the literature on state-formation in the majority world. In one such text, dealing with sub-Saharan Africa, the authors argue that 'whole regions have become virtually independent, probably for the foreseeable future, from all central control' (Bayart, Ellis and Hibou 1999: 19–20). As a result, the state becomes an almost superficial entity, leading to a split in society between 'a legal edifice which is the partner of multilateral institutions and Western governments, and the real fabric of society' (Bayart, Ellis and Hibou 1999: 20). The state does not remain empty, but rather integrates into society; it does this, however, not through hegemony, but through hidden networks of informal elites and power-brokers. The result is the emergence of states which have strong, but tangled, social roots, operating as 'shadow' or 'rhizome' states enmeshed in broad, complex social networks (Bayart, Ellis and Hibou 1999: 47, 81, 88). Clientelism and electoral systems act as mediations, plugging the state into informal power networks (Bayart, Ellis and Hibou 1999: 48). Externally imposed reforms disappear into this web of deceptions and networks, and flows thus escape any political locus (Bayart, Ellis and Hibou 1999: 97). At the limit, Africa even becomes impossible to denumerate (Bayart, Ellis and Hibou 1999: 116). Economic power tends to shift to decentred networks linked to segmentary communities, more networked even than traditional mafias. In short, a state emerges which is not itself the locus of social meaning, but a kind of fiction, hiding informal power (concentrated in shadowy elites or diffused through networks) that constructs the actual integrative force of society. Even within the state, one does not always find Laclauian hegemony.

Conclusion: why not radical democracy

So what are the conclusions of all this? First and foremost, that Laclau and Mouffe's claims about the necessity, inevitability and constitutivity of certain social logics are false. They are falsified by an extensive literature on social movements that shows many cases in which these logics do not operate. This is an important analytical point for those studying social movements, and has implications for the most basic ontological postulates of Laclauian theory.

Secondly, this rebuttal of the political inevitability of despotic signification also has political implications. The political implication of Laclauian theory is extremely restrictive; it basically proclaims that there is only one game in town, that of despotic signification, representation and hegemony. This forecloses on a range of possibilities which in fact arise in social movements but which are ruled out in principle on this kind of reading. The opening of the analytical field

153

also opens up a wider range of political and social options. Of course it is still open to Laclauians to claim that radical democracy by means of despotic signification is the best of the options available; but they do so in a political field which is no longer reduced to one game (or to radical democracy versus totalitarianism or fantasmatic fullness), but which includes everything from hidden transcripts and shadow states to stateless societies and networked swarms.

The purpose of this chapter has been to provide a critique, not a complete alternative theory. We have attempted elsewhere to begin to theorise what horizontalism involves in concrete terms,[16] something which is also being attempted by others (Day 2005, Holloway 2002). A few brief comments are in order, however. Firstly, the possibility of avoiding despotic signification can be effectively theorised in terms of the Deleuzian distinction between arborescent apparatuses (which do require such a signifier) and rhizomes (which do not). The adoption of rhizomatic and horizontal social relations helps to diffuse discursive construction in such a way as to reduce the risk of despotic signification arising.

While avoiding arborescence, horizontal movements do not, of course, avoid contingency, but they handle it in a different way, elaborating it in the forms of affinities and smooth space instead of trying to ward it off through despotic signification. They avoid 'the political' in the Mouffean sense, and in the sense of Kropotkin's 'political principle'. But they are not 'apolitical' in the sense of being without contestation, deliberation and power. They tend, however, to reject the negative, dominatory power of statist and hierarchical relations in favour of a type of power which is constructed contingently and horizontally, and which attempts to avoid rigid arrangements and constitutive exclusions. This idea of two types of power is not new. One finds this distinction in Foucault, and especially Deleuze's reading of Foucault; in Hardt and Negri's distinction between constitutive and constituted power, Castoriadis's instituting and instituted imaginaries, Kropotkin's social and political principles, Benjamin's law-destroying (as opposed to law-creating or upholding) violence and Holloway's distinction between power-over and power-to. We think the rejection of hierarchical domination is necessary, but not sufficient, to eliminate oppression in everyday life. This still leaves an entire field of possibilities in terms of what strategies can be developed to further enrich rhizomatic relations. Bakhtinian dialogism and a Derridean/Spivakian ethics of openness are examples of constructive strategies of affirmative power which help to combat exclusions.

The situation might become clearer if we contrast Mouffe's endorsement of Schmitt with the rather different positions of Walter Benjamin, Herbert Marcuse and Giorgio Agamben. Benjamin pursued an ongoing debate with Schmitt, for instance in his *Theses on the Philosophy of History*. Thesis Eight states that: 'The tradition of the oppressed teaches us that the "state of emergency" in which we live is not the exception but the rule'.[17] This echoes Schmitt's suggestion that social and legal order are founded on a moment of exception. The difference between Benjamin and Schmitt, however, is substantial, because Schmitt invokes the 'state of emergency' as a way of maintaining the power of law and social order even when these are collapsing – in other words, law is to be defended through its own suspension. For Benjamin, in contrast, the awareness of contingency is not pegged back onto a defence of fixed structures, but is supposed to open onto new utopian possibilities. In other words, both Schmitt and Benjamin enter a space where the social order becomes contestable, but Schmitt tries to maintain the order in the face of its own contestability, whereas Benjamin's point is to use this contestability to undermine the existing social system. Agamben has repeated this kind of criticism recently, using the state's reliance on states of exception to attack its very existence and instead call for utopian imaginings of a 'coming community' in relation to autonomist politics (Agamben 1993, 2005). Marcuse, in his critique of totalitarianism, denounces decisionism as irrationalist, as 'justification by mere existence', and as misrepresenting political issues as existential. Further, its socio-political role is concealed. 'Although these sacrifices are made at the "brink of meaninglessness", they have nonetheless a concealed, very "rational" purpose: factually and ideologically stabilizing the current system of producing and reproducing life' (Marcuse 1988: 30–1).

The different positions on states of exception do not occur in a vacuum. The duality between endorsing and denouncing the state's reliance on exception can be linked more broadly to the duality between active and reactive (or micro-fascist) forms of desire in the work of Deleuze and Guattari – whereas Schmitt's work is a micro-fascist reinscription of order into contingency, Benjamin's project has the characteristics of an escape, of a line of flight from the disaster of modernity. Laclau and Mouffe are here in a continuity with Schmitt (explicitly so in Mouffe's case), whereas horizontalism derives more from Benjamin and Agamben, who can be typified as horizontalist theorists.

We feel in particular that what Day calls the 'logic of affinity' offers an ethically and socially attractive alternative to logics of despotic signification. Affinity and non-representation leave open possibilities of interrelations that are ruled out by Laclauian hegemony. One example is dialogue in the Bakhtinian sense. In Bakhtinian dialogue, 'utterly incompatible elements . . . are distributed among several worlds . . . within several complete fields of vision of equal value' (Bakhtin 1984: 12). Bakhtinian dialogue is impossible within a Laclauian framework because it lacks a despotic signifier; its very possibility is conditioned on the suspension or abolition of this signifier. It creates the possibility of listening and communicating across borders; in this way, it opens up possibilities for overcoming the imposition of voicelessness on indigenous peoples, disempowered social groups and people who are different in various ways, even of other species and the biosphere, without this taking the form of an equivalence or a radical exclusion. In this way it realises a Derridean openness to otherness, to the possibility of another unrecognised exclusion to overcome, far more effectively than a Laclauian approach which ultimately returns to the state and its 'moment of decision'.

Notes

1. Laclau explicitly states that 'people need *an* order, and the actual content of it becomes a secondary situation' (1996a: 44). See also Laclau and Zac (1994) for a particularly systematic statement of Laclau's pro-order sentiments.
2. See, for instance, the essays in Howarth et al. (2000) applying Laclauian theory to social movements such as Latin American populism, inter-war French fascism, Green ideology and Irish Republicanism; Stavrakakis (2001); Norval (1996).
3. See Kropotkin (2002), Clastres (1989), Sahlins (1972), Lee and DeVore (1978), Barclay (1982) and Turnbull (1987).
4. 'The !Kung of the Kalahari Desert', http://www.ucc.uconn.edu/~epsadm03/kung.html based on Shostak (1981).
5. Robert Redfield, cited at http://anthro.palomar.edu/social/soc_2.htm.
6. anon. (1999), 'Rumble in the jungle. Fighting for freedom in West Papua' [RJ], *Do or Die* 8: 231, 230, 232.
7. From OPM/TPN Communiqué 1/12/99, cited http://www.angelfire.com/zine2/blackstarnorth/tribalwar.html.
8. Hakim Bey, 'The Temporary Autonomous Zone', at http://www.t0.or.at/hakimbey/taz/taz3a.htm.

9. Feral Faun (1988), 'Feral Revolution', http://www.insurgentdesire.org.uk/feralrevolution.htm.
10. See, for instance, Guattari (1995), Curtis et al. (2000) and Jim Sinclair (2005), 'Autism Network International: The Development of a Community and its Culture', http://web.syr.edu/~jisincla/History_of_ANI.html.
11. See Scott (1985), Galvan (2004), Hecht and Simone (1994: 14–15); Lomnitz (1977); Chatterjee (1993), Fantasia (1988) and Kotkin (1997).
12. The most extensive documenting of evidence is in the six-volume 'Bavaria Project' by Martin Broszat et al., *Bayern in der NS-Zeit* (Munich/Vienna, 1977–83). See also Peukert (1988). Fulbrook (1997) explicitly discusses East German everyday life in terms of *Resistenz*. See Kotkin (1997) for discussion of the Soviet Union.
13. See Andrew Robinson (2005), 'The Rhizomes of Manipur', work in progress, available at www.nottingham.ac.uk/iaps/Manipur%20illustrated.pdf.
14. See, for example, Workers' Solidarity, 'Interview with Subcomandante Marcos', 11 May 1994; archived at http://flag.blackened.net/revolt/mexico/ezln/anmarin.html.
15. See, for example, Robinson (2005b), Nun (1996), Nemeth (1980) and Adamson (1980).
16. See Robinson (2004), Robinson and Tormey (2005) and Tormey (2006).
17. Walter Benjamin (1940), 'On the Concept of History/Theses on the Philosophy of History', http://www.leedstrinity.ac.uk/depart/media/staff/ls/WBenjamin/CONCEPT2.html, accessed October 2007.

Friends and Enemies, Slaves and Masters: Fanaticism, Wendell Phillips and the Limits of Agonism

Joel Olson

Fanaticism presents one of the most important political problems since 11 September 2001. Curiously, however, this subject has so far largely evaded scrutiny by political theorists. The rise in extremist activity since the end of the Cold War is often noted and decried, but contemporary democratic theorists have yet to analyse extremism as a political category. This is true even of the branch of theory usually referred to as 'agonistic democratic theory', which maintains that conflict is a permanent, central and potentially useful feature of democratic politics. Current debates between deliberative and agonistic models of democracy concern whether public deliberation is irreducibly agonistic or whether it should strive conceptually for consensus. Yet this debate obscures what these two branches of democratic theory share. Despite an appreciation for the role of conflict in politics, agonistic democratic theory's approach to political conflict is quite similar to its purportedly conflict-averse rival. That is, like deliberative models, agonistic theories overwhelmingly focus on conflict that takes place among parties who share a common liberal ethical and political framework that provides the principles and rules within which legitimate political contest takes place. Contemporary democratic theory does not much analyse challenges to this framework. To the extent that it does, it overwhelmingly understands them as a threat to democracy. Democratic theory lacks an account of fanaticism, then, because it tends to focus on conflicts between parties who share a liberal framework and largely ignores conflicts over the framework itself – which is precisely the terrain that tends to breed zealots. As a result, democratic theory has yet to grapple with one of the key political problems of the twenty-first century.

This narrow focus also leads democratic theorists to assume that extremism is inherently anti-democratic, since it rejects the 'official' framework of political engagement. This assumption, however, presumes the inherent justice of that framework. Fanaticism often undermines democracy when parties share the same ethico-political framework within which to resolve their disagreements. This is not necessarily true, however, when the parties dispute the justice of the framework itself. In such conflicts, zealotry can sometimes be a democratic tool when it rallies public opinion to expand the citizen body or its power. In struggles over the framework within which politics takes place, zealotry can be useful to radical democrats as well as reactionaries.

A theory that accounts for struggles between competing ethico-political frameworks and the role of extremism in them, then, can expand and enrich contemporary democratic thought beyond the boundaries of agonism. One key source for such a theory, I argue, is the work of the great abolitionist agitator Wendell Phillips. With his fellow radicals in the American Anti-Slavery Society (AAS), Phillips sought to deepen American democracy through what theorists would now call agonistic participation. Yet the function of such contentious 'talk', as Phillips called it, was not to bring citizens together onto the same playing field. Rather, it was to *divide* the public sphere into friends (slaves and abolitionists) and enemies (masters) and to encourage conflict between them. By mobilising public opinion in such a Manichean fashion, Phillips used fanaticism as a strategy for hegemony. Rather than assume the necessity of a common playing field, he sought to pit an abolitionist framework against the slave masters' framework in order to install the former as the new 'common sense' of American public opinion. By drawing lines between friends and enemies, repudiating compromise and pressuring the political middle to choose between slaves and masters, Phillips's fanaticism insisted that American liberty and equality could not exist alongside slavery. That this argument seems blatantly obvious today proves there can be democratic potential in the fanatical encouragement of intractable conflict.

My argument begins by explaining how liberal theory tends to view conflict as a problem of accommodating diverse opinions within a political community. Using Carl Schmitt's critique of liberalism and his friends/enemies notion of politics, I show how this perspective tends to ignore conflicts over liberal principles themselves. In other words, liberal theory tends to focus on disagreements among parties who share a common moral and political framework and much less so on conflicts over the framework itself. This focus is reproduced in agonistic democratic theory. Through a critique of the work of Chantal Mouffe, I argue that such theory sidesteps the problem of irreconcilable conflict in politics. The failure to theorise conflict over the framework of political engagement leads agonistic democrats to ironically commit the very same 'evasion of the political' they criticise deliberative models for doing. It also leads them to accept the view that fanaticism is inherently undemocratic even though it is a conflict-based form of political engagement that would seem to merit their closer attention.

I then turn to the work of Phillips to outline an alternative approach to the study of democracy, conflict and extremism. In his fight against the Slave Power, Phillips does not presume a model of democracy in which individuals interact within the perimeter of a consensually agreed-upon ethico-political framework, nor does he try to construct such a framework. Rather, he accepts that conflict is often over the framework itself. Through an interpretation of Phillips's speeches on the power of public opinion, I argue that the purpose of political discourse or 'talk' for him is to reshape public opinion, and that doing so requires increasing political conflict rather than moderating it. For Phillips, the purpose of talk is to agitate public opinion until a new moral and political 'common sense' that reflects principles of justice can be forged. Talk is a means to achieve hegemony by dividing the public into friends and enemies and attacking the latter. I demonstrate the strategic nature of Phillips's notion of talk through an analysis of some of his key speeches during the Civil War.

The democratic potential of this approach is evident in Phillips's attack on the US Constitution as a pro-slavery document. In this attack he draws uncompromising lines between friends and enemies of the slave. Yet he does so in a way that radically redefines American citizenship to include African Americans and to recognise the democratic power of Black agency. Ironically, Phillips reveals the contingency of liberty, equality and democracy (and thus their susceptibility to radical transformation) through his uncompromising commitment to anti-slavery and anti-racist principles. Like Mouffe, he recognises the essentially contested nature of these concepts. Yet he does not seek to create a consensus on the use of these ideals as the moral and political grounds upon which debate takes place, as Mouffe does. Instead, he seeks to *divide* the nation into those who support sham liberty and those who support real freedom. I conclude by sketching the boundaries of a democratic extremism. Only when conflict is between ethico-political frameworks and only when fanaticism seeks to expand ordinary people's participation in political affairs, I suggest, is it likely to contribute to democratic struggles.

Conflict and liberalism

Fanaticism, extremism or zealotry (I use the terms interchangeably here) is often regarded as an individual temperament, a condition caused by desperation and/or psychological instability that drives a person to engage in political activity that goes well beyond the mainstream. Suicide bombers and other terrorists are the archetype of this temperament.[1] It is much less recognised that fanaticism is also a strategy to achieve power. It is this specifically political notion of fanaticism that I am concerned with here. Zealotry is the political mobilisation of the refusal to compromise. It is an approach to politics that divides the world into friends and enemies in order to mobilise people in the service of a cause one is passionately committed to. It is a form of engagement that seeks not to come to terms with an opponent but to defeat it.[2]

Democratic theory's difficulty in understanding political zealotry begins with a tension in liberal democracies. A distinguishing feature of liberal democracies is freedom of opinion. In addition, like any state, liberal regimes must ensure a stable political community. The tension results when opinion threatens stability. How is it possible to conserve the polity while permitting the expression of ideas that threaten the cohesion and stability of the polity? This tension is well recognised by liberal theorists. Diversity of opinion is crucial for them because it respects individual liberty and generates ideas that can lead to social progress. Yet it can also disrupt the stability upon which freedom and progress rest. As Richard Bellamy writes, 'Pluralism is both the life-blood of democracy and its greatest challenge' (1999: 115). It is the double-edged sword of liberalism.

For liberals like Bellamy this is an enduring tension that democracies must constantly attend to. For critics of liberalism, however, it is an irresolvable contradiction that undermines the efficacy of liberalism in building stable states. As the conservative legal scholar Carl Schmitt argues, liberalism rests on a plurality of ideas produced through the process of open discussion. Democracy, meanwhile, requires a set of commonly held ideas among citizens, and must exclude ideas that jeopardise citizens' unity. Further, while liberalism presumes universal equality, democracy is necessarily exclusionary. That is, democracy presumes equality among equals (i.e. among citizens) but inequality between unequals (i.e. between citizens and non-citizens). Universal equality under liberalism is practically meaningless, Schmitt argues, because it is attached to no substantive power and it provides no substantive power. When everyone is equal, equality is a grand but empty gesture. Democracy does give equality substance, however, because it insists on certain exclusions (between citizens and non-citizens) that make equality meaningful for citizens. Ironically, inequality and exclusion, not free discussion and pluralism, make equality material. 'Equality is only interesting and valuable politically so long as it has substance, and for that reason at least the possibility and the risk of inequality' (Schmitt 1985a: 9). Thus, Schmitt argues, liberalism and democracy are irreconcilable. Liberalism rests on discussion and openness – heterogeneity. Democracy rests on a community constituted by exclusions – homogeneity. Democracy requires a homogeneity that the heterogeneity of liberalism perpetually undermines.

Schmitt's critique of liberalism is important because it illuminates the framework within which liberal democratic theory tends to analyse political conflict. Liberal theorists tend to presume that political contention can be settled through models and techniques that moderate disagreement. There need be no fundamental, irresolvable conflicts; political cohesion is possible so long as parties are willing to negotiate and compromise. For Schmitt, this optimism fails to recognise the essentially dichotomous and antagonistic nature of politics. He argues that politics at its most elemental is an activity that divides the world into friends and enemies, with the potential of physical combat between them. 'Friends' are those with whom one shares a common identity, while an enemy is 'the other, the stranger' who is 'existentially something different and alien' from oneself and one's friends (Schmitt 1996: 26). Politics reflects the human tendency to distinguish between friends and enemies, a formulation in which combat is not inevitable but always latent. 'War is neither the aim nor the purpose nor even the very content of politics. But as an ever present possibility it is the leading presupposition which determines in a characteristic way human action and thinking and thereby creates a specifically political behaviour' (Schmitt 1996: 34). Liberalism, he charges, denies the inevitability of enemies. It assumes that no one need be excluded from the public sphere and that the potential for conflict need not be omnipresent. The essence of liberal politics is not conflict between friends and enemies but the resolution of differences among 'the people', who are all potential friends.

Liberal theorists, in consequence, tend to concentrate on conflicts in which the competing parties are not irreconcilably opposed because they share a similar conception of the 'rules' by which conflict is played out. That is, liberal theory tends to focus on conflicts that take place within the same ethico-political framework, by which I mean the principles, rules, values and norms that structure how members of a polity express and resolve differences with each other. Parties may compete with each other on the political field, but they do not fight over the nature of the field itself. In regards to liberalism, this field is constituted by the values of individual liberty and equality. As Chantal Mouffe argues, liberal democracy requires a consensus among adversaries regarding these values (1999b: 756). While all must hold to these values, they nevertheless give rise to multiple meanings and interpretations, as there is no single absolute definition of them. Thus, the polity is constituted by a commitment to liberty and equality as well as by disagreement over their meaning and implementation (Mouffe 2000: 102). Schmitt's theory of politics, on the other hand, suggests a more expansive view of conflict. For him, conflict may take place not just within the same ethico-political framework but also over the legitimacy of the framework itself. His model assumes no consensus on basic political values.

Liberal democratic theory typically disregards understandings of politics such as Schmitt's for being overly simplistic. A 'friends versus enemies' model leaves little room for the subtleties of politics and fails to recognise that conflict is always contingent and amenable to compromise. The aim of liberal democratic theory is rather to moderate conflict so as to preclude a friends/enemies dichotomy. It regards the emergence of Manichaeism as a failure of politics rather than its essence. As a result, when liberal theory does confront such conflict, frequently its first reaction is to exclude those who encourage it. For example, Bellamy writes, 'A politics of reciprocity excludes fanatics who scorn the necessity of justifying themselves to others in terms the addressees can recognise, and insist instead that the truth can only be perceived if one adopts their creed. Negotiation with such persons has no point because they do not themselves acknowledge the need for it. Crucially, they fail to demonstrate equal concern and respect for the opinion of others' (1999: 107).

Bellamy's argument ignores the fact that fanatics such as Ian Paisley in Northern Ireland and Jean-Marie Le Pen in France regularly participate in democratic politics. It is unclear how a politics of reciprocity would exclude them. And even if it is possible to exclude them, these actors do not suddenly disappear from the stage. It is legitimate for a theory to exclude enemies of its ethico-political framework from deliberations in order to preserve its integrity. Nevertheless, it must still consider the implications of such exclusion. Unfortunately, agonistic democratic theory has little to say about conflict between competing frameworks, tending to concentrate on conflict within a common, typically liberal, ethico-political framework. Even agonistic theories, ironically, do not sufficiently appreciate the role of conflict in politics. Not surprisingly, they are frequently uncomfortable with the zealots such conflicts sometimes produce.

Agonism and the limits of 'friendly enemies'

One of the central concerns of agonistic democratic theory regards what Bonnie Honig calls 'the displacement of politics', or the attempt by various sorts of political theories to remove discord, conflict, resistance and struggle from politics. Contemporary liberal, communitarian and deliberative democratic theories, for example, construct a notion of politics as 'stabilizing moral and political subjects, building consensus, maintaining agreements, or consolidating communities and identities' (Honig 1993: 2). These 'virtue' theories of politics seek to displace conflict by conceptualising politics as administration, regulation, consensus and juridical settlement. Thus, they 'tend to remove politics from the reach of democratic contest' (Honig 1993: 4).

What is needed, Honig argues, is a theory of democratic politics that accommodates conflict rather than contains it. Agonistic theories of democracy hold that conflict and power are the essence of democracy. Neither deliberation nor compromise nor a communal consensus on the good life can ever completely drive power from politics. The task is not to reduce or eliminate conflict but to transform it so that it enhances democratic life rather than threatens it. As Honig puts it, agonistic theories of democracy 'converge on one point: they are critical of attempts to still the unruly conflicts and contests of democratic politics for fear that the result must be violations of freedom, plurality, tolerance, individuality, or community' (Honig 1993: 14). What Jacques Rancière refers to as 'the political suppression of politics' can only be countered by a resolutely agonistic political theory in which conflict is a recognised and appreciated feature of the democratic process rather than a problem to be deliberated away (Rancière 1995).

Nevertheless, agonistic democratic theories place limits on political contestation that go largely unacknowledged. This is evident in the work of one of the most prominent theorists of agonistic democracy, Chantal Mouffe. Like Honig, Mouffe is concerned with the 'evasion of the political' in contemporary political philosophy. Rationalist, universalist, individualist thinking, she argues, evades politics because it does not recognise that antagonism is inherent to the public sphere (Mouffe 1993). Following Schmitt, Mouffe accepts that conflict between friends and enemies is the defining feature of politics. Yet she recognises that such a conception of the political poses a challenge for radical democrats like her who believe in pluralism, political liberalism and social democracy – all of which, Schmitt argues, denies a friends/enemies framework (Schmitt 1996; Schwab 1989).

To resolve this tension, Mouffe holds that democrats need to recognise, with Schmitt, that conflict is the 'crucial category of politics'. But this need not lead to authoritarian conclusions, as it did for him. Conflict can be healthy for a democratic public sphere if *antagonism* can be transformed into *agonism*. An antagonism, Mouffe argues, takes place between *enemies*, or 'persons who have no common symbolic space'. Agonism, however, involves conflict with an *adversary* whom one struggles with but respects and therefore does not seek to destroy. An adversary, paradoxically, is a 'friendly enemy'. It consists of 'persons who are friends because they share a common symbolic space but also enemies because they want to organize this common symbolic space in a different way' (Mouffe 2000: 13).

The challenge for Mouffe, then, is to develop a politics that creates this 'common symbolic space' and thereby enables 'legitimate dissent among friends' (Mouffe 1999a: 5). Enemies have nothing in common. Their only recourse is combat. Yet combat is not inevitable because enmity is not immutable. Mouffe argues that who counts as a 'friend' and who counts as an 'enemy', as well as the relations between them, are socially constructed. Thus, it is possible to renegotiate tensions between them in ways that do not lead to the kind of mortal combat that Schmitt foresees. The creation and acceptance of common 'ethico-political principles' by the contending parties transforms the very nature of political conflict and makes a friends/enemies conception of politics compatible with pluralism, liberty and equality:

> The adversary is in a certain sense an enemy, but a legitimate enemy with whom there exists a common ground. Adversaries fight against each other, but they do not put into question the legitimacy of their respective positions. They share a common allegiance to the ethico-political principles of liberal democracy. However, they disagree about their meanings and their forms of implementation, and such a disagreement is not one that could be resolved through rational argument. Hence the antagonistic element in the relationship. Conceived in such a way, liberal-democratic politics can be seen as a consistent and never fully achieved enterprise to diffuse the antagonistic potential present in human relations. (Mouffe 1999a: 4)

Rather than eliminate conflict, the task of agonistic democratic theory is to create a common ethico-political framework within which conflict can take place.

Mouffe's emphasis in her recent work has been to theorise the transformation of antagonism into agonism and to emphasise the need for a 'shared adhesion' to the principles of liberty and equality (Mouffe 2000: 102). But she has not much considered the possibility of a failure to develop a common ethico-political framework between contending parties. In other words, she has much to say about adversaries but little to say about enemies proper. Further, as Monique Deveaux (1999) notes, agonistic democrats as a whole have surprisingly little to say about such entrenched conflicts.[3] Yet such conflicts are surely crucial for democratic theorists to understand. What if, for example, one of the parties in a conflict refuses to adhere to a liberal framework because, it claims, it violates its cultural tenets? Or what if one of the parties agrees with the principles of liberty and equality but accuses the other party of fatally compromising them? Wendell Phillips, for example, cherished liberty and equality but declared these concepts as articulated in the US Constitution to be a sham due to the clauses that protected slavery. Despite a shared republican philosophy, he held that it was impossible to turn abolitionists and slave masters into 'friendly enemies'. Antagonistic conflict was unavoidable even though the parties ostensibly shared a common ethico-political framework.

Mouffe does not totally ignore conflicts between groups that do not share a common framework, yet on those occasions when she does address them she almost always regards them as a threat to democracy. She alludes to the break-up of the former Yugoslavia along ethnic lines, terrorism after 9/11 and the actions of the religious right in the United States as examples of when antagonism fails to turn into agonism and friends/enemies conflict becomes destructive (see Mouffe 2001, Mouffe 2005b and Angus 2005, respectively). The way to deal with such conflict, she argues, is to exclude from the public sphere those who do not share the 'ethico-political values of liberty and equality for all'. Her notion of a radical and plural democracy 'requires discriminating between demands which are to be accepted as part of the agonistic debate and those which are to be excluded. A democratic society cannot treat those who put its basic institutions into question as legitimate adversaries' (Mouffe 2005a: 120).

It is legitimate for Mouffe to exclude on principle those who do not share her ethico-political framework; indeed, maintaining the integrity of her liberal framework requires that she do so. Yet it is still necessary to consider the implications of such exclusions. Two questions emerge in particular. First, who will do the excluding? The decision to exclude is inevitably a political one, yet nowhere does Mouffe provide for an authority who will determine when a party has violated the commitment to liberty and equality and must therefore be excluded. Absent such an authority, the decision would most likely be taken by the hegemon, which obviously has an interest in defining threats to a liberal and egalitarian framework to its advantage. (Slave masters, for example, argued that abolitionists threatened their liberties as property owners and as whites and therefore did not deserve a voice in the public sphere, so they tried to suppress the latter through censorship and harassment.) Second, it is unlikely that the excluded will accept their exclusion silently. What sorts of struggles might such exclusions result in? In other words, the necessity of exclusion compels the question: what are the implications for democratic theory regarding struggles over the ethico-political framework within which politics takes place? What happens when antagonistic conflict breaks out in the agonistic polity?

These questions relate to the struggle for hegemony, but Mouffe generally does not place her democratic theory in the context of hegemonic struggles. It might seem strange to argue this, given Mouffe and Ernesto Laclau's seminal work *Hegemony and Socialist Strategy* (1985). However, as Jules Townshend (2004) notes in his overview of Mouffe and Laclau's impact on political theory, Mouffe's post-*Hegemony* work has not much engaged the concept. One place she does address the relationship between hegemony and agonistic democratic theory is in her recent book *On the Political*. There she repeats the argument from *Hegemony* that politics is a struggle between political projects seeking hegemony. Yet throughout the book she constrains hegemonic conflict to those struggles that take place within a common ethico-political framework (2005a: 32–3, *passim*). She does not examine hegemonic struggles over the nature and content of the liberal egalitarian framework, nor does she consider struggles that ostensibly take place within such a framework but are nevertheless irreconcilable – such as that between republican masters and republican abolitionists.

Mouffe insists that only an agonistic political theory can properly acknowledge the central role of conflict in politics and reconcile it with democracy. Yet she constructs her theory by blurring the categories of friend and enemy and thereby diluting her notion of political conflict. Turning 'enemies' into 'adversaries' by redefining conflict from a struggle between friends and enemies to a conflict among friends (or 'friendly enemies') is a clever theoretical move. Yet it ultimately shunts irreducible antagonism. As a result, Mouffe's theory is closer to sophisticated theories of deliberative democracy that account for conflict among citizens than she acknowledges.[4] Mouffe criticises deliberation for being based on a consensus model of politics, yet by her own account an agonistic democratic theory rests on a 'conflictual consensus' in which the contending parties consent to a common framework within which all other issues are to be debated (Mouffe 1999b: 756).

The enemy ultimately disappears in Mouffe's political theory, but not in politics. Some enemies cannot be turned into friends, and some conflicts are inherently antagonistic. When parties conflict over the very ethico-political framework within which debate takes place, they have reached the horizon of deliberation. The only option left is struggle. Often, such struggles produce zealots. To analyse effectively fanaticism and intractable political conflict in the wake of 9/11, then, we need to go beyond current democratic theory. Examining the struggle against slavery in the United States is useful in this regard, for it was a struggle in which questions of fanaticism and the role of conflict in politics were hotly debated. One of the most eloquent, fiery and popular thinkers on these matters was the radical abolitionist Wendell Phillips. The speeches of Phillips suggest new ways to think about extremism and the role of conflict in politics. For as with Schmitt, Phillips held a friends/enemies view of politics, yet unlike the German thinker, he used such a perspective to advance a radical notion of democracy.

Phillips and the hegemony of public opinion

Wendell Phillips was one of the leading figures of the radical wing of the abolitionist movement led by William Lloyd Garrison. Born in 1811 to a prominent Boston family, he rejected the expectations of his patrician lineage and joined the unpopular abolitionist movement in 1837 at the urging of his soon-to-be wife, Anne Greene. He quickly became a leader in the movement. A masterful public speaker, he and Frederick Douglass were probably the most popular orators of the nineteenth century. (He delivered his most famous speech, 'The Lost Arts', over two thousand times.) Phillips was a leading American radical from the 1830s through the Civil War, Reconstruction and the post-war labour movement until his death in 1884 (Stewart 1986).

Shaping public opinion is the central objective of Phillips's political philosophy and his primary weapon in doing so is what he calls 'talk'. 'What is talk?' he asks in a speech at the onset of the Civil War. 'Why, it is the representative of brains. And what is the characteristic glory of the nineteenth century? That it is ruled by brains, and not by muscle; that rifles are gone by, and ideas have come in; and, of course in such an era, talk is the fountain-head of all things' ('Suffrage for Woman', s.2, 118).[5] Even in the midst of the Civil War he believes that talk is the pre-eminent influence on politics in the nineteenth century. The abolitionists are 'the all-talk party', for they seek to abolish slavery by turning Northern public opinion against it. 'The age of bullets is over,' Phillips says. 'The age of men armed in mail is over. The age of thrones has gone by. The age of statesmen . . . is over. The age of thinking men has come. With the aid of God, then, every man I can reach I will set *thinking* on the subject of slavery. [Cheers]' ('Public Opinion', s.1, 50).

As the above quotes suggest, Phillips epitomises an Enlightenment faith in the power of reason to triumph over coercion. At first brush, then, his views on talk and public opinion might seem to embody precisely the sort of liberal naiveté that Schmitt is so critical of. But Phillips is different, for he does not view talk as a replacement for power so much as a form of power itself. Phillips's goal is to create a new abolitionist, anti-racist public opinion and he sees his principal weapon in this struggle as talk. The purpose of talk, as he understands it, is not to turn enemies into adversaries. Rather, it is to win the struggle between friends and enemies, slaves and masters, apostles of justice and traders in human flesh. In other words, *Phillips does not employ talk to moderate conflict but to increase political agitation.*

This is evident in Phillips's famous speech on John Brown's raid on Harpers Ferry, given just two weeks after the assault in 1859. In it Phillips provides perhaps his most radical philosophical defence of public opinion and the power of talk. He begins the speech by saying:

> Insurrection of thought always precedes the insurrection of arms. The last twenty years [referring to the abolitionist movement] have been an insurrection of thought. We seem to be entering on a new phase of this great American struggle. It seems to me that we have never accepted – as Americans, we have never accepted our own civilization. We have held back from the inference which we ought to have drawn from the admitted principles which underlie our life . . . The idea on the other side of the water [Europe] seems to be, that man is created to be taken care of by somebody else. God did not leave him fit to go alone; he is in everlasting pupilage to the wealthy and the educated . . . The Old World, therefore, has always distrusted the average conscience, – the common sense of the millions. It seems to me the idea of our civilization, underlying all American life, is, that men do not need any guardian. We need no safeguard. Not only the inevitable, but the best power this side of the ocean, is the unfettered average common sense of the masses. ('Harpers Ferry', s.1, 263–4)

Humans need no guardian. They can determine for themselves the right and true path, which they do by talking with others. The autonomy and independence that lies at the heart of American civilisation, Phillips claims, is founded on the power of public opinion. Phillips is proud of this yet he is also gravely concerned, for public opinion is currently supportive of or indifferent to slavery. For over twenty years the abolitionists have sought an 'insurrection of thought' regarding slavery, yet white Americans have refused to listen. This stiff-necked people have refused to accept the fundamental meaning of American democracy. But John Brown has changed that! He has exposed the true aim of the Slave Power, which is nothing less than the destruction of republican government itself. As a result, white Northerners are finally coming to see what the radical abolitionists have long argued: slavery threatens democracy for whites as well as Black people, for the North as well as the South. The fruit of the abolitionists' longstanding commitment to moral suasion is John Brown – and Virginia's apoplectic reaction to his deed. Both shall turn public opinion toward the just ('Harper's Ferry', s.1, 286–8).

'Our aim is to alter public opinion' ('Philosophy of the Abolition Movement', s.1, 110). The purpose of talk is to abolitionise public opinion in order to defeat the Slave Power and bring about a radical reconstruction of American society. Such talk certainly includes rational argument, deliberation and agonistic contest – this is evident in the Garrisonians' willingness to allow anyone to speak at their public events, including mob participants and pro-slavery voices (Mayer 1998). Yet the essential function of talk for Phillips is *agitation*, not the construction of a common ethico-political framework. Agitation is the moulding of public opinion through contentious talk in order to shape the laws and customs of a society ('Daniel O'Connell', s.2, 396). 'The work of the agitator,' Richard Hofstadter (1948: 136) explains, 'consists chiefly in talk; his function is . . . to influence the public mind in the interest of some large social transformation'. Phillips seeks to use agitation to construct a new, more democratic ethico-political framework, from which the reorganisation of democratic institutions will follow (Phillips 1865). Talk as agitation is not an end in itself, as Schmitt claims regarding liberal discussion. Rather, it is a means to achieve hegemony, by which I mean the struggle between dominant and subordinate groups to rule by defining the 'common sense' of a society (Gramsci 1971). Hegemony presumes a struggle between two different ethico-political frameworks, or two different sorts of 'common sense', rather than conflict that takes place within a common framework.

Phillips seeks to create a new common sense by using agitation to construct utterly opposing abolitionist and pro-slavery frameworks and encouraging conflict between them. His goal is not to turn enemies into adversaries but to foster two hostile camps. In a May 1863 speech he provocatively constructs a principle he calls 'the North', which represents equality, free speech, freedom of religion and democracy. The principle of 'the South', meanwhile, represents censorship, religious oppression, a sham democracy and an 'aristocracy of the skin' ('State of the Country', s.1, 534). 'That South,' Phillips thunders, 'is to be annihilated . . . This country will never know peace nor union until the South (using the words in the sense I have described) is annihilated, and the North is spread over it' ('State of the Country', s.1, 534–5). There is little evidence of a desire for a 'conflictual consensus' here, even as civil war rages. In another speech, Phillips blasts the Lincoln administration for its early conduct of the war. As of August 1862, Phillips notes, Lincoln was still publicly denying that the Civil War was a war to end slavery.[6] Until Lincoln recognises that this is a war over 'the principles of Liberty', its outcome is in doubt.[7] 'The war can only be ended by annihilating that oligarchy which formed and rules the South and makes the war, – by annihilating a state of society,' Phillips insists. Yet 'our present policy neither aims to annihilate that state of things we call "the South", made up of pride, idleness, ignorance, barbarism, theft, and murder, nor to replace it with a substitute. Such an aimless war I call wasteful and murderous' ('The Cabinet', s.1, 451). Lincoln must not sit on the fence any longer. He must recognise that this war is a struggle for hegemony between competing ethico-political frameworks, identify his friends and his enemies, and act accordingly to defeat 'the South' and install 'the North' as the new national common sense.

The aim of anti-slavery agitation is not to overcome this North–South dualism but to deepen it. 'Now, wherever there is the war of ideas, every tongue takes a side. There is no neutrality. Even silence is not neutrality; but he who speaks a word of sympathy to his brother-man is on the side of humanity and progress' ('Kossuth', s.2, 44). Abolitionist agitators are catalysts who crystallise politics into hostile camps of abolition and slavery, right and wrong, salvation and sin, democracy and tyranny – and force people to decide between them. This Manichean approach to politics would seem to go against the spirit of much of contemporary democratic theory, yet it was clearly part of a radically democratic strategy. Phillips is perhaps naive in his faith that talk can replace bullets in hegemonic struggle, but his theory of agitation reflects a hardnosed political calculation that making radical abolitionism the new 'common sense' requires a struggle framed in the fanatical terms of friends against enemies.[8]

The Civil War led to the end of slavery, citizenship for African Americans and the (unfulfilled) possibilities of Reconstruction. Though much of this was undone by white reaction, these victories ultimately paved the way for universal citizenship. For all his fanatical rhetoric and agitation, then, one might be tempted to see Phillips's work as consolidating liberal democracy rather than radicalising it. Such a conclusion, however, would miss the radically democratic potential of Phillips's politics. This potential is evident in an 1844 pamphlet he edited entitled *The Constitution, A Pro-Slavery Compact* (Phillips 1969). The pamphlet largely consists of excerpts from debates of the 1787 constitutional convention, various state constitutional conventions and the First US Congress, all of which show that, counter to those moderate abolitionists who argue that the Constitution is anti-slavery, the framers of the United States deliberately protected slavery in constructing the new nation. The Constitution is thus a 'covenant with death and an agreement with hell', as Garrison put it, that should be dissolved along with the Union it created and replaced by a new republic of non-slaveholding states that refuse to be complicit in the sin of slavery. Disunion, as the Garrisonians called it, was a radical strategy to abolish slavery by urging the North to secede from the South (rather than vice versa) and repudiate the Constitution for objectively protecting slavery.

In calling for the break-up of the United States, disunion radically redefined American citizenship. This is evident in the 'Address of the Executive Committee of The American Anti-Slavery Society to the Friends of Freedom and Emancipation in the U. States', written by Phillips and passed at the 1844 annual meeting of the society to announce disunionism as its official position.[9] Contrary to popular opinion in both North and South, which held that Black people are incapable of citizenship, the address boldly asserts that slaves are Americans who are held as slaves by other Americans and who are denied their God-given freedom by the US Constitution. 'Three millions of the *American people* are crushed under the American Union!' booms the address. 'They are held as slaves . . . the government is their enemy' (Phillips 1969: 110, emphasis added). Abolitionists must atone for living under a government that is in thrall to the Slave Power by making the struggle of the slave their own. 'Their stripes are inflicted on our bodies, their shackles are fastened on our limbs, their cause is ours!' In order to end such oppression abolitionists must act alongside the slaves to overthrow the government. 'The Union which grinds them to the dust rests upon us, and with them we will struggle to overthrow it!' (Phillips 1969: 110). Disunionism is the means to overthrow the government. It turns slaves into Americans and masters into tyrants and enemies. As the AAS slogan adopted at that meeting declares, 'Equal Rights for All—No Union with Slaveholders!'

Solidarity with the enslaved is also evident in Phillips's speeches defending Black agency. Phillips never viewed slaves and free Black people as helpless victims or suppliant benefactors of white efforts. Instead, anticipating W. E. B. Du Bois's argument in his classic *Black Reconstruction* (1992), he argues that African Americans are the key to winning the Civil War, abolishing slavery and reconstructing democracy. In December 1861 he states, 'My opinion is, that the blacks are the key to our position . . . He that gets them wins, and he that loses them goes to the wall. [Applause.] At present they are the only Unionists' ('War for the Union,' s.1, 434). Such a position requires Phillips to challenge the 'common sense' racial attitude of the

North in his day, which is that slavery is wrong but Black people are nevertheless inferior to whites. He does this cleverly. That month Phillips began lecturing on Toussaint L'Ouverture, the leader of the Haitian Revolution. It quickly became one of his most popular speeches. The reason for his choice of topic was transparent to his audience: to attack anti-Black racism by paying tribute to Black agency. Placing L'Ouverture alongside great figures of history like Mohammed, Napoleon, Cromwell and John Brown, Phillips acknowledges that L'Ouverture 'had a vein of religious fanaticism, like most great leaders' ('Toussaint L'Ouverture,' s.1, 477). Yet L'Ouverture is greater than Cromwell and Napoleon, for their genius was limited to military exploits or tainted by racism. Only Brown is of similar stature, for he also recognised that Black courage is central to any victory for American liberty ('Toussaint L'Ouverture,' s.1, 491). Phillips's hagiography of L'Ouverture is calculated to push white Northern opinion from a moderate anti-slavery position to a radical vision of racial equality.

By redefining American citizenship, Phillips and his comrades demonstrate the contingent nature of equality, liberty and republicanism. Disunionism reveals that these are not eternal concepts handed down by the Founders but politically contested articulations that are subject to refinement and rearticulation through struggle. Further, fanaticism makes this reconceptualisation of democracy possible. Like Mouffe, Phillips and his comrades employ agonistic deliberation: 'We believe that the effect of this movement [for disunion] will be . . . to create discussion and agitation throughout the North' (Phillips 1969: 111). Yet their agonism does not presuppose a common ethico-political framework. Rather, they seek to challenge existing notions of equality and liberty in order to *divide* the nation into those who support the sham republicanism of 'the South' and those who support the real freedom of 'the North'. The aim of the disunion campaign is 'to convulse the slumbering South, like an earthquake' and to 'attack the slave power in its most vulnerable point, and to carry the battle to the gate' (Phillips 1969: 111). It is also to win a sceptical white North over to Phillips's principle of the North: abolition, racial equality, universal citizenship, agonism. In inciting controversy and drawing lines between friends and enemies, the radical abolitionists reimagined equality, liberty and democracy in the North as well as the South. Their uncompromising opposition to slavery and racial prejudice, interestingly, enabled this new imaginary. Theirs was an unyielding absolutism that never lapsed into dogma. By making

174

some principles absolute they revealed the contingent nature of others, and in so doing created opportunities to deepen democracy. Phillips's fanaticism may have consolidated liberal democracy, but it also raised the possibility of going beyond it.

While undoubtedly a product of the Enlightenment, Phillips's faith in political talk retains a Machiavellian moment. He insists that 'the moral suasion of public opinion', mobilised by uncompromising principles and fanatical tactics, is key to the creation of a more democratic society. By conceiving of talk as part of a struggle for hegemony, Phillips expands the boundaries of democratic theory beyond its focus on conflict within a common ethico-political framework. He enriches and extends such theory by suggesting ways in which democratic participation can be employed – and employed fanatically – to win struggles over the terms of political engagement itself.

The boundaries of democratic extremism

This is not to say that fanaticism is always or even usually democratic, of course. Extremism certainly can be put toward anti-democratic ends and often has been, as the history of this short century already attests. Nor is this to deny the importance of compromise and moderation in any stable democratic society. Rather, an analysis of Phillips helps distinguish between those sorts of fanaticism that are likely to further democracy and those that are likely to undermine it. When opposing sides in a conflict share the same ethico-political framework, agonistic theory provides a radically democratic approach to political engagement. This model is also valuable when it seems possible to forge a common framework out of contending ones, for like liberty and equality, ethico-political frameworks are politically and historically contingent constructions that are subject to negotiation when the involved parties are willing to do so. (This, one could argue, is what took place with the National Party and the African National Congress in South Africa in the 1990s, parties that represented two opposed frameworks but negotiated an end to the very apartheid system the National Party had created.)

When disputing parties employ competing ethico-political frameworks, however, and when at least one side has no desire to make the compromises needed to construct a common framework, then the horizon of agonistic theory has been reached. This is the realm of intractable conflict, in which the objective is not to create 'friendly enemies' but to defeat one's opponent and to install one's framework

175

as the 'common sense' of a society. In such a realm, the potential for fanaticism exists because it is precisely a strategy to achieve hegemony by mobilising friends against enemies through an irresolute refusal to compromise. Islamist groups such as the Taliban and Al-Qaeda have made use of zealotry in this way, as have certain elements of the US anti-abortion movement in the 1980s and 1990s (Mason 2002; Risen and Thomas 1998).

Yet as the radical abolitionists show, the mobilisation of the refusal to compromise is not inherently undemocratic. Rather, it is an approach to politics that can be used by any party. Zealotry coalesces the forces in a conflict, defines its poles, makes the strongest possible case for one pole against the other and pushes the moderate centre to choose sides. In so doing, it shapes the political centre itself. This approach can be useful for democratic forces in struggles in which opposing sides do not share the same ethico-political framework. When zealotry is put in the service of a more democratic 'common sense', as it was for the radical abolitionists, then it contributes to democracy.[10] For this reason, fanaticism should be evaluated according to the same criteria radical democrats use to assess other forms of political activity: does it expand the ability of ordinary people to participate in those affairs that affect their daily life?

A critical understanding of zealotry can expand and enrich agonistic theories beyond their self-imposed boundaries. Extremism is neither a vice nor a virtue but an approach to politics that often emerges in times of profound social and political tension. Democratic theory must speak to these times. Hence the value of Wendell Phillips. By making agonistic participation part of a struggle for hegemony and by employing a friends/enemies framework in a democratic context, this thinker, a man of the nineteenth century by any criteria, can help us better understand and engage in the twenty-first.

Notes

Thanks to Lisa Disch, Chad Levin, Adrian Little, Moya Lloyd, Joseph Lowndes, David Plotke, Sam Chambers, Aurelian Craiutu and David Schlosberg for their comments on drafts of this article. Thanks also to Katrina Taylor for research assistance.

1. Fanaticism is often associated with terrorism but the two are distinct phenomena. Terrorism is a tactic; it is the use of violence to instil fear in a target population. Fanaticism is a strategy; it is political activity, driven by an ardent devotion to a cause, which seeks to draw lines along

a friends/enemies dichotomy in order to mobilise friends and moderates in the service of that cause. Such a strategy may or may not use terror tactics. Terrorists are often zealots, but zealots are not necessarily terrorists.

2. I analyse this notion of fanaticism further in Olson 2007.

3. For example, Rancière (1995) argues that conflict (particularly class conflict) is at the heart of democratic politics, yet his notion of class conflict is not a clash of 'two hostile camps' as it is for Marx. Rather, it is the means through which a democratic political community is constituted. The objective of class struggle is not to create a new world but rather for the workers to prove 'that they truly belong to the society, that they truly communicate with all in a common space' (Rancière 1995: 48). Connolly's work is also similar to Mouffe's in this regard, as he acknowledges (Connolly 1995: 128 fn. 19). His ethos of 'critical responsiveness' calls for an attitude of generosity toward others in the negotiation and renegotiation of identities that is politics. In such engagements one can be firm and principled but must always consider the possibility that 'I could be wrong'. Yet his approach toward 'fundamentalists' (those who refuse to acknowledge the contestable nature of their fundamental beliefs) presumes a common liberal ethico-political framework. For example, he urges pro-choice and pro-life positions to each respect the articulation of the opposing position, if not the position itself (Connolly 1995: 130). This is an admirable notion but something we should hardly expect absolutists on either side of the issue to agree to. This is also quite similar to Gutmann and Thompson's (1997) notion of 'reciprocity', which suggests that the differences between deliberative and agonistic theories are not so great. I am very sympathetic to Mouffe's, Rancière's and Connolly's efforts to create a common ethico-political framework within which healthy agonistic conflict takes place. Yet this project is different from considering hegemonic struggles over the framework itself.

4. Knops (2007) makes a similar point.

5. Phillips's major speeches are collected in two series of *Speeches, Lectures, and Letters*, published in 1863 and 1891, respectively. When citing his speeches, I will provide the title of the speech and indicate the series from which it came. A selection of his speeches is available in a collection edited by Ignatiev (Phillips 2001).

6. Phillips did not know that Lincoln was at that time deliberating with his cabinet on when to issue his Preliminary Emancipation Proclamation.

7. The slaves already recognised that this was a war between freedom and slavery, Phillips notes. A friend at Port Royal relayed to him that slaves did not run from artillery rounds when they struck nearby because, they explained, 'we knew they were not meant for us' ('The Cabinet,' s.1, 449).

8. Phillips's strategy to achieve hegemony by dividing public opinion is in

many ways akin to Laclau and Mouffe's notion of the 'logic of equivalence' in *Hegemony and Socialist Strategy* (1985). The logic of equivalence, they explain, creates a 'simplification of political space' that divides the public sphere into 'two antagonistic fields' in a struggle for hegemony. The 'logic of difference', meanwhile, increases the complexity and diversity of society rather than simplifying and dividing it. A radical and plural democracy, they argue, must constantly tack between these logics of polarisation and plurality (Laclau and Mouffe 1985: 127–34. See also Laclau 2005b).

9. The address is included in Phillips 1969. As an official statement of the American Anti-Slavery Society (of which Phillips was an executive committee member), the address lists no specific author. However, the presentation and style of argument is clearly Phillips's. Further, shortly after this address was published Phillips wrote another pamphlet, *Can An Abolitionist Vote or Take Office Under the United States Constitution?* (Phillips 1845), which makes many of the same points as this address and uses much of the same evidence. In addition, Phillips's biographer, James Brewer Stewart, has confirmed Phillips's authorship of the address for me in a personal correspondence.

10. I discuss the factors tending to produce a democratic zealotry in more detail in Olson 2007.

9

The Northern Ireland Paradox

Adrian Little

We are always writing the history of the same war, even when we are
writing the history of peace and its institutions. (Foucault 2003: 16)

Introduction

In recent years there has been a growth in literature attempting to
relate the political analysis of Northern Ireland with contemporary
themes in democratic theory. These contributions highlight numerous
areas of overlapping concern such as the possibilities for conflict resolution (Horowitz 2002; McGarry and O'Leary 1996, 2008; O'Flynn
2004), the role of deliberative democracy in understanding justice
(O'Neill 2000, 2002; Newey 2002; Little 2003a) and the different
interpretations of the 'problem' in Northern Ireland (Finlayson 2006;
Vaughan-Williams 2006). These works have helped to fill a breach in
the literature on Northern Ireland because for many years it was
treated as a unique society which was divorced from the normal pre-
occupations of democratic theory. In demonstrating that political philosophy can contribute considerable insight into the analysis of
politics in Northern Ireland, this literature has served a very useful
purpose, although questions remain over the wisdom of applying
liberal ideas of democracy to the situation in Northern Ireland (Little
2004, 2003b). Perhaps, then, given these questions, the politics of
Northern Ireland and its future might be debated in terms of the limitations of the democratic paradigm and, in particular, the contribution that theories of radical democracy might be able to offer to our
understanding of the problems that Northern Ireland engenders.

This chapter outlines the basic tenets of radical democratic theory,
the reasons why it can provide an innovative reading of the Northern
Ireland conflict and its implications for future political developments
in the province. What will become clear is the contribution of radical
democratic thought in describing and understanding contemporary

political arrangements in Northern Ireland; radical democracy is endorsed as a means of explaining the Northern Irish political paradigm. At the same time, however, this descriptive contribution is not accompanied with a predictive dimension that would help to explain the directions in which Northern Irish democracy is moving. This is a justifiable position insofar as radical democracy tends to question the terms in which meta-narratives of appropriate political organisation are constructed and challenge theories of democracy which put forward an 'institutional fix' to contemporary liberal democratic organisation. Less defensible, though, is the failure of radical democracy to provide a strategic conception of the development of a radical democratic politics and, in particular, the reluctance to critically analyse the foundations upon which theories of democracy are established.

Radical democratic theory offers a valuable interpretive method of comprehending the nature of politics in Northern Ireland and, simultaneously, the conflict in the province and its management provide interesting insights for the practical implications of radical democracy. This is why Northern Ireland provides such a meaningful test case for radical democratic theory (Clohesy 2000). The irony of this development should not be lost. The Belfast Agreement of 1998 was widely regarded as the dawning of a new democratic era in Northern Ireland in both the popular and the academic literature.[1] This response emanated from an overarching feeling of relief that a degree of 'normality' was being established within the Northern Irish polity. No longer was the sphere of Northern Irish politics to be dominated by the simple majority with the provision in the accord to establish new power-sharing arrangements (Wilford 2001).[2] While the Northern Ireland Assembly (established in the Agreement) would clearly be an innovative institution, the democratic basis of these arrangements was open to interpretation (Little 2004). Although Northern Ireland probably required a power-sharing system, the very nature of consociational democracy has been the subject of considerable debate (Lijphart 1977; Taylor 2008). Thus, while the settlement was driven by political practicalities and contingent imperatives, its democratic credentials were much more debatable.

Part of the problem with the enactment of the Belfast Agreement is the problematic understanding of democracy that drove the process of political agreement in Northern Ireland (Little 2004; Bourke 2003). Not surprisingly, then, given the difficult conditions on the ground, the progress of democracy in the last ten years has not been smooth.[3] This is not particularly problematic from a radical democratic viewpoint which recognises the unlikelihood (or impossibility) of establishing political procedures that can grapple with all modern social complexities. However, it is the ideals of liberalism rather than radical democracy that have underpinned the Agreement and methods of explaining political developments since its inception. Yet, the practice of democracy in Northern Ireland is certainly distinct from prevailing liberal ideal-types. This has given rise to perceptions of stalemate and a political impasse in Northern Ireland when, arguably, a radical democratic perspective may help us to comprehend the 'normality' of the situation.

The paradox here is that the further away from the ideal-type of the Belfast Agreement that Northern Ireland moves, perhaps the closer it moves to the 'normal' working of democracy. Radical democracy helps us to understand this while simultaneously challenging the liberal democratic paradigm that continues to dominate political discourses over the future of Northern Ireland. I contend that an awareness of how Northern Ireland fits within the radical democratic paradigm sheds new light on political developments there and challenges some of the dominant arguments that are put forward to explain contemporary and future options in the province. An example of this was the way in which support for the Agreement (which supposedly enshrined democracy) withered in the harsh light of political exigencies and contingencies that constrained political choices in Northern Ireland at the start of this century.[4] However, rather than being considered a backward step, these developments are comprehensible when viewed through the lens of radical democracy. Thus, the various retreats from democracy in Northern Ireland in the last ten years emanate from misconceptions about the operation of democracy rather than any withdrawal from democratic engagement *per se.*

These comments help to explain the descriptive power of radical democracy as an interpretive strategy in contemporary political analysis. It invokes a set of ideas that challenge the presuppositions of many of the dominant theories of contemporary politics and in particular the over-determination of conceptual signifiers in liberal democracy such as liberty, rights and the rule of law. Radical democracy understands democracy as an inevitably unfinished project – a political ideal that can never be attained and which contains the seeds of its own incompletion. However, radical democratic theory needs to be more explicit about the inconclusive nature of the pursuit of the founding principles of democratic theory such as popular sovereignty and the rule of the people. By failing to address these conceptual underpinnings of democracy more directly, radical democracy is left open to the criticism that it fails to provide any kind of institutional alternative to the liberal models it rejects. On the contrary, radical democracy needs to emphasise the idea of the inevitable incompletion of democracy, the exclusions it always engenders and, thus, the constitutive failure at the heart of any democratic polity (Little 2008a, 2008b). In short, radical democracy needs to highlight its critique of democracy to a similar extent as it invokes the limitations of liberal models of democratic politics.

Towards a radical democratic paradigm?

The rise of radical theories of democracy in the last ten years has problematised the dominant liberal and deliberative models of democracy in contemporary political theory. These theories associated *inter alia* with Mouffe (2000, 2005a), Connolly (1995, 2005b), Laclau (2005b) and Rancière (1999, 2006) have provided valuable rebuttals of the central tenets that underpin liberal democratic orthodoxy and have instead pointed to the inevitability of conflict and disagreement and their implications for social organisation. Thus, instead of envisaging democracy as a sphere of political harmony or the construction of consensus, theories of radical democracy point to the unavoidable dissension that exists in complex, multicultural societies. The central argument is the difficulty of establishing universal agreement in pluralistic, conflict-ridden society and the problems associated with the preoccupation with consensus and rationality in liberal democratic theory (Little 2007).

To this extent it is fairly clear, given the growing volume of literature in the field, what radical theories of democracy oppose. Their rejection of liberal democracy has been fluently articulated and the outlines of an alternative paradigm are beginning to emerge. At the same time, however, radical democratic theorists have been sceptical of challenges suggesting that they need to outline alternative institutional arrangements to augment their critical view of democracy. This reluctance to grapple with issues of institutional design is, while understandable, something of a hostage to fortune. It leaves radical democracy open to criticisms that it offers no palpable alternative to the dominant order or that it is merely an intellectual project with little to offer the organisation of real democratic societies.[5] Moreover, it facilitates claims that it amounts to little more than a radicalised form of liberalism. While there are reasons to regard these absences as justifiable in terms of the objectives that radical democracy is trying to achieve, it is incumbent on its advocates to demonstrate the applicability of radical democracy to everyday life. If radical democracy potentially offers new ways of thinking about the future of democratic politics, then it is important to draw out what these implications might be (Little 2002a, 2002c).

To ascertain the relevance of radical democracy to Northern Ireland, it is important to outline some basic claims which underpin radical democratic theories. While, given its breadth and fluidity, it is difficult to pin down a definition of radical democracy, some central claims can be identified. The list here is certainly not exhaustive but it provides a flavour of radical democratic argumentation. Thus, the main contentions in this chapter revolve around the following issues:

- Rather than focusing on political institutions and procedures, radical democracy makes us think in terms of a democratic paradigm;
- That the procedures and rules of democratic conduct are not stable but instead fluctuate and evolve over the course of time;
- That attempts to specify the rules and/or procedures of democracy are an obstacle to democratic progress rather than facilitating it;
- That any consensus over democratic processes is transitory and contingent;
- Thus the inclusion of political actors in democratic processes is an issue of political judgement so that actors or their opponents may question the propriety of their participation at different times;
- That democracy is always at least partially conflictual and that it should not be envisaged as the means through which violence and conflict are eradicated;
- That the democratic pursuit of equality is sometimes compromised by or in tension with the liberal goal of freedom.

Taken together these themes in radical democratic analysis paint a starkly contrasting picture to many of the normative assumptions of democratic theory and the discourses which underpin contemporary politics in Northern Ireland. Insofar as it opposes such traditional understandings of democracy, we can at least understand the claims of radicalism in radical democratic theory (even if we do not wholly concur with them). These theoretical arguments ask pertinent questions of the process by which the dominant rhetoric of democracy has emerged in contemporary politics and suggest that there is greater utility in alternative approaches. To highlight this it is worth outlining the claims above in a little more detail.

The first claim is perhaps one that immediately offends the sensibilities of many democratic theorists. Here we come up against the tendency to view democracy in terms of the political institutions and procedures that it involves. In orthodox democratic theories, then, democracy can be pinned down in normative terms and political theorists can design and implement procedures to embody these normative goals. Moreover, in a positivist sense, we can then ascertain the extent to which any given society is democratic by assessing the degree to which their political processes meet the objectives of democracy. The intuitive attraction (to some people at least!) of these approaches is reflected in populist discourses of democracy and the rhetoric employed by political actors to advance the desirability of the export of Western liberal democratic structures to other 'non-democratic' parts of the world (Carothers 2002, 2004; Little 2008a). Radical democratic thinkers, on the other hand, regard the types of procedures and institutions in a given society to be a matter of political debate. There is no universal definition of democracy that can be parachuted into societies and superimposed upon the political divisions and structures which characterise them. Instead, it is better that we think of democracy as a paradigm in which a range of different democratic arguments can be brought to bear in working out the ways in which democratic politics – conceived in traditional terms as political equality and the 'rule of the people' – can be institutionalised (Mouffe 2000). Moreover, the institutions that are established are not impervious to the changing dynamics and context of society so that the democratic institutions which are appropriate at one particular point will not necessarily be those most apt on a different occasion (and certainly not in a different society). For this reason, radical democratic thinkers see democracy as a paradigm – a way of thinking about political organisation that advances some notion of political equality, popular sovereignty and the rule of the people without prescribing the best methods in which that can be achieved.

These arguments feed into a broader critique of the consensus-driven ideas that underpin political liberalism and deliberative democracy. One of the strongest points articulated by radical democratic theorists is that the pursuit of consensus or the demand that there is consensus over political procedures in orthodox democratic theories is a serious obstacle to democratic progress in many societies.

Moreover, the pursuit of consensus is also seen as a way of excluding oppositional voices to the dominant perspectives on democracy so that politics does not operate in a suitably inclusive manner. While, indeed, there may well be arguments that are not deemed to be appropriate in democracies (for example, those in favour of racial vilification), the reification of democratic procedures such that any oppositional voice which challenges the structures of democracy is deemed inappropriate is the thin end of a substantial wedge. As Jacques Rancière has argued, this form of organisation is not an instantiation of democracy but a means of policing democracy to ensure that oppositional voices are kept on the margins of political argument (Rancière 1999, 2006; Little 2007). For Rancière, the demand for consensus equates to the disappearance of politics as the objective of rational agreement closes down spaces for political engagement (Rancière 1999). Thus, according to this line of argument, democratic processes are impeded and rendered extremely partial by the focus on democratic procedures and the goal of consensus. A vision of democracy freed from consensual objectives and procedures is much more open to political engagement across difference than one which attempts to ring-fence the political and prevent the articulation of oppositional ideas to democratic procedures. The radical democratic conception is one which allows for more fluidity and dynamic change in the way we understand political structures and the transitory nature of political agreements. It comprehends the need for contingent notions of democracy and the fragile way in which polities are held together in complex societies. While its inability to articulate a model or prototype for democracy can therefore be seen as a weakness, it is simultaneously a strength in allowing for the political to reflect social and cultural change.

Not only is the substance of democratic agreement open to challenge and development, but also the interlocutors and parties to political accords will change over time. There is a widespread recognition in radical democratic theory that 'the political' is populated by a wide range of political groups with varying arguments and viewpoints (Little 2002a). At any one time, however, this same polity will exclude other people and perspectives that have views that are deemed to be beyond the pale, most frequently in contemporary politics, because they promote homophobia and/or racism. While radical democracy strives for widespread inclusion, it acknowledges that sometimes there are views that are not accepted within the political domain; thus democracy is always characterised by inevitable exclusions. In this sense, there will always be groups on the margins of political engagement and there may be times at which their participation in democratic decision-making is not deemed acceptable. Clearly, this alludes to the potential for the sinister exclusion of oppositional viewpoints (Rancière 1999) but it also should recognise that at times groups may exclude themselves because they disagree with the course of debate or its likely outcomes. In this sense, whilst radical democrats encourage an open, pluralist sphere of politics, they also recognise that such a sphere of politics is always surrounded by barriers which may be difficult to surmount. The sphere of democratic politics is never completely open, although it is fair to say that radical democrats want to broaden the space for a wider range of political actors than they perceive to be the case in contemporary political liberalism. Nonetheless a perfectly open polity is never wholly achievable in radical democratic thinking and the forging of democratic institutions is inevitably exclusive.

Finally, for the purpose of this analysis, radical democrats point to the unavoidability of conflict in democratic politics and, even more importantly, the inability of democracy to eradicate such conflict and establish consensus. While partial agreements are attainable, such is the nature of political disagreement that characterises complex, pluralistic societies that such accords should be regarded as temporary and contingent. This is what Mouffe alludes to as a 'conflictual consensus' (Mouffe 2000). According to this perspective, the propensity for disagreement is inherent to the democratic political condition. In this situation all agreements should be regarded as transient and subject to challenge, reform and change. Mouffe sees the demands of liberty and equality which underpin the two elements of the liberal democratic equation as potentially in tension with one another. While there may be ways to reconcile competing demands in specific instances, there is also plentiful opportunity for tensions and contradictions to emerge. Hence, where these concepts are accommodated within a political agreement, there should be no assumption that conflict is precluded. Changing social, economic or cultural conditions can shift the context in which such agreements develop. Moreover, the shifting arguments of political actors can lead to an invalidation of previous agreements by contemporary players on the democratic stage. This ongoing tension and the problem of its management are inherent to radical theories of democracy in such a way as to ensure that politics is understood to be in a permanent state of dynamic flux. In the next section I work out some of the implications of these insights for understanding contemporary Northern Irish politics.

Northern Ireland: towards a radical democratic analysis

In this section I outline some of the events which have recently animated Northern Irish politics before going on to assess the extent to which they can be explained coherently within the radical democratic paradigm. As noted in the introduction, the prevailing model of democracy in Northern Ireland has been that of consociationalism. In its simplest terms, consociational democracy is construed in terms of power-sharing whereby multiple representatives of both sides of a social divide are united in a grand coalition in an executive. Minorities have a veto on decision-making to prevent stronger social factions from dominating the political agenda and reforging the democratic process to reflect their majority status (for more detail see Taylor 2008). To a certain extent, the Northern Ireland Assembly constructed through the Belfast Agreement reflects this model. It was intended that this system would reward political parties that were prepared to countenance moderation and power-sharing as opposed to those who maintained more exclusionary, isolationist platforms. In Northern Ireland consociationalism has taken the form of pursuing a consensus on the middle ground through appealing to moderate wings of both sides of the ethno-national divide. The focus on 'parallel consent' (Wilford 2001; Little 2004) as the foundation of decision-making was a mechanism that was intended to suck political parties and their supporters from the margins to the centre ground of political consensus.[6]

The progress of the institutions established through the Belfast Agreement has been chequered. After an initial delay while political parties prevaricated about their establishment, the bodies were set up and became operational. For the first time in its history, Northern Ireland was governed primarily by internal, cross-community institutions which harnessed majority support in the province. However, in the intervening period, it has been beset by difficulties and its existence has been the source of considerable political dispute and unrest. This has led to a number of suspensions of the institutions with power reverting to the British government under the auspices of the Secretary of State for Northern Ireland. The most recent of these suspensions was in place from October 2002 to May 2007 – a duration that calls into question whether the model of democracy constructed for Northern Ireland was at work at all. Moreover, many people within Northern Ireland have seemed relatively content with direct rule and electoral evidence over the last ten years suggests that (especially within unionist communities) they were increasingly voting for parties which were less rather than more likely to coalesce on some imagined consensual middle ground.

Seen through the light of an historically informed democratic theory, these developments are perhaps unsurprising. As Richard Bourke has argued, Northern Ireland has not just been the focus of a practical political conflict; it has also been a battleground of political ideas (Bourke 2004). The meaning of democracy has been obfuscated by concerns over whether institutionalising democracy would renew majoritarian government.[7] This fear reflects the years of unionist rule before 1972 where democracy was partly the basis of the problem as the unionist regime employed democratic discourses to marginalise the minority nationalist population. The tendency to view democracy in these majoritarian terms has continued and is evident in the obsession in Northern Irish politics with demography, population trends and constitutional issues. Whilst this may be explicable, it is a shallow reflection of the breadth and depth of issues currently under the microscope of democratic theory. Bourke contends that this narrow view of democracy has helped to breed defensive forms of unionism and has narrowed the nationalist focus on demographic change.

The question, then, is whether radical theories of democracy help to break us out of the constraints of this rather narrow conception of democracy. Clearly, there are ways in which Northern Ireland fits quite comfortably within the radical democratic paradigm. After all, not only is it a polity constructed around a conception of conflict, but also a society in which understandings of the unavoidable nature of disagreement prevail. Indeed, in some sections of Northern Irish society the imprint of violence (either as victim or perpetrator) can be viewed as a sign of authenticity in terms of people's identifications (Maynes 2003: 23). Thus, violence, either through its perpetration or its experience as a victim, is a central force in political identity and the biographies of political parties and actors. Perhaps, then, we should not be surprised that this imprint of violence has marked the way in which democracy is often invoked in Northern Ireland (Little 2006). In these discourses democracy is the obverse of violence and the progress of democratic politics was about ending violence. At this point, however, we see discourses in Northern Ireland moving away from radical theories of democracy. For the latter, conflict and

188

violence are an unavoidable part of 'the political' in a society marked by high levels of disagreement whereas, in Northern Ireland, democracy is often conceived primarily as a way of resolving violent conflict. Thus, whilst Northern Ireland appears susceptible to radical democratic political analysis, quite frequently such a view of the nature of democracy is not operative.

It is also clear that the traditional focus of democratic theory on the nature of democratic political institutions is evident in current Northern Irish politics. Controversy over the provisions of the Belfast Agreement have been a staple of Northern Irish political debate since 1998 as is the extent to which the stipulations of the Agreement have been met and whether they should continue to frame the political paradigm. However, this situation does not invalidate radical democratic analysis of Northern Ireland. Instead, we can learn lessons from the overt challenge to agreed political mechanisms and institutions in the province; indeed, this situation demonstrates the contested nature of democratic institutions and the need to legitimise them over time through change and reform in response to alterations in the particular political culture. To this extent, at least, Northern Ireland is comprehensible within a radical democratic paradigm even if the nature of political institutions and constitutional issues remain the focus of political debate. Insofar as the basic conditions of democracy are the stuff of political debate in Northern Ireland, then it remains clearly within the kinds of parameters established in radical democratic theory.

It follows from this that attempts to determine consociationalism or power-sharing as the defining features of Northern Irish democracy are open to question. The fact that such methods have been the strategies developed to deal with the contemporary political situation in no way entails that this need always be the case. Shifts in the context of Northern Ireland, for example the changing nature of the European Union, could have an important bearing on the nature of the Northern Irish polity (Little 2008b). Indeed, already the nature of consociationalism has had its democratic credentials questioned (Dixon 2001). This, in itself, does not invalidate consociationalism as a theory of democracy – although there might be reasons for doing so – but it does suggest that there must be scope to challenge the prevailing political institutions and their legitimacy in a changing social and cultural context. In this sense the Belfast Agreement is a point of departure on what democracy in Northern Ireland might look like in the future rather than enshrining that particular vision.

Part of this uncertainty about the future shape of a democratic polity in Northern Ireland lies in the shifting fortunes of political actors over time and the exclusion – either forced or voluntary – of some parties and groups. The make up of the polity has a fundamental impact on the nature of political engagement. Thus, for example, although a pivotal dimension of the 1990s peace process in Northern Ireland was concerned with ending violent engagement especially on the part of the Provisional Irish Republican Army (PIRA), it was also concerned with shoring up a centrist agenda by playing on the strength of the leading parties on either side of the ethno-nationalist divide. The Ulster Unionist Party (UUP) and the Social Democratic and Labour Party (SDLP) respectively represented the moderate wings of unionism and nationalism and, as the largest parties, held considerable sway in the shaping of the political agenda in the 1990s. Not surprisingly, then, when the institutions provided for in the Agreement were established, the positions of First Minister and Deputy First Minister were occupied by these two parties. At the same time, however, electoral support was beginning to leak from these parties and, ten years on from the Agreement, it is clear that they have haemorrhaged substantial elements of their support. In the current situation, the political agenda in Northern Ireland is concerned with achieving accommodation between the Democratic Unionist Party (DUP) and Sinn Féin (SF) as respectively the two largest parties. This is a fundamentally different task given the more radical agendas pursued by these parties. Put simply, the theoretical model designed to shore up the centre ground of Northern Irish politics has been overtaken by the electoral reality that increasingly more people have voted for more radical parties. This demonstrates the way in which the fluidity and dynamism that characterises radical democracy is significant in assessing practical scenarios, not least the fact that the fluctuating nature of political beliefs in a society has a fundamental bearing on the ways in which those societies can approach issues of political accommodation.

A corollary to this point is the exclusion of some parties or groups from the sphere of political engagement. Radical democracy implies that such exclusions are inevitable and it is clear that for many years Sinn Féin was perceived to be beyond the pale for other parties in Northern Ireland and the two governments when it came to formal political engagement. It took – and indeed is still taking – a long process of negotiation and persuasion for SF to convince its opponents of the rectitude of its place in formal political processes. In that time other groups associated with political violence have been welcomed into the political fold, been excluded by the two governments or, in the case of some smaller loyalist parties, have excluded themselves on the grounds that the formal political process appeared to be offering them little reward.[8] In this sense Northern Ireland is an excellent example of the changing political agents that comprise a democratic polity. Of course, some parties have much greater longevity and authority than others but that does not prevent them being usurped by traditionally less authoritative competitors, as was the case with the DUP supplanting the UUP.

Northern Irish politics is clearly informed by the centrality of conflict to political life in a way that helps to reinforce the radical democratic argument. However, the extent to which this is viewed as a normal state of affairs is more contentious. Northern Ireland, like many other societies, labours under the pretension that the normal state of democracy is one where violence and conflict is supplanted by peaceful forms of political disagreement. While the reduction in violence that accompanied the Belfast Agreement is undoubtedly welcome, the 'normality' of this situation is more of a matter of contention. Northern Ireland should not be viewed as a 'place apart' insofar as, according to radical democratic theory, all societies contain sources of disagreement and potential violence; the extent to which they manage to contain such violence is a matter of political contingency and the capacity of people – both ordinary and elite – to reach some form of accommodation across difference. Northern Ireland fits a radical democratic model insofar as there is little impetus for consensus or a 'rational' solution. Instead, there is an awareness of the competition of rationalities and their fundamental differences. Thus, there is a greater likelihood that the conflictual nature of democracy will be understood, although that has not prevented more orthodox understandings of democracy prevailing in Northern Ireland as we shall see.

In the light of these points we can see that several key aspects of contemporary Northern Irish politics resonate with the radical democratic model. This is not to say of course that such thinking is accepted as the most appropriate way to view political debates in the province but it does imply that the situation in Northern Ireland is not so radically different that it can only be viewed within its own special framework. Instead, it offers lessons about how radical democratic thinking might be employed to cast light on other conflictual political scenarios. Whilst some commentators contend that the resort to violence and paramilitarism are 'parallel exit strategies' from politics (Maynes 2003: 34), perhaps it is more accurate to see them as withdrawals from the existing mode of democracy coupled with the inability to see partial objectives being achieved through that system. Hence, the radical democratic imagination of democracy is one that is always marked by a certain ambivalence whereby some groups see little of benefit through participation in formal political mechanisms. Thus, we can see how the focus on the end of violence and paramilitarism as a precursor to democracy is a misreading of the nature of the politi-cal. Such an 'end' to violence is never possible and the demand for such an end point signifies the emergence of a vicious circle. As Augusteijn reminds us, it 'is ultimately not even important whether the republi-can commitment to democracy can be defined as just rhetorical. What is crucial is that they believe in it and that it determines their actions and long-term strategy' (Augusteijn 2003: 21).

Radical democracy moves us away from idealistic notions of democracy as a sphere of relatively harmonious democratic engage-ment towards recognition that politics is inherently conflictual and sometimes violent. While the rhetorical discourses concerning vio-lence and opposition play a significant role in the paradigmatic framing of Northern Irish politics, they can simultaneously help to obfuscate the prevailing conditions. In short, whilst Northern Ireland fits within a radical democratic paradigm, traditional and orthodox conceptions of democracy tend to hold much more sway in under-standing politics in the province. From the perspective of radical democracy, this embodies a retreat from democracy.

Northern Ireland and the retreat from democracy?

The establishment of consociational institutions in Northern Ireland was clearly intended as a means of 'normalising' democratic politics (albeit through the use of unusual democratic institutions). When the devolved institutions have been operational, it is clear that some of the traditional intransigencies have broken down and that, in some cases, policy has become more significant than ethno-national alle-giances.[9] At the same time, however, it is equally clear that during the operation of the Northern Ireland Assembly sectarian divisions have always been apparent and sometimes at the surface of political debate. In this sense, the creation of democratic institutions did not suddenly wash away deeply ingrained social and cultural differences. The discomfort within unionism at the prospect of sharing power with nationalists, SF in particular, was never surmounted. While the SDLP was in the ascendancy in nationalist circles power-sharing was perhaps more palatable, but the electoral rise of SF made benign interpretations of the nationalist agenda much harder for unionists to swallow.

The difficulties of enacting democracy in divided societies should help to sustain radical democratic analyses. The waxing and waning of unionist support for the Belfast Agreement in Northern Ireland is evidence of the fluidity of democracy and the changing perspectives of groups on the operation of democracy. The prevailing attitude within Northern Ireland has been described variously as a culture of fatalism by Arthur Aughey (2005) or as being mired in 'an orgy of self-pity' by Paul Bew (2000). The significance of these claims lies in the fact that they come from commentators commonly associated with unionism. While for many years unionism traded upon a promotion of 'ambiguous equilibrium' (Dixon 2001) as a means of staving off nationalist advances, the post-Agreement situation is one where unionism has been forced to adopt a much more vigorous and aggressive rebuttal of the political situation. Except that where once they had the violent campaign of the IRA to sustain their reluctance to enter into democratic engagement, those reasons are becoming less and less sustainable.

At the same time, however, the moral absolutism of the DUP and its rejection of more radical understandings of democracy have clearly reaped electoral dividends. Just as SF has made its case for electoral recognition and found favour with the nationalist electorate since the 1990s, the DUP has advanced at the expense of the UUP. With the electorate at least, the reluctance of the DUP to enter into democratic engagement with its largest opponent on the nationalist wing of Northern Irish politics has harnessed considerable support. The moral absolutism in which the DUP couched its rejection of interaction with SF clearly touched a nerve in unionist communities. Having overtaken the UUP as the largest unionist party in the Northern Ireland Assembly elections of November 2003, the DUP almost wiped it out in the Westminster election of May 2005. However, the difficulty for the DUP came in the aftermath of its electoral success and its eventual agreement to form a government involving SF but this is a difficulty entirely consistent with radical democratic analyses.

Why might the situation in Northern Ireland in the last ten years be regarded as a retreat from democracy? At least in its radical formulation, democracy surely allows for periods of engagement and disengagement as a normal flow of democratic interaction between opposing groups. In this sense, the growing support for SF and the DUP is not a problem in itself. After all, radical democracy appears to thrive on notions of contention and critique generated by opposing forces and the process of transforming antagonisms into workable agonistic politics (Mouffe 2000). In Northern Ireland, though, while recent events might suggest that the construction of such an agonistic politics is on the agenda, the extent to which adversaries have accepted the legitimacy of alternative positions held by their opponents is questionable. Indeed, in Northern Ireland after the Belfast Agreement, there appeared to be increasing moral certitude within large sections of the unionist community generally and the DUP in particular about the undesirability of their opponents and their propensity to resort to means of illegitimate violence. In this sense, at least, there appears to be something of a retreat from the possibilities of democracy in the period since the late 1990s in Northern Ireland.[10]

Radical democracy seeks to challenge popular discourses and the overarching political rhetoric that seems gripped by a dichotomy between democracy and violence. These discourses are criticised for overlooking the co-existence of violence and democratic politics in most liberal democratic societies (Little 2006). Arguably, this highlights the problems of consociational systems which attempt to shore up consensus and the middle ground by presenting a model of democracy which has a tenuous relationship with most operational democracies. Ultimately, the success of the Northern Irish peace process as a democratic project cannot be guaranteed by appealing to political elites alone; instead, it requires more stringent efforts to develop realistic discourses of democracy amongst ordinary people. This reflects the magnitude of the task – elite political initiatives are insufficient to establish democratic practice in Northern Ireland or elsewhere. The failing of the consociational model has been in appealing to political elites and the middle ground rather than addressing the demands and issues which affect the everyday lives of people in Northern Ireland. A concern for the latter does not provide a clear pathway to the establishment of democracy in Northern Ireland, but it does identify the territory on which a reversal from the retreat from democracy might be conducted.

Conclusion

A radical democratic approach to Northern Irish politics needs to be understood more in terms of the imperfections of democracy than has

THE NORTHERN IRELAND PARADOX

hitherto been the case. Instead, democracy has been viewed as the light at the end of the dark tunnel of the violence that characterised 'the Troubles'. Insofar as the Belfast Agreement was supposed to embody a new era of democracy, it has been a failure. However, as an exemplar of the fragile, contingent nature of democratic agreements and their transient relationship with conflictual societies it has much to teach us. Rather than viewing the Belfast Agreement as the encapsulation of democratic politics, it should be regarded as the starting point from which we might reconsider what democratic politics amounts to. This suggests that we need to treat claims of conflict resolution through such agreements with some care. The democratic process, viewed from the radical democratic perspective, is – at best – one of conflict management and hopefully transformation.

It is for this reason that it can be argued that Northern Ireland exemplifies aspects of radical democracy in action. Due to the ubiquitous nature and awareness of disagreement, politics in Northern Ireland does not engage in the consensual masquerade to the same extent as other liberal democratic polities. This is not to say that the tropes of liberal democratic argument do not hold sway in Northern Ireland – as we have seen they most certainly do – but that politics there perhaps come closer to the idea of a 'conflictual consensus' (Mouffe 2000) than in more orthodox liberal democratic politics. In other words, agreements in Northern Ireland are inherently infused with the propensity for disagreement to break out and political actors are acutely aware of the contingent nature of the accords that are forged. Ironically, then, and perhaps unwittingly, political actors in Northern Ireland often do operate in a manner commensurate with some of the principles of radical democracy. While it would be too strong to describe them as radical democrats, the awareness of intractable difference, political conflict and the contingency of agreements and consensus ensures that many politicians in Northern Ireland operate in ways that are more akin to radical democracy than tends to be the case in less openly divided polities.

Put simply, this chapter contends that we need to understand the imperfections and shortcomings of democracy. This is the case in all liberal democratic societies although the point is more apparent when we use examples of more radically conflictual situations like Northern Ireland. The imperfect notion of democracy provides us with greater scope to investigate the difficulties of political transformation especially where this involves a radical challenge for the social and cultural foundations of society. This is not a situation which has evolved in Northern Ireland in recent years. Instead, we have an exemplar of a democratic paradox: the establishment of democratic criteria which act as an obstacle to the realisation of democratic politics. This is evident in the creation of political institutions under the Belfast Agreement which have been operational less frequently than the old system of direct rule from Westminster since their establishment. These institutions, founded on the principles of democratic self-government, implement a variety of procedures which are questionable on democratic grounds (Little 2004). In Northern Irish political discourse there is insufficient awareness of the imperfections or failings of democracy, that is, the conflict and antagonism which such mechanisms engender. Northern Ireland, however, still labours under the pretence that democracy is the solution to the management of social conflict. As long as such an idealistic vision of democracy prevails, then it is more difficult to imagine a workable democracy in Northern Ireland. Indeed, it is a recipe for the continuation of the tendency to construct unrealistic models of democracy that act as an impediment to political progress. In short, in mainstream political discourses, the idea of democracy is so misunderstood that it has now become as big an impediment to the management of Northern Ireland's political divisions as it is a part of the solution.

To conclude, the example of Northern Ireland demonstrates some of the deficiencies in radical democratic theory as well as its strengths. The weaknesses of *liberalism* are apparent in the politics of Northern Ireland and radical democratic theory but the failings and inevitable inconclusiveness of *democracy* is rarely addressed in either.[11] Radical democracy is a useful prism through which to understand and interpret Northern Irish politics but it is not equipped with the wherewithal to provide an alternative democratic model. This lacuna is not necessarily problematic for radical democracy if it is able to make clear that any democratic system will be deficient and incomplete. Thus, a radical democratic paradigm is one that recognises the shortcomings of democracy and the inevitable exclusions that it engenders and therefore the need for continual critical analysis of democracy in whatever complex context it is operating. In other words, the absence of a normative platform in radical democracy (and hence a clear strategic direction) is not a weakness if it can make clear that it is democracy itself rather then merely its liberal interpretation which is at the root of the problem. This does not entail the rejection of democracy but instead a stronger, bolder democratic perspective that is reinforced by a radical view of its inadequacies.

Notes

1. The Belfast Agreement was signed in 1998 as the culmination of the peace process that had been ongoing through the 1990s. It is regarded as the symbolic ending of 'the Troubles' that had blighted Northern Irish society since the late 1960s. The Agreement harnessed the support of the British and Irish governments as well as three of the four major political parties in the North as well as many of the smaller parties. Its provisions are broadly consociational although the extent of this is a matter of some dispute in the academic literature (see O'Leary 1999, Dixon 2001, Taylor 2008 and Wilford 2001).
2. From its formation through the 1920 Government of Ireland Act to the proroguing of the Northern Irish parliament by the British government in 1972, Northern Ireland, though nominally democratic, had been governed by the main Unionist party and discrimination against nationalists was widespread.
3. At the time of writing the institutions that were established through the Belfast Agreement have been mothballed for longer periods of time than they have been operational.
4. The Agreement was partly designed to shore up the middle ground and build up a consensus dominated by the more moderate parties on either side of the ethno-national divide, namely the Ulster Unionist Party and the Social Democratic and Labour Party. In the aftermath of the Agreement both of these parties lost significant electoral ground to the more radical elements of their communal constituency, the Democratic Unionist Party and Sinn Féin respectively.
5. As a counterbalance to that argument, this chapter demonstrates that Northern Ireland embodies aspects of radical democratic theory in its political practice.
6. In the Assembly members have to designate themselves as 'nationalist', 'unionist' or 'other'. In this way it is possible to gauge whether there is majority support on both sides of the ethno-national divide for a proposed course of action. For critical reflection on the process of designation, see Little 2004, 2008b.
7. This misappropriation of the meaning of democracy is widespread in contemporary liberal democratic politics rather than being particular to the conditions of Northern Ireland (Rancière 2006).
8. For example, in 1998 the Ulster Democratic Party (linked to the Ulster Defence Association) withdrew from the political process.
9. A useful example is in the area of post-primary education and the reaction to the 2001 Burns Report. In his time as Education Minister, Martin McGuinness of Sinn Féin backed the ending of selection for schools following the 'Eleven plus' examination whereby the successful qualified for grammar schools while the remainder were allocated places in

secondary schools. The move harnessed majority support in Northern Ireland but it was also fiercely criticised by many unionist politicians in particular. The controversy around the issue thus reflected both the breaking down and the reification of ethno-national political division. See http://education.guardian.co.uk/specialreports/grammarschools/story/0,,1703537,00.html for further details.

10. The reformation of the power-sharing executive in 2007 might be seen as an example of agonism in practice although, equally, it might be regarded as an unholy alliance between fundamental antagonists in pursuit of strategic political objectives. Both readings are consistent with radical democratic analysis.

11. For exceptions, see Bourke (2003) in the Northern Irish literature and Laclau (2005b) in radical democratic theory.

Conclusion

Adrian Little and Moya Lloyd

The theories of radical democracy outlined, analysed and criticised in this book reflect a diverse body of thought. Radical democracy is characterised by its heterogeneity and, as a result, it invokes and embraces a politics of contingency and contestation. This makes it a fascinating object of study but also an elusive one. Radical democracy emphasises a vibrant, dynamic conception of politics that ensures that the object of analysis is never settled, uncontested or static. On this account the criticism that radical democracy does not spell out an institutional alternative to current or past forms of democratic politics misses the point; the theoretical foundations of the idea of radical democracy suggest that radical democracy can never be 'achieved'. Rather, it thrives on the exposition of the exclusions, inequalities and injustices that have historically characterised democratic politics and which continue to do so. Thus, when we say that radical democratic politics can never be achieved, we simultaneously recognise that democracy can be more or less radical. Most of the theorists analysed in this book subscribe in one form or another to the view that a more radically democratic politics is possible through the process of exposing and challenging the exclusionary limits of mainstream democratic theory and practice. Nonetheless *a more* radical democratic politics is never conceived as *the* radical democratic politics because the methodological underpinnings of this theoretical stance imply that any political institutional arrangements need to be further contested to unveil exclusionary tendencies.

The architectural spaces of radical democracy

The contributions to this book make clear that the notion of political space in radical democracy is multi-faceted and that the institutional architecture is difficult to specify. Radical democracy focuses on the micro-politics of individual concerns and matters that many liberal democratic theories have sought to consign to the private sphere. At the same time, however, radical democracy addresses a range of more public issues from the radical concerns aired by social movements and pressure groups on both the national and international level, through to the nature of political discourse and its impact in higher echelons of government. This demonstrates that there is not a singular space in which radical democracy operates. A radical democratic theory must recognise that focusing on one level of political engagement – be that micro, meso or macro – is incomplete because the interactions on any one of those levels are always affected by developments in the others. The dynamic nature of radical democratic theory is such that it needs to understand the ongoing process of disruption and reshaping that takes place in all political interactions. Even if it was possible to clearly delineate the different levels and spaces of democracy (which is highly debatable), these spaces can never be hermetically sealed. Thus, engagements on any level are permanently in flux as they are challenged and unsettled in other spheres of democratic interaction.

Although, as James Martin points out, radical democracy has often been linked to the politics of civil society, he is correct to argue that this is only one dimension of a theoretical approach that challenges a multiplicity of spaces in which democracy is thought to operate. Certainly, the work of Laclau and Mouffe engages with debates around new social movements and the problems associated with overly statist or economistic forms of radical politics. However, though it may try to open up neglected spaces for democratic politics, radical democracy can never wholly escape the traditional arenas and institutions in which democracy is enacted. Thus, while the arguments in this book have highlighted the spatial nature of radical democratic theory, they must also recognise the ways in which radical democratic politics needs to engage with the traditional institutional foundations of democracy. For some, such as Andrew Robinson and Simon Tormey, this insight demonstrates the way in which radical democracy remains wedded to statist conceptions of democracy – a situation which they believe seriously impedes the radical credentials which radical democracy lays claim to.

For other contributors, though, the spatial metaphors invoked by radical democratic theory provide a fertile breeding ground for serious rethinking of democratic politics. On this account, the impact that a spatialised conception of democracy has on traditional models which have tended to concentrate on either institutional structures or the nature of political agency in democratic societies (e.g. individuals, communities, pressure groups, social movements, political parties, global movements and so forth) is more fundamental. The spatial dimension of radical democratic theory sets it apart from the dominant tradition in democratic theory of seeking an 'institutional fix' to the practice of democratic societies. Indeed, post-structuralist conceptions of radical democracy challenge the very basis upon which such theorising can take place. In this sense, radical democracy criticises and undermines assumptions about the geographical space in which democracy can be enacted, the composition and means of deciding the 'people' (i.e. the supposedly sovereign body) and, as a result, the legitimacy of institutions that are often presented in a justificatory fashion as the way of ensuring that theoretical conceptions of democracy are enacted in political practice (Rancière 2006, Laclau 2005).

In different ways Andrew Schaap and Adrian Little argue that, as well as the sharp light provided by transgressive forms of political action, the limitations of liberal democratic politics are also (and perhaps more acutely) demonstrated by the attempt to reclaim the territory on which liberal democratic politics have been established. Therefore, it is not only in the wholesale rejection of liberal democratic institutions that a radical democratic politics can be established; rather the attempt to disrupt liberal democracy by unveiling its exclusions can be advanced by direct engagement with the principles and institutions that liberal democracies use to legitimise their structures. As Mark Wenman makes clear, such a process of disrupting and rearticulating the justificatory principles of liberal democracy can also be conducted on a global level where 'empty signifiers' can potentially be addressed anew and subjected to new hegemonic enterprises. And, as Moya Lloyd and Birgit Schippers demonstrate in their engagement with the work of Judith Butler, there is always a possibility of resignifying established political practices to inspire new hegemonic understandings. That said, the strategy of resignification is obviously fraught with the dangers of shoring up established meanings and understandings. In a sense, then, this is a perfect example of the contingency of radical democratic theory.

What this discussion exemplifies is the unsettled architectural space that radical democracy both occupies and advocates. This reinforces the centrality of understanding the multiplicity of arenas in which radical democratic politics can be conducted. For radical democrats, then, it is not only the open exclusion of certain voices that is at issue in challenging the liberal democratic paradigm.

Recognition of this policing of political agency must be accompanied by recognition of the policing of political spaces. This spatial dimension is pivotal to a full understanding of the reluctance of radical democrats to seek out the 'institutional fix' to the problems of liberal democracy. Indeed, this reluctance to specify the kinds of institutional arrangements that provide the foundations of other theories of democracy is both justifiable and consistent with the various methodological approaches that radical democracy invokes. In particular, the post-structuralist conceptions of radical democracy that have been the centrepiece of the analyses in this book are highly critical of institutional blueprints given their demands for deep contextualisation and the primacy of dynamic change. On this understanding the premise of institutional design encapsulating the idea of radical democracy is highly problematic. These points noted, however, it is worth pointing to an ambiguity in radical democratic theory about the role of the state. Perhaps the closest that radical democrats have come to a normative explanation of their stance on the state is William Connolly's radical pluralism (2005a). As fruitful as Connolly's perspective is, it is still a highly theoretical conception of the state which makes little attempt to grapple with the nuts and bolts of institutional politics. Thus, while the state is a pivotal institution (or set of pivotal institutions) in conceptions of radical democracy, it plays a fluid and fluctuating role in most radical democratic theories.

It is clear that civil society is an important space for radical democratic politics but this is a space that is never clearly delineated. Thus, most radical democratic theorists recognise the blurring of the lines between the state and civil society. Often civil society may be a privileged site in terms of the articulation of radical critiques of the prevailing order but it is a site that articulates with the state and overlaps with it. However, if the state and civil society cannot be clearly delineated, then it is clear that the state has a fundamental role to play in radical democratic politics – a role that is unlikely to be wholly benign. For this reason radical democracy cannot present an unadulterated picture of civil society or a conception of the relationship between the state and civil society that is purely functional. Instead, both the state and civil society are central to radical democratic politics in ways which may both assist and hinder the course of radical democracy. Approaches such as that of Robinson and Tormey are probably correct to emphasise the need to recognise the spectre of a potentially *dirigiste* state in radical democratic theories but it is also important to comprehend the ways in which state institutions might shore up radical democracy (although it would be unrealistic to expect anarchist theories to take this on board).

It is therefore important to recognise the difficulties in establishing a radical democratic theory of the state not least because there is no clear picture of democracy itself. This leaves radical democracy open to critics who argue that it is not sufficiently distinguished from the liberal democratic state to warrant the label 'radical'. Most of the chapters in this book have argued in one way or another against this reading of radical democracy but it is important to recognise that, in recent years, a radical critique of radical democracy has begun to emerge.

The radical critique of radical democracy

Radical democratic theory, especially that which has emerged in the tradition of post-structuralism and Laclau and Mouffe's *Hegemony and Socialist Strategy*, has articulated a theory of democracy that unsettles and disrupts the dominant theories and practices of liberal democracy. However, in recent years, an increasing number of commentators from the continental philosophy and anarchist traditions have sought to challenge the radical credentials of radical democracy (Butler, Laclau and Žižek 2000, Agamben 2005). From this perspective radical democracy may challenge orthodox models of liberal democracy but, in failing to present a coherent alternative, remains locked into the trajectory established by the liberal democratic paradigm. Thus, according to this view, radical democracy offers a shift within the liberal democratic perspective but no clean break from it. According to this account, it is then beset by exactly the same problems as liberal democracy albeit potentially mitigated to some extent.

Our contention in this book has been that there is an important distinction to be made between the critical theory tradition of radical democracy as evinced in the work of commentators such as Habermas and Young, and the post-structuralist variant articulated by Laclau and Mouffe and inspired by theorists like Foucault and Derrida. Where the former does remain within the liberal democratic tradition, we contend that, whatever its limitations, the latter approach has the potential to shift us towards a more radical interpretation of radical democracy. This, we contend, is an approach that embodies a more critical stance towards democracy itself, that is, it recognises that radical democratic theory is not concerned with finding a more pure or genuine form of democracy but that all theories of democracy suffer the problem of appealing to 'the people' or a form of popular sovereignty that can never be perfectly encapsulated. Crucially, then, radical democracy is concerned not only with the critique of the liberal dimension of liberal democracy – it also challenges the democratic part of this equation. This is why deconstruction is such a pivotal technique for radical democratic analysis; it allows a thoroughgoing critique of both liberalism and democracy without resorting to a wholesale rejection of either. The radical aspect lies in the disruption of the very terms and language of democratic discourse rather than a critique of democracy where the issue is merely how to practice democracy better.

This brings us back to a crucial point made at the outset of the book. The idea of democracy and what we expect of it lies at the heart of these debates. In analysing democracy many within the critical theory tradition of democratic analysis have sought to rethink the tools of democracy in such a way as to construct democracy as a way of debating and then reaching agreement about the rational course of action. In the work of commentators like Habermas this dynamic is so important that universal agreement on the rational course of action is the desired objective (at least metaphorically if not practically). Most democratic theories are less ambitious but the need to ameliorate disagreements remains a prominent aspect of contemporary democratic theory. While the critical theory tradition of democratic analysis subscribes to this view of the importance of the consensual dimension of democracy, post-structuralist accounts of radical democracy are sceptical if not openly critical of rationalism and the pursuit of consensus. This helps to explain why the critical theory tradition is drawn towards the possibilities of agonism as a means of negotiating social and political conflict and political negotiation as a means of overcoming social division and the asymmetries of power that contribute to their reproduction. Post-structuralist accounts, on the other hand, seek to explain and reflect the dynamics of power that contribute to the construction of rationality and consensus and thus the problems that remain even after an agonistic model of politics has been constructed. While radical democracy may attempt to apprehend forms of social power to invigorate new hegemonic enterprises, forms of power are elusive and resistant to such processes, meaning that the 'project' of radical democracy is always incomplete. Nonetheless the attempt to engage in a hegemonic project with the mechanisms of democracy may shift the boundaries of the democratic paradigm in more or less radical directions.

Thus, while there are many variations within radical democratic politics, there are important distinctions to be made between those that regard democratic politics as something to be improved through institutional reform, and those who want to problematise the language of democratic discourse itself. In the latter case, disagreement and upheaval are fundamental to democratic politics, whereas the former perspective regards such disputes as ultimately resolvable. While all conflicts may, strictly speaking, be resolvable, this does not mean that in certain circumstances this is possible or even desirable.

What characterises the post-structuralist account of radical democracy, then, is not only an understanding of the primacy of disagreement and conflict to democratic politics but its positive embrace of those disputes. For post-structuralist radical democrats, democracy should be understood in terms of the necessity of contestation. This entails an understanding of contestation that goes beyond the mere existence of a multiplicity of views emanating from social pluralism; rather, it invokes a more thoroughgoing conception of disagreement that sees challenges to the prevailing hegemonic order as the lifeblood of democracy. In different ways, Alan Finlayson and Joel Olson explain the centrality of critical and oppositional discourses to the framing of the parameters of particular democratic entities. Thus, while radical democracy may be concerned with a hegemonic enterprise, the nature of that project is open to question. This is a process that is enhanced by the conflict of competing rhetorical discourses because there is no agreement among radical democratic theorists as to what radical democracy should look like. It pertains to a way of understanding democracy in a critical fashion rather than trying to outline a blueprint of what radical democracy should look like.

It is in this spirit that we envisage democracy as a fugitive condition whereby we need to recognise the transient nature of its structures and its characteristic elusiveness (Wolin 1994b). Against static conceptions of democracy, we argue that democracy should be conceived as complex and defined by a process of constant reinvention. This dimension of reinvention is pivotal to radical conceptions of democracy because it potentially inspires and legitimises attempts to disrupt the prevailing order at any given time. Therefore, radical democratic politics embrace contestation and disagreement as fundamental dimensions of any democratic order; it is the degree of openness to such conflict that should enable us to make judgements as to whether polities are more or less democratic (although those judgements will also be the sources of further dispute). Ultimately, though, radical democracy invokes a politics of renewal whereby democratic societies are understood to be subject to critical interventions and alive to the possibility of perpetual reconstruction. This, we argue, provides radical democracy with an open-ended dimension whereby the 'promise' of democracy is continually invoked to inspire contestation and challenges to existing institutional structures. Radical democratic theory invokes a conflictual conception of politics that animates democracy and construes it as eternally open to change and improvement. The implications of this are clear: if democracy *is* in a fugitive condition, radical democracy openly suggests that it does not need to be apprehended.

Bibliography

Adamson, W. L. (1980) *Hegemony and Revolution*, Berkeley: University of California Press.

Agamben, G. (1993) *The Coming Community*, Minneapolis: University of Minnesota Press.

Agamben, G. (2005) *State of Exception*, Chicago: University of Chicago Press.

Alquati, R. (1974) 'The Network of Struggles in Italy', unpublished paper.

Althusser, L. (1977) *For Marx*, London: Verso.

Ang, I. (1985) *Watching 'Dallas'*, London: Methuen.

Angus, I. (2005) 'An Interview with Chantal Mouffe and Ernesto Laclau', http://www.ianangus.ca/cp1.htm, accessed 14 June 2005.

Archibugi, D., Held, D. and Kohler, M. (1998) *Re-imagining Political Community: Studies in Cosmopolitan Democracy*, Cambridge: Polity Press.

Arendt, H. (1991) *On Revolution*, Harmondsworth: Penguin.

Arononwitz, S. (1994) 'The Situation of the Left in the United States', *Socialist Review*, vol. 23, no. 3, pp. 5–79.

Ashbee, E. (2007) 'Polyamory, Social Conservatism and the Same-Sex Marriage Debate in the US', *Politics*, vol. 27, no. 2, pp. 101–7.

Aughey, A. (2005) *The Politics of Northern Ireland: Beyond the Belfast Agreement*, London: Routledge.

Aughey, A. (2001) 'Learning from "The Leopard"', in R. Wilford (ed.) *Aspects of the Belfast Agreement*, Oxford: Oxford University Press.

Augusteijn, J. (2003) 'Political Violence and Democracy: An Analysis of Tensions within Irish Republican Strategy, 1914–2002', *Irish Political Studies*, vol. 18, no. 1, Summer, pp. 1–26.

Bacchi, C. L. and Beasley, C. (2002) 'Citizen bodies: is embodied citizenship a contradiction in terms?', *Critical Social Policy*, vol. 22, no. 2, pp. 324–52.

Baird, R. M. and Rosenbaum, S. E. (eds) (2004) *Same-Sex Marriage: the Moral and Legal Debate*, 2nd edition, Amherst, NY: Prometheus Books.

Baker, G. (2002) *Civil Society and Democratic Theory: Alternative Voices*, London: Routledge.

Baker, G. and Chandler, D. (eds) (2006) *Global Civil Society: Contested Futures*, London: Routledge.

Bakhtin, M. (1984) *Problems of Dostoevsky's Poetics*, Minneapolis: University of Minnesota Press.

Balibar, É. (2002) *Politics and the Other Scene*, London: Verso.

Balibar, É. (2004) *We, the People of Europe? Reflections on Transnational Citizenship*, Princeton: Princeton University Press.

Barber, B. (1984) *Strong Democracy: participatory politics for a new age*, Berkeley: Berkeley University Press.

Barclay, H. (1982) *People without Government: An Anthropology of Anarchy*, St Louis: Left Bank Books.

Barry, A., Rose, N. and Osborne, T. (eds) (1996) *Foucault and Political Reason: Liberalism, Neo-Liberalism and Rationalities of Government*, London: UCL Press.

Barry, B. (2001) *Culture and Equality: An Egalitarian Critique of Multiculturalism*, Cambridge, MA: Harvard University Press.

Bayart, J.-F., Ellis, S. and Hibou, B. (1999) *The Criminalization of the State in Africa*, Oxford: James Currey/International African Institute.

Baynes, K. (1995) 'Democracy and the Rechtstaat: Habermas's *Faktizität and Geltung*', in Stephen K. White (ed.) *The Cambridge Companion to Habermas*, Cambridge: Cambridge University Press.

Beasley, C. and Bacchi, C. (2000) 'Citizen Bodies: embodying citizens – a feminist analysis', *International Feminist Journal of Politics*, vol. 2, no. 3, pp. 337–58.

Bellamy, R. (1999) *Liberalism and Pluralism: Toward a Politics of Compromise*, London: Routledge.

Benhabib, S. (1995a) 'Feminism and Postmodernism', in S. Benhabib et al., *Feminist Contentions: A Philosophical Exchange*, London: Routledge, pp. 17–34.

Benhabib, S. (1995b) 'Subjectivity, Historiography, and Politics', in S. Benhabib et al., *Feminist Contentions: A Philosophical Exchange*, London: Routledge, pp. 107–25.

Benhabib, S., Butler, J., Cornell, D. and Fraser, N. (1995) *Feminist Contentions: A Philosophical Exchange*, London: Routledge.

Bennett, J. (2005) 'In Parliament with Things', in L. Tønder and L. Thomassen (eds) *Radical Democracy: Politics between Abundance and Lack*, Manchester: Manchester University Press.

Bennett, J. (2007) 'Edible Matter', *New Left Review*, 45, May–June, pp. 133–45.

Berman, M. (1983) *All That is Solid Melts Into Air: The Experience of Modernity*, London: Verso.

Bew, P. (2000) 'The Belfast Agreement of 1998: From Ethnic Democracy to a Multicultural, Consociational Settlement', in M. Cox et al. (eds) *A Farewell to Arms? From 'Long War' to Long Peace in Northern Ireland*, Manchester: Manchester University Press.

Bhabha, H. K. (1992) 'Postcolonial Authority and Postmodern Guilt', in L. Grossberg, C. Nelson and P. Treichler (eds), London: Routledge, pp. 56–66.

Bhabha, H. (1994) *The Location of Culture*, London: Routledge.

Bieler, A., Bonefeld, W., Burnham, P. and Morton, A. (eds) (2006) *Global Restructuring, State, Capital and Labour*, New York: Palgrave.

Bohman, J. (1998) 'The Coming of Age of Deliberative Democracy', *Journal of Political Philosophy*, 4, pp. 418–43.

Bologna, S. (1980) 'The Tribe of Moles', in S. Lottringer and C. Marazzi (eds) *Italy: Autonomia – Post-Political Politics*, New York: Semiotext(e), 1980.

Bornstein, K. (1994) *Gender Outlaw: On men, women and the rest of us*, London: Routledge.

Bourdieu, P. (2002) *Language and Symbolic Power*, Cambridge: Polity Press.

Bourke, R. (2003) *Peace in Ireland: The War of Ideas*, London: Pimlico.

Brown, M. P. (1997) *RePlacing Citizenship: Aids Activism and Radical Democracy*, London: The Guilford Press.

Burchell, G., Gordon, C. and Miller, P. (1991) *The Foucault Effect: Studies in Governmentality*, Chicago: University of Chicago Press.

Burnyeat, M. (1994) 'Enthymeme: The Logic of Persuasion', in David J. Furley and Alexander Nehemas (eds) *Aristotle's Rhetoric: Philosophical Essays*, Princeton: Princeton University Press, pp. 3–55.

Butler, J. (1990) *Gender Trouble: Feminism and the Subversion of Identity*, London: Routledge.

Butler, J. (1992) 'Contingent Foundations: Feminism and the Question of "Postmodernism"', in J. Butler and J. W. Scott (eds) *Feminists Theorize the Political*, London: Routledge, pp. 3–21.

Butler, J. (1993) *Bodies that Matter: On the Discursive Limits of 'Sex'*, London: Routledge.

Butler, J. (1996) 'Universality in Culture', in Martha C. Nussbaum *For the Love of Country?*, ed. Joshua Cohen, Boston: Beacon Press, pp. 45–52.

Butler, J. (1997a) *Excitable Speech: A Politics of the Performative*, London: Routledge.

Butler, J. (1997b) *The Psychic Life of Power: Theories in Subjection*, Stanford: Stanford University Press.

Butler, J. (1998) 'Left Conservatism II', *theory & event*, vol. 2, no. 2.

Butler, J. (1999a) *Gender Trouble: Feminism and the Subversion of Identity*, Anniversary edition, London: Routledge.

Butler, J. (1999b) *Subjects of Desire: Hegelian Reflections in Twentieth Century France*, 2nd edition, New York: Columbia University Press.

Butler, J. (2000a) 'Restaging the Universal: Hegemony and the Limits of Formalism', in J. Butler, E. Laclau and S. Žižek (2000) *Contingency, Hegemony, Universality*, London: Verso, pp. 11–43.

Butler, J. (2000b) 'Competing Universalities', in J. Butler, E. Laclau and S. Žižek (2000) *Contingency, Hegemony, Universality*, London: Verso, pp. 136–81.

Butler, J. (2000c) 'Dynamic Conclusions', in J. Butler, E. Laclau and S. Žižek (2000) *Contingency, Hegemony, Universality*, London: Verso, pp. 263–80.

Butler, J. (2000d) 'Changing the Subject: Judith Butler's Politics of Radical Resignification. An Interview with Gary A. Olsen and Lynn Worsham', *JAC*, vol. 20, no. 4, pp. 727–65.

Butler, J. (2000e) *Antigone's Claim: Kinship between Life and Death*, New York: Columbia University Press.

Butler, J. (2001) 'The End of Sexual Difference?', in Elisabeth Bronfen and Misha Kavka (eds) *Feminist Consequences: Theory for the New Century*, New York: Columbia University Press, pp. 414–34.

Butler, J. (2002) 'Bodies and power, revisited', *Radical Philosophy*, no. 114, pp. 13–19.

Butler, J. (2004a) *Undoing Gender*, London: Routledge.

Butler, J. (2004b) 'Changing the Subject: Judith Butler's Politics of Radical Resignification', in Sarah Salih (ed. with Judith Butler) *Judith Butler Reader*, Oxford: Blackwell, pp. 325–56.

Butler, J. (2004c) *Precarious Life*, London: Verso.

Butler, J., Laclau, E. and Žižek, S. (2000) *Contingency, Hegemony, Universality: Contemporary Dialogues on the Left*, London: Verso.

Card, C. (1996) 'Against marriage and motherhood', *Hypatia*, vol. 11, no. 3, pp. 1–23.

Card, C. (2007) 'Gay Divorce: Thoughts on the Legal Regulation of Marriage', *Hypatia*, vol. 22, no. 1, pp. 24–38.

Carothers, T. (2002) 'The End of the Transition Paradigm', *Journal of Democracy*, vol. 13, no. 1, January, pp. 5–21.

Carothers, T. (2004) *Critical Mission: Essays on Democracy Promotion*, Washington, DC: Carnegie.

Carver, T. and Chambers, S. (2008) *Judith Butler and Political Theory: Troubling Politics*, London: Routledge.

Chambers, S. (2003) *Untimely Politics*, Edinburgh: Edinburgh University Press.

Chambers, S. (2004) 'Giving Up (on) Rights? The Future of Rights and the Project of Radical Democracy', *American Journal of Political Science*, vol. 48, no. 2, pp. 185–200.

Chambers, S. (2007a) 'Normative Violence after 9/11: Rereading the Politics of Gender Trouble', *New Political Science*, vol. 29, no. 1, pp. 43–60.

Chambers, S. (2007b) ' "An Incalculable Effect": Subversions of Heteronormativity', *Political Studies*, vol. 55, no. 3, pp. 656–79.

Chambers, S. (2008) *The Queer Politics of Television*, London: I. B. Tauris.

Chambers, S. (1996) *Reasonable Democracy: Jürgen Habermas and the Politics of Discourse*, Ithaca: Cornell University Press.

Chatterjee, P. (1993) *The Nation and its Fragments*, Princeton: Princeton University Press.

Chesters, G. (2006) *Another World is Possible: Social Movements Confronting Capital and the State*, London: Pluto Press.

Chesters, G. and Walsh, I. (2006) *Complexity and Social Movements: Protest at the Edge of Chaos*, London: Routledge.

Christodoulidis, E. (2001) 'The Aporia of Sovereignty: On the Representation of the People in Constitutional Discourse', *King's College Law Journal*, no. 12, pp. 111–33.

Christodoulidis, E. (2007) 'Against Substitution: The Constitutional Thinking of Dissensus', in M. Loughlin and N. Walker (eds) *The Paradox of Constitutionalism: Constituent Power and Constitutional Form*, Oxford: Oxford University Press.

Clastres, P. (1989) *Society Against the State*, New York: Zone.

Clohesy, A. M. (2000) 'Provisionalism and the (im)possibility of justice in Northern Ireland', in D. Howarth et al. (eds) *Discourse Theory and Political Analysis: Identities, Hegemonies and Social Change*, Manchester: Manchester University Press.

Cohen, J. and Arato, A. (1992) *Civil Society and Political Theory*, Cambridge, MA: MIT Press.

Cohen, J. and Rogers, J. (1995) *Associations and Democracy*, London: Verso.

Connolly, W. (1991) *Identity/Difference: Democratic Negotiations of the Political Paradox*, Ithaca: Cornell University Press.

Connolly, W. (1995) *The Ethos of Pluralization*, Minneapolis: University of Minnesota Press.

Connolly, W. (2002) *Neuropolitics*, Minneapolis: Minnesota University Press.

Connolly, W. (2005a) *Pluralism*, Durham, NC: Duke University Press.

Connolly, W. (2005b) 'The Evangelical-Capitalist Resonance Machine', *Political Theory*, vol. 33, no. 6, 2005, pp. 869–86.

Coole, D. (2007) 'Experiencing Discourse: Corporeal Communicators and the Embodiment of Power', *British Journal of Politics and International Relations*, vol. 9, no. 3, pp. 413–33.

Cox, R. (1991) 'Social Forces, States and World Orders: Beyond International Relations Theory', in R. Little and M. Smith (eds) *Perspectives on World Politics*, 2nd edition, London: Routledge.

Critchley, S. and Marchart, O. (2004) 'Introduction', in Simon Critchley and Oliver Marchart (eds) *Laclau: a critical reader*, London: Routledge, pp. 1–13.

Curtis, T., Dellar, R., Leslie, E. and Watson, B. (eds) (2000) *Mad Pride: A Celebration of Mad Culture*, London: Spare Change Books.

Day, R. J. F. (2005) *Gramsci is Dead: Anarchist Currents in the Newest Social Movements*, London: Pluto Press.

DeLanda, M. (1997) *A Thousand Years of NonLinear History*, London: Zone Books.

Deleuze, G. (1994) *Difference and Repetition*, New York: Columbia University Press.

Deleuze, G. (2001) *Pure Immanence: Essays on Life*, New York: Zone Books.

Deleuze, G. and Guattari, F. (1987) *A Thousand Plateaus*, London: Continuum.

Derrida, J. (1976) *Of Grammatology*, Baltimore: The Johns Hopkins University Press.

Derrida, J. (1991) 'Signature Event Context', in P. Kamuf (ed.) *A Derrida Reader: Between the Blinds*, London: Harvester Wheatscheaf, pp. 82–111.

Derrida, J. (1994) *Specters of Marx: The State of the Debt, the Work of Mourning, and the New International*, translated by Peggy Kamuf, New York and London: Routledge.

Deveaux, M. (1999) 'Agonism and pluralism', *Philosophy and Social Criticism*, vol. 25, no. 4, pp. 1–22.

Dillon, M. (2000) 'Poststructuralism, Complexity and Poetics', *Theory, Culture & Society*, vol. 17, no. 5, pp. 1–26.

Disch, L. (1999) 'Judith Butler and the Politics of the Performative', *Political Theory*, vol. 27, no. 4, pp. 545–59.

Dixon, P. (2001) *Northern Ireland: The Politics of War and Peace*, London: Palgrave.

Doel, M. (1999) *Poststructuralist Geographies: The Diabolical Art of Spatial Science*, Edinburgh: Edinburgh University Press.

Dow, C. (2000) 'Aborginal Tent Embassy: Icon or Eyesore?', Social Policy Group, Parliament of Australia, http://wopared.parl.net/Library/pubs/chron/1999-2000/2000chr03.htm, accessed 28 September 2006.

Dryzek, J. (2002) *Deliberative Democracy and Beyond: Liberals, Critics, Contestations*, Oxford: Oxford University Press.

Du Bois, W. E. B. (1992) *Black Reconstruction in America 1860–1880*, New York: Atheneum.

Epstein, B. (1996) 'Radical Democracy and Cultural Politics: What about Class? What about Political Power?', in D. Trend (ed.) *Radical Democracy: Identity, Citizenship and the State*, London: Routledge.

Esposito, R. (2006) *Communitas: Origine e destino della comunitá*, 2nd edition, Turin: Einaudi.

Ettelbrick, P. (2004) 'Since When Is Marriage A Path To Liberation?', in Andrew Sullivan (ed.) *Same-Sex Marriage: Pro and Con: A Reader*, 2nd edition, New York: Vintage Books, pp. 122–8.

Falk, R. (1999) *Predatory Globalisation: A Critique*, Cambridge: Polity Press.

Fantasia, R. (1988) *Cultures of Solidarity*, Berkeley: University of California Press.

Farrar, C. (1988) *The origins of democratic thinking: the invention of politics in classical Athens*, Cambridge: Cambridge University Press.

Favell, A. (1993) 'James Coleman: Social Theorist and Moral Philosopher', *American Journal of Sociology*, vol. 99, no. 3, pp. 590–613.

Ferguson, A. (2007) 'Gay Marriage: An American and Feminist Dilemma', *Hypatia*, vol. 22, no. 1, pp. 39–57.

Finlayson, A. (2003) *Making Sense of New Labour*, London, Lawrence and Wishart.

Finlayson, A. (2006) 'What's the Problem? Political Theory, Rhetoric and Problem-Setting', *Critical Review of International Social and Political Philosophy*, vol. 9, no. 4, December, pp. 541–57.

Finlayson, A. and Martin, J. (2006) 'Poststructuralism', in C. Hay, M. Lister and D. Marsh (eds) *The State: Theories and Issues*, London: Palgrave, pp. 155–71.

Foley, G. (2001) 'Black Power in Redfern: 1968–1972', accessed at: http://www.kooriweb.org/foley/essays/essay_1.html, last viewed 29 June 2007.

Foucault, M. (1977) *Discipline and Punish: The Birth of the Prison*, London: Allen Lane.

Foucault, M. (1980) *Power/Knowledge: Selected interviews and other writings 1972–1977*, Brighton: Harvester Press.

Foucault, M. (1989) *Madness and Civilisation*, London: Routledge.

Foucault, M. (1991) 'Governmentality', in G. Burchell, C. Gordon and P. Miller (eds) *The Foucault Effect: Studies in Governmental Rationality*, Hemel Hempstead: Harvester Wheatsheaf.

Foucault, M. (2002) 'Pastoral Power', in *Power: Essential Works of Foucault Vol. 3*, Harmondsworth: Penguin.

Foucault, M. (2003) *Society Must be Defended*, Harmondsworth: Penguin.

Foucault, M. (2007) *Security, Territory, Population. Lectures at the Collège de France, 1977–78*, Basingstoke: Palgrave.

Fraser, N. (1995a) 'False Antitheses', in Seyla Benhabib et al., *Feminist Contentions: A Philosophical Exchange*, London: Routledge, pp. 59–74.

Fraser, N. (1995b) 'Pragmatism, Feminism, and the Linguistic Turn', in Seyla Benhabib et al., *Feminist Contentions: A Philosophical Exchange*, London: Routledge, pp. 157–71.

Fraser, N. (1997) *Justice Interruptus: Critical Reflections on the 'Postsocialist' Condition*, London: Routledge.

Fulbrook, M. (1997) *Anatomy of a Dictatorship: Inside the GDR 1949–89*, Oxford: Clarendon.

Gagarin, M. and Woodruff, P. (eds) (1995) *Early Greek Political Thought from Homer to the Sophists*, Cambridge: Cambridge University Press.

Galvan, D. C. (2004) *The State Must Be Our Master of Fire: How Peasants Craft Culturally Sustainable Development in Senegal*, Berkeley: University of California Press.

Gasché, R. (2004) 'How Empty Can Empty Be? On the place of the universal', in Simon Critchley and Oliver Marchart (eds) *Laclau: a critical reader*, London: Routledge, pp. 17–34.

Geoghegan, V. (1995) *Ernst Bloch*, London: Routledge.

Giddens, A. (1999) *Runaway World: How Globalization is Shaping Our Lives*, London, Profile Books.

Gilbert, K. (1993) *Aboriginal Sovereignty: Justice, the Law and Land*, Canberra: Burrambinga Books.

Gill, S. (2000) 'Towards a Postmodern Prince? The Battle in Seattle as a Moment in the New Politics of Globalisation', *Millennium*, vol. 29, no. 1, pp. 131–40.

Gilroy, P. (1993) *The Black Atlantic. Modernity and Double Consciousness*, London: Verso.

Glynos, J. (2003) 'Radical Democratic Ethos, or, What is an Authentic Political Act?', *Contemporary Political Theory*, vol. 2, no. 2, pp. 187–208.

Graff, E. J. (2004) *What is Marriage For?*, with foreword by Richard Goldstein, Boston: Beacon Press.

Gramsci, A. (1971) *Selections from the Prison Notebooks*, edited and translated by Quintin Hoare and Geoffrey Nowell Smith, New York: International.

Gramsci, A. (1988) 'Prison Writings', in D. Forgacs (ed.) *A Gramsci Reader*, London: Lawrence and Wishart.

Grassi, E. (2001) *Rhetoric as Philosophy: The Humanist Tradition*, Carbondale: Southern Illinois University Press.

Guattari, F. (1995) 'La Borde: A Clinic Unlike Any Other', in *Chaosophy*, New York: Semiotext(e), pp. 187–208.

Gutmann, A. and Thompson, D. (1996) *Democracy and Disagreement*, Cambridge, MA: Harvard University Press.

Habermas, J. (1990) 'Discourse Ethics: Notes on a Program of Philosophical Justification', in *Moral Consciousness and Communicative Action*, Cambridge, MA: MIT Press.

Habermas, J. (1996) *Between Facts and Norms: Contributions to a Discourse Theory of Law and Democracy*, Cambridge, MA: MIT Press.

Habermas, J. (1998) 'On the Internal Relation between the Rule of Law and Democracy', in *The Inclusion of the Other*, Cambridge, MA: MIT Press.

Habermas, J. (2001) 'Constitutional Democracy: A Paradoxical Union of Contradictory Principles?', *Political Theory*, vol. 29, no. 6, pp. 766–81.

Habermas, J. (2002) 'On Legitimation Through Human Rights', in P. De Grieff and C. Cronin (eds) *Global Justice and Transnational Politics*, Cambridge, MA: MIT Press.

Haddock, B., Roberts, P. and Sutch, P. (eds) (2006) *Principals and Political Order: The Challenge of Diversity*, London: Routledge.

Hampshire, S. (1999) *Justice is Conflict*, London: Duckworth.

Hann, C. and Dunn, E. (1996) *Civil Society: Challenging Western Models*, London: Routledge.

Hardt, M. and Negri, A. (2001) *Empire*, Cambridge, MA: Harvard University Press.

Hecht, S. and Simone, A. M. (1994) *Invisible Governance: The Art of African Micropolitics*, New York: Autonomedia.

Hegel, G. W. F. (1967) *The Philosophy of Right*, Oxford: Oxford University Press.

Held, D. (1993) 'Democracy: From City-states to a Cosmopolitan Order?', in D. Held (ed.) *Prospects for Democracy: North, South, East, West*, Cambridge: Polity Press.

Held, D. (1995) *Democracy and the Global Order: From the Modern State to Cosmopolitan Governance*, Cambridge: Polity Press.

Held, D. and McGrew, A. (2002) *Globalisation/Anti-Globalisation*, Cambridge: Polity Press.

Higgins, N. P. (2005) *Understanding the Chiapas Rebellion: Modernist Visions and the Invisible Indian*, Austin: University of Texas Press.

Hirst, P. Q. and Thompson, G. (1996) *Globalisation in Question: the International Economy and the Possibilities of Governance*, Cambridge: Polity Press.

Hofstadter, R. (1948) *The American Political Tradition*, New York: Alfred A. Knopf.

Holloway, J. (2002) *Change the World Without Taking Power*, London: Pluto Press.

Honig, B. (1993) *Political Theory and the Displacement of Politics*, Ithaca: Cornell University Press.

Honig, B. (2001) 'Dead Rights, Live Futures: A Reply to Habermas's "Constitutional Democracy"', *Political Theory*, vol. 29, no. 6, pp. 792–805.

Honig, B. (2007) 'Between Decisionism and Deliberation: Political Paradox in Democratic Theory', *American Political Science Review*, vol. 101, no. 1, pp. 1–17.

hooks, b. (1994) *Outlaw Culture: Resisting Representation*, London: Routledge.

Horowitz, D. (2002) 'Explaining the Northern Ireland Agreement: The Sources of an Unlikely Constitutional Consensus', *British Journal of Political Science*, vol. 32, no. 2, pp. 193–220.

Howarth, D., Norval, A. and Stavrakakis, Y. (eds) (2000) *Discourse Theory and Political Analysis: Identities, Hegemonies, and Social Change*, Manchester: Manchester University Press.

Ivanitz, M. (2002) 'Democracy and Indigenous Self-Determination', in A. Carter and G. Stokes (eds) *Democratic Theory Today*, Cambridge: Polity Press.

Jenkins, F. (2001) 'The Heeding of Differences: On Foreclosure and Openness in a Politics of the Performative', *Constellations*, vol. 8, no. 3, pp. 364–75.

Joyce, P. (2003) *The Rule of Freedom: Liberalism and the Modern City*, London: Verso.

Kaldor, M. (2003) *Global Civil Society: An Answer to War*, Cambridge: Polity Press.

Kalyvas, A. (2005) 'Popular Sovereignty, Democracy and the Constituent Power', *Constellations*, vol. 12, no. 2, pp. 223–44.

Kant, I. (1991a) 'Idea for a Universal History with a cosmopolitan Intent', in H. Reiss (ed.) *Kant Political Writings*, Cambridge: Cambridge University Press.

Kant, I. (1991b) 'Perpetual Peace: A Philosophical Sketch', in H. Reiss (ed.) *Kant Political Writings*, Cambridge: Cambridge University Press.

Kant, I. (1991c) 'An Answer to the Question "What is Enlightenment?" ', in H. Reiss (ed.) *Kant: Political Writings*, Cambridge: Cambridge University Press, pp. 54–60.

Karagiannis, N. and Wagner, P. (2005) 'Towards a Theory of Synagonism', *The Journal of Political Philosophy*, vol. 13, no. 3, pp. 235–62.

Keane, J. (1998) *Civil Society: Old Images, New Visions*, Cambridge: Polity Press.

Keane, J. (2003) *Global Civil Society?* Cambridge: Cambridge University Press.

Keenan, A. (2003) *Democracy in Question*, Palo Alto: Stanford University Press.

Kennedy, D. (2002) 'The Critique of Rights in Critical Legal Studies', in W. Brown and J. Halley (eds) *Left Legalism/Left Critique*, Durham, NC: Duke University Press.

Kennedy, G. (1991) 'Introduction', in Aristotle, *The Rhetoric*, Oxford: Oxford University Press.

Kerruish, V. and Purdy, J. (1998) 'He "Look" Honest – Big White Thief', *Law/Text/Culture*, vol. 4, no. 1, pp. 146–65.

Knops, A. (2007) 'Debate: Agonism as Deliberation: On Mouffe's Theory of Democracy', *The Journal of Political Philosophy*, vol. 15, no. 1, pp. 115–26.

Kotkin, S. (1997) *Magnetic Mountain: Stalinism as a Civilisation*, Berkeley: University of California Press.

Kropotkin, P. (1902) *Mutual Aid: A Factor in Evolution*, accessed at dwardmac.pitzer.edu/Anarchist_Archives/kropotkin/mutaidcontents.html.

Kymlicka, W. (1996) *Multicultural Citizenship: A Liberal Theory of Minority Rights*, Oxford: Oxford University Press.

Laclau, E. (1990) *New Reflections on the Revolution of our Time*, London: Verso.

Laclau, E. (1996a) *Emancipation(s)*, London: Verso.

Laclau, E. (1996b) 'Death and Resurrection of the Theory of Ideology', *Journal of Political Ideologies*, vol. 1, no. 3, pp. 201–20.

Laclau, E. (1999) 'Hegemony and the Future of Democracy', *JAC*, vol. 19, no. 1, pp. 1–34.

Laclau, E. (2000) 'Identity and Hegemony: the Role of Universality in the Constitution of Political Logics', in J. Butler, E. Laclau and S. Žižek, *Contingency, Hegemony, Universality*, London: Verso.

Laclau, E. (2001) 'Democracy and the Question of Power', *Constellations*, vol. 8, no. 1, pp. 3–14.

Laclau, E. (2003) 'Can Immanence Explain Social Struggles?', in *Diacritics*, vol. 31, no. 4, pp. 3–10.

Laclau, E. (2005a) 'The Future of Radical Democracy', in L. Tønder and L. Thomassen (eds) *Radical Democracy: Between Abundance and Lack*, Manchester: Manchester University Press.

Laclau, E. (2005b) *On Populist Reason*, London: Verso.

Laclau, E. and Mouffe, C. (1985) *Hegemony and Socialist Strategy: Towards a Radical Democratic Politics*, London: Verso.

Laclau, E. and Mouffe, C. (2001) *Hegemony and Socialist Strategy*, 2nd edition, London: Verso.

Laclau, E. and Zac, L. (1994) 'Minding the Gap: The Subject of Politics', in E. Laclau (ed.) *The Making of Political Identities*, London: Verso.

Laursen, J. C. (1986) 'The Subversive Kant: The Vocabulary of "Public" and "Publicity" ', *Political Theory*, vol. 14, no. 4, pp. 584–603.

Lee, R. B. and DeVore, I. (1978) *Kalahari Hunter-Gatherers: Studies of the !Kung San and their Neighbours*, New York: Harvard University Press.

Lefort, C. (1986) *The Political Forms of Modern Society: Bureaucracy, Democracy, Totalitarianism*, Cambridge, MA: MIT Press.

Lefort, C. (1988) *Democracy and Political Theory*, Minneapolis: University of Minnesota Press.

Lennon, K. (2006) 'Making life livable. Transsexuality and bodily transformation', *Radical Philosophy*, no. 140, pp. 26–34.

Lijphart, A. (1977) *Democracy in Plural Societies*, London: Yale University Press.

Lindahl, H. (2007) 'Constituent Power and Reflexive Identity: Towards an Ontology of Collective Selfhood', in M. Loughlin and N. Walker (eds) *The Paradox of Constitutionalism: Constituent Power and Constitutional Form*, Oxford: Oxford University Press.

Linklater, A. (1998) *The Transformation of Political Community: Ethical Foundations of the Post-Westphalian Era*, Cambridge: Polity Press.

Little, A. (2002a) *The Politics of Community: Theory and Practice*, Edinburgh: Edinburgh University Press.

Little, A. (2002b) 'Feminism and the Politics of Difference in Northern Ireland', *Journal of Political Ideologies*, vol. 7, no. 2, pp. 163–77.

Little, A. (2002c) 'Community and Radical Democracy', *Journal of Political Ideologies*, vol. 7, no. 3, pp. 369–82.

Little, A. (2003a) 'The Problems of Antagonism: Applying Liberal Political Theory to Conflict in Northern Ireland', *British Journal of Politics and International Relations*, vol. 5, no. 3, pp. 373–92.

Little, A. (2003b) 'Multiculturalism, Diversity and Liberal Egalitarianism in Northern Ireland', *Irish Political Studies*, vol. 18, no. 2, pp. 23–39.

Little, A. (2004) *Democracy and Northern Ireland: Beyond the Liberal Paradigm*, London: Palgrave.

Little, A. (2006) 'Theorizing Violence and Democracy: The Case of Northern Ireland', *Theoria*, no. 111, pp. 62–86.

Little, A. (2007) 'Between Disagreement and Consent: Unravelling the Democratic Paradox', *Australian Journal of Political Studies*, vol. 42, no. 1, March, pp. 143–59.

Little, A. (2008a) *Democratic Piety: Complexity, Conflict and Violence*, Edinburgh: Edinburgh University Press.

Little, A. (2008b) 'Sunningdale for Slow Learners? Towards a Complexity Paradigm', in R. Taylor (ed.) *Consociational Theory: McGarry/O'Leary and the Northern Ireland Conflict*, London: Routledge.

Lloyd, M. (2005a) *Beyond Identity Politics: feminism, power, and politics*, London: Sage.

Lloyd, M. (2005b) 'Butler, Antigone and the State', *Contemporary Political Theory*, vol. 4, no. 4, pp. 451–68.

Lloyd, M. (2007a) *Judith Butler: from norms to politics*, Cambridge: Polity Press.

Lloyd, M. (2007b) 'Radical Democratic Activism and the Politics of Resignification', *Constellations*, vol. 14, no. 1, pp. 129–46.

Lomnitz, L. (1977) *Networks and Marginality: Life in a Mexican Shantytown*, New York: Academic Press.

Lyotard, J.-F. (1984) *The Postmodern Condition: a report on knowledge*, Manchester: Manchester University Press.

McGarry, J. and O'Leary, B. (1996) *The Politics of Antagonism*, 2nd edition, London: Athlone.

McGarry, J. and O'Leary, B. (2008) 'Power Shared After the Death of Thousands', in R. Taylor (ed.) *Consociational Theory: McGarry/O'Leary and the Northern Ireland Conflict*, London: Routledge.

MacKinnon, C. A. (1996) *Only Words*, Cambridge, MA: Harvard University Press.

McNay, L. (1999) 'Subject, Psyche and Agency: The Work of Judith Butler', *Theory, Culture & Society*, vol. 16, no. 2, pp. 175–93.

McNay, L. (2000) *Gender and Agency: Reconfiguring the Subject in Feminist and Social Theory*, Cambridge: Polity Press.

Marcos, Subcomandante (2001) *Questions and Swords*, El Paso: Cinco Puntos Press.

Marcuse, H. (1998) *Negations*, London: Free Association Books.

Marx, K. (1983) 'A Contribution to the Critique of Political Economy', in E. Kamenka (ed.) *The Portable Karl Marx*, Harmondsworth: Penguin.

Marx, K. (1987) 'On the Jewish Question', in D. McLellan (ed.) *Karl Marx: Selected Writings*, Oxford: Oxford University Press.

Mason, C. (2002) *Killing for Life: The Apocalyptic Narrative of Pro-Life Politics*, Ithaca: Cornell University Press.

Mathiesen, T. (1965) *The Defenses of the Weak: A Sociological Study of a Norwegian Correctional Institution*, London: Tavistock.

Matza, D. (1964) *Delinquency and Drift*, New York: John Wiley and Sons.

Maus, I. (2002) 'Liberties and Popular Sovereignty: On Jürgen Habermas's Reconstruction of the System of Rights', in R. von Schomberg and K. Baynes (eds) *Discourse and Democracy: Essays on Habermas's Between Facts and Norms*, Albany: State University of New York Press.

May, J. and Thrift, N. (2001) *Timespace: Geographies of Temporality*, London: Routledge.

Mayer, H. (1998) *All on Fire: William Lloyd Garrison and the Abolition of Slavery*, New York: St. Martin's Griffin.

Maynes, P. (2003) 'Understanding Violence', *Soundings*, Issue 22, Winter, pp. 29–36.

Mill, J. S. (1985) *On Liberty*, London: Penguin.

Mills, C. (2000) 'Efficacy and Vulnerability: Judith Butler on Reiteration and Resistance', *Australian Feminist Studies*, vol. 15, no. 32, pp. 265–79.

Mills, C. (2003) 'Contesting the Political: Butler and Foucault on Power and Resistance', *The Journal of Political Philosophy*, vol. 11, no. 3, pp. 253–72.

Modood, T. and Favell, A. (2003) 'Multiculturalism', in Alan Finlayson (ed.) *Contemporary Political Theory: A Reader and Guide*, Edinburgh: Edinburgh University Press, pp. 484–522.

Motha, S. (2002) 'The Sovereign Event in a Nation's Law', *Law and Critique*, no. 13, pp. 311–38.

Mouffe, C. (1979a) 'Hegemony and Ideology in Gramsci', in C. Mouffe (ed.) *Gramsci and Marxist Theory*, London: Routledge.

Mouffe, C. (1979b) 'Introduction: Gramsci Today', in C. Mouffe (ed.) *Gramsci and Marxist Theory*, London: Routledge.

Mouffe, C. (1993) *The Return of the Political*, London: Verso.

Mouffe, C. (1995) 'Democracy and Pluralism: A Critique of the Rationalist Approach', *The Cardozo Law Review*, vol. 16, no. 5, pp. 1533–45.

Mouffe, C. (1996a) 'Radical Democracy or Liberal Democracy', in D. Trend (ed.) *Radical Democracy: Identity, Citizenship and the State*, London: Routledge.

Mouffe, C. (1996b) 'Democracy, Power, and the "Political" ', in S. Benhabib (ed.) *Democracy and Difference: Contesting the Boundaries of the Political*, Princeton: Princeton University Press.

Mouffe, C. (ed.) (1999a) *The Challenge of Carl Schmitt*, London: Verso.

Mouffe, C. (1999b) 'Deliberative Democracy or Agonistic Pluralism?', *Social Science Research*, vol. 66, no. 3, pp. 745–58.

Mouffe, C. (2000) *The Democratic Paradox*, London: Verso.

Mouffe, C. (2001) 'Every Form of Art Has a Political Dimension', *Grey Room*, 2, Winter, pp. 98–125.

Mouffe, C. (2005a) *On the Political*, London: Routledge.

Mouffe, C. (2005b) 'Schmitt's Vision of a Multipolar World Order', *The South Atlantic Quarterly*, vol. 104, no. 2, pp. 245–51.

Muldoon, P. (2006) ' "The Very Basis of Civility": On Reconciliation, Agonism and Conquest', unpublished manuscript.

Nancy, J.-L. (1991) *The Inoperative Community*, ed. P. Connor, Minneapolis: University of Minnesota Press.

Negri, A. and Hardt, M. (1994) *Labor of Dionysus: Critique of the State Form*, Minneapolis: University of Minnesota Press.

Nemeth, T. (1980) *Gramsci's Philosophy*, Brighton: Harvester.

Newey, G. (2002) 'Discourse rights and the Drumcree Marches: A Reply to O'Neill', *The British Journal of Politics and International Relations*, vol. 4, no. 1, pp. 75–97.

Newman, S. (2007) *Unstable Universalities: Poststructuralism and Radical Politics*, Manchester: Manchester University Press.

Norval, A. J. (1996) *Deconstructing Apartheid Discourse*, London: Verso.

Norval, A. (2001) 'Radical Democracy', in P. B. Clarke and J. Foweraker (eds) *Encyclopedia of Democratic Thought*, London: Routledge.

Norval, A. (2004) 'Democratic Decisions and the Question of Universality: Rethinking Recent Approaches', in S. Critchley and O. Marchart (eds) *Laclau: A Critical Reader*, London: Routledge.

Norval, A. (2007) *Aversive Democracy: Inheritance and Originality in the Democratic Tradition*, Cambridge: Cambridge University Press.

Nun, J. (1996) 'Elements for a Theory of Democracy: Gramsci and Common Sense', *Boundary 2*, Special Issue, vol. 14, no. 3, Spring, pp. 197–229.

Oakeshott, M. (1975) 'Civil Association', in *On Human Conduct*, Oxford: Oxford University Press.

Oakeshott, M. (1991) *On Human Conduct*, Oxford: Clarendon.

O'Flynn, I. (2004) 'Why Justice Can't Have It All, In Reply to O'Neill', *Ethnicities*, vol. 4, no. 4, pp. 545–61.

O'Leary, B. (1999) 'The Nature of the Agreement', *Fordham Journal of International Law*, vol. 22, no. 4, pp. 1628–67.

Olson, J. (forthcoming) 'The Freshness of Fanaticism: The Abolitionist Defense of Zealotry', *Perspectives on Politics*.

O'Neill, S. (2002) 'Democratic Theory with Critical Intent: Reply to Newey', *The British Journal of Politics and International Relations*, vol. 4, no. 1, pp. 98–114.

O'Neill, S. (2000) 'Liberty, Equality and the Rights of Cultures: the Marching Controversy at Drumcree', *The British Journal of Politics and International Relations*, vol. 2, no. 1, pp. 26–45.

Parekh, B. (2000) *Rethinking Multiculturalism: Cultural Diversity and Political Theory*, London: Macmillan.

Passavant, P. A. and Dean, J. (2001) 'Laws and Societies', *Constellations*, vol. 8, no. 3, pp. 376–89.

Pateman, C. (1989) *The Disorder of Women: Democracy, Feminism and Political Theory*, Cambridge: Polity Press.

Patton, P. (2001) 'Reconciliation, Aboriginal Rights and Constitutional Paradox in Australia', *The Australian Feminist Law Journal*, vol. 15, no. 1, pp. 25–40.

Peukert, D. J. K. (1988) *Inside Nazi Germany: Conformity, Opposition and Racism in Everyday Life*, Harmondsworth: Penguin.

Phillips, A. (1993) *Democracy and Difference*, Cambridge: Polity Press.

Phillips, W. (1845) *Can an Abolitionist Vote or Take Office Under the United States Constitution?*, New York: American Anti-Slavery Society, http://www.gutenberg.org/files/11274/11274-h/11274-h.htm#AE13vote, accessed 11 September 2005.

Phillips, W. (1863) *Speeches, Lectures, and Letters*, first series, Boston: James Redpath.

Phillips, W. (1865) *Remarks of Wendell Phillips at the Mass Meeting of Workingmen in Faneuil Hall, Nov. 2, 1865*, Boston: Voice Printing and Publishing.

Phillips, W. (1891) *Speeches, Lectures, and Letters*, second series, Boston: Lee and Shepard.

Phillips, W. (ed.) (1969) *The Constitution, A Pro-Slavery Compact*, New York: Negro Universities Press.

Phillips, W. (2001) *The Lesson of the Hour: Wendell Phillips on Abolition & Strategy*, ed. Noel Ignatiev, Chicago: Charles H. Kerr.

Piven, F. F. and Cloward, R. (1977) *Poor People's Movements: Why they Succeed, How they Fail*, New York: Pantheon Books.

Puwar, N. (2004) 'Thinking about making a difference', *British Journal of Politics and International Relations*, vol. 6, no. 1, pp. 65–80.

Rancière, J. (1995) *On the Shores of Politics*, London: Verso.

Rancière, J. (1999) *Disagreement: Politics and Philosophy*, Minneapolis: University of Minnesota Press.

Rancière, J. (2001) 'Ten Theses on Politics', *Theory and Event*, vol. 5, no. 3.

Rancière, J. (2004) 'Who is the subject of the rights of man?', *South Atlantic Quarterly*, vol. 103, no. 2/3, pp. 297–310.

Rancière, J. (2006) *Hatred of Democracy*, London: Verso.

Rawls, J. (1993) *Political Liberalism*, New York: Columbia University Press.

Richards, I. A. (1936) *The Philosophy of Rhetoric*, Oxford: Oxford University Press.

Risen, J. and Thomas, J. L. (1998) *Wrath of Angels: The American Abortion War*, New York: Basic Books.

Robinson, A. (2004) 'Constructing Revolutionary Subjectivities', *Utopian Studies*, vol. 15, no. 2, pp. 141–72.

Robinson, A. (2005a) 'The Political Theory of Constitutive Lack: A Critique', *Theory and Event*, vol. 8, no. 1 (March–April).

Robinson, A. (2006b) 'Towards an Intellectual Reformation: The Critique of Common Sense and the Forgotten Revolutionary Project of Gramscian Theory', *Critical Review of International Social and Political Philosophy*, vol. 8, no. 4, pp. 469–82.

Robinson, A. and Tormey, S. (2005) ' "Horizontals", "Verticals" and the Conflicting Logics of Transformative Politics', in P. Hayden and C. el-Ojeili (eds) *Confronting Globalisation: Humanity, Justice and the Renewal of Politics after Postmodernism*, Basingstoke: Palgrave Macmillan, pp. 208–26.

Robinson, S. (1994) 'The Aboriginal Embassy: An Account of the Protests of 1972', *Aboriginal History*, vol. 18, no. 1, pp. 49–63.

Robson, R. (2007) 'A Mere Switch or a Fundamental Change? Theorizing Transgender Marriage', *Hypatia*, vol. 22, no. 1, pp. 58–70.

Rose, N. (1999) *Powers of Freedom: Reframing Political Thought*, Cambridge: Cambridge University Press.

Rosenfeld, M. (1995) 'Law as Discourse: Bridging the Gap Between Democracy and Rights', *Harvard Law Review*, no. 108, pp. 1163–89.

Ross, D. (2004) *Violent Democracy*, Cambridge: Cambridge University Press.

Rousseau, J.-J. [1762] (1997) 'The Social Contract', in *The Social Contract and Other Later Political Writings*, ed. Victor Gourevitch, Cambridge: Cambridge University Press.

Rummens, S. (2006) 'The Co-originality of Private and Public Autonomy in Deliberative Democracy', *The Journal of Political Philosophy*, vol. 14, no. 4, pp. 469–81.

Sahlins, M. (1972) *Stone Age Economics*, Berlin: Walter de Gruyter.

Schaap, A. (2006) 'Agonism in Divided Societies', *Philosophy and Social Criticism*, vol. 32, no. 2, pp. 255–77.

Schaap, A. (forthcoming 2009) 'The Absurd Proposition of Aboriginal Sovereignty', in A. Schaap (ed.) *Law and Agonistic Politics*, Aldershot: Ashgate.

Schecter, D. (2000) *Sovereign States or Political Communities? Civil Society and Contemporary Politics*, Manchester: Manchester University Press.

Scheuerman, W. E. (1999) 'Between Radicalism and Resignation: Democratic Theory in Habermas's *Between Facts and Norms*', in Peter Dews (ed.) *Habermas: A Critical Reader*, Oxford: Blackwell.

Schmitt, C. (1985a) *The Crisis of Parliamentary Democracy*, translated by Ellen Kennedy, Cambridge, MA: MIT Press.

Schmitt, C. (1985b) *Political Theology*, translated by George Schwab, Cambridge, MA: MIT Press.

Schmitt, C. (1996) *The Concept of the Political*, translated by George Schwab, Chicago: University of Chicago Press.

Schwab, G. (1989) *The Challenge of the Exception: An Introduction to the Political Ideas of Carl Schmitt between 1921 and 1936*, 2nd edition, Westport, CT: Greenwood Press.

Scott, J. C. (1977a) 'Protest and Profanation', *Theory and Society*, vol. 4, no.1, pp. 1–38.

Scott, J. C. (1977b) 'Protest and Profanation', *Theory and Society*, vol. 4, no. 2, pp. 211–46.

Scott, J. C. (1985) *Weapons of the Weak*, New Haven: Yale University Press.

Scott, J. C. (1990) *Domination and the Arts of Resistance*, New Haven: Yale University Press.

Shostak, M. (1981) *Nisa: The life and words of a !Kung woman*, New York: Random House.

Singer, D. (1970) *Prelude to Revolution: France in May 1968*, London: Jonathan Cape.

Skinner, Q. (2002) *Visions of Politics Volume 1: Regarding Method*, Cambridge: Cambridge University Press.

Smith, A. M. (2001) 'Words that Matter: Butler's *Excitable Speech*', *Constellations*, vol. 8, no. 3, pp. 390–9.

de Souza, L. M. T. M. (2002) 'A Case Among Cases, A World Among Worlds: The Ecology of Writing Among the Kashinawa in Brazil', *Journal of Language Identity and Education*, vol. 1, no. 4, pp. 261–78.

de Souza, L. M. T. M. (2003) 'Voices on Paper: Multimodal Texts and Indigenous Literacy in Brazil', *Social Semiotics*, vol. 13, no. 1, pp. 29–42.

de Souza, L. M. T. M., (2004) 'Remapping Writing: Indigenous Writing and Cultural Conflict in Brazil, *English Studies in Canada*, vol. 30, no. 3 (2004), pp. 4–16.

Sparks, H. (1997) 'Dissident Citizenship: Democratic Theory, Political Courage, and Activist Women', *Hypatia*, vol. 12, no. 4, pp. 74–110.

Spelman, E. V. (1982) 'Woman as Body: Ancient and Contemporary Views', *Feminist Studies*, vol. 8, no. 1, pp. 109–31.

Starr, A. (2000) *Naming the Enemy: Anti-Corporate Movements Confront Globalisation*, London: Zed Books.

Stavrakakis, Y. (2001) 'Religious populism and political culture: the Greek case', *South European Society and Politics*, vol. 7, no. 3, pp. 29–52.

Stewart, J. B. (1986) *Wendell Phillips: Liberty's Hero*, Baton Rouge: Louisiana State University Press.

Stone, A. (2004) 'Towards a Genealogical Feminism: A Reading of Judith Butler's Political Thought', *Contemporary Political Theory*, vol. 4, no. 1, pp. 4–24.

Sullivan, A. (ed.) (2004) *Same-Sex Marriage: Pro and Con: A Reader*, 2nd edition, New York, Vintage Books.

Taylor, C. (1995) 'Irreducibly Social Goods', in *Philosophical Argument*, Cambridge, MA: Harvard University Press.

Taylor, R. (ed.) (2008) *Consociational Theory: McGarry/O'Leary and the Northern Ireland Conflict*, London: Routledge.

Tester, K. (1992) *Civil Society*, London: Routledge.

Thomassen, L. (2007) 'Beyond Representation?', *Parliamentary Affairs*, vol. 60, no. 1, pp. 111–26.

Thompson, E. P. (1963) *The Making of the English Working Class*, New York: Victor Gollancz.

Tønder, L. and Thomassen, L. (eds) (2005a) 'Introduction: Rethinking Radical Democracy between Abundance and Lack', in *Radical Democracy: Politics between Abundance and Lack*, Manchester: Manchester University Press.

Tønder, L. and Thomassen, L. (eds) (2005b) *Radical Democracy: Politics between Abundance and Lack*, Manchester: Manchester University Press.

Tormey, S. (2004) *Anti-Capitalism: A Beginners Guide*, Oxford: Oneworld.

Tormey, S. (2006) 'Not in my Name: Deleuze, Zapatismo and the Critique of Representation', *Parliamentary Affairs*, vol. 59, no. 1, pp. 138–54.

Townshend, J. (2004) 'Laclau and Mouffe's Hegemonic Project: The Story So Far', *Political Studies*, vol. 52, no. 2, pp. 269–89.

Trend, D. (ed.) (2006) *Radical Democracy: Identity, Citizenship and the State*, London: Routledge.

Tully, J. (2000) 'The Struggles of Indigenous Peoples for and of Freedom', in D. Ivison, P. Patton and W. Sanders (eds) *Political Theory and the Rights of Indigenous Peoples*, Cambridge: Cambridge University Press.

Turnbull, C. M. (1987) *The Forest People*, New York: Simon and Schuster.

Valentine, J. (2001) 'The Hegemony of Hegemony', *History of the Human Sciences*, vol. 14, no. 1, pp. 88–104.

Vaneigem, R. (1994) *The Movement of the Free Spirit*, New York: Zone.

Van Roermund, B. (1997) *Law, Narrative and Reality: An Essay in Intercepting Politics*, Dordrecht: Kluwer.

Van Roermund, B. (2003) 'Sovereignty: Unpopular and Popular', in N. Walker (ed.) *Sovereignty in Transition*, Oxford: Hart Publishing.

Vaughan-Williams, N. (2006) 'Towards a Problematisation of the Problematisations that Reduce Northern Ireland to a Problem', *Critical Review of International Social and Political Philosophy*, vol. 9, no. 4, December, pp. 513–26.

Vázquez-Arroyo, A. Y. (2004) 'Agonized Liberalism: The Liberal Theory of William E. Connolly', *Radical Philosophy*, 127 (September/October), pp. 8–19.

Virilio, P. (1991) *Desert Screen: War at the Speed of Light*, New York: Continuum.

Walzer, M. (1992) 'The Civil Society Argument', in C. Mouffe (ed.)

Dimensions of Radical Democracy: Pluralism, Citizenship, Community, London: Verso.

Ward, C. (1992) 'Anarchy in Milton Keynes', *The Raven*, 18, vol. 5, no. 2, April–June, pp. 116–31.

Warner, M. (1999) *The Trouble with Normal: Sex, Politics, and the Ethics of Queer Life*, Cambridge, MA: Harvard University Press.

Warren, M. (1989) 'Liberal Constitutionalism as Ideology: Marx and Habermas', *Political Theory*, vol. 17, no. 4, pp. 511–34.

Warren, M. E. (2001) *Associations and Democracy*, Princeton: Princeton University Press.

Waterford, J. (1992) 'We're Already Home', *Canberra Times*, 25 January, pp. 1–2.

Wenman, M. (2003) 'Laclau or Mouffe? Splitting the Difference', *Philosophy and Social Criticism*, vol. 29, no. 5, pp. 581–606.

Whelan, F. (1983) 'Prologue: Democratic Theory and the Boundary Problem', in J. R. Pennock and J. W. Chapman (eds) *Liberal Democracy*, New York: New York University Press.

Widder, N. (2004) 'The Relevance of Nietzsche to Democratic Theory: Micropolitics and the Affirmation of Difference', *Contemporary Political Theory*, vol. 3, no. 2, pp. 188–211.

Widder, N. (2005) 'Two routes from Hegel', in L. Tønder and L. Thomassen (eds) *Radical Democracy*, Manchester: Manchester University Press, pp. 32–49.

Wilford, R. (ed.) (2001) *Aspects of the Belfast Agreement*, Oxford: Oxford University Press.

Williams, J. (2005) *Understanding Poststructuralism*, Stocksfield: Acumen.

Wintemute, R. (2005) 'From "Sex Rights" to "Love Rights": Partnership Rights as Human Rights', in N. Bamforth (ed.) *Sex Rights: The Oxford Amnesty Lectures 2002*, Oxford: Oxford University Press, pp. 186–224.

Wolin, S. (1994a) 'Norm and Form: The Constitutionalising of Democracy', in J. P. Eueben, J. R. Wallach and J. Ober (eds) *Athenian Political Thought and the Representation of American Democracy*, Ithaca: Cornell University Press.

Wolin, S. (1994b) 'Fugitive Democracy', *Constellations*, vol. 1, no. 1, pp. 11–25.

Young, I. M. (1990) *Justice and the Politics of Difference*, Princeton: Princeton University Press.

Young, I. M. (1996) 'Communication and the Other: Beyond Deliberative Democracy', in S. Benhabib (ed.), *Democracy and Difference: Contesting the Boundaries of the Political*, Princeton: Princeton University Press, pp. 120–36.

Young, I. M. (2000) *Inclusion and Democracy*, Oxford: Oxford University Press.

Young, I. M. (2001) 'Activist Challenges to Deliberative Democracy', *Political Theory*, vol. 29, no. 5, pp. 670–90.

Zerilli, L. (1998) 'This Universalism Which Is Not One', *Diacritics*, vol. 28, no. 2, pp. 3–20, http://www.mi2.hr/radioActive/past.txt/03.03.zerelli.thisuniversalismwhichisnotone.html (accessed 24/11/04).

Index

AAS (American Anti-Slavery Society), 159, 178n
abolitionists, 176; *see also* slavery
Aborigines, 55–7, 69, 71, 72n
accommodationism, 13, 14, 15–18, 19, 20, 22
adoption, 41, 46
Africa, 146, 152–3, 175
African Americans, 173
Agamben, G., 155
aggregationism, 13, 14, 15, 18, 19, 20, 22, 25, 31, 94
agitation, 171–2
agonism, 14, 30, 53, 59, 60, 70, 109, 112, 158, 159, 160, 164–8, 176, 194, 204; *see also* conflict
AIDS activism, 75, 85
Al-Qaeda, 176
Alquati, R., 148
Althusser, L., 118
American Civil War, 171–2
anarchy, 68, 141, 147
ANC (African National Congress), 175
Ang, I., 147
animal welfare laws, 16
antagonism, 21, 25, 60, 70, 97, 107, 109, 110, 120, 136, 137, 138, 196
  into agonism, 165, 166–7, 194
  constitutive, 25
anti-capitalism, 116, 128, 133, 149, 150
anti-colonialism, 85
Anzaldúa, G., 37
appropriation, 80, 82–3
Arato, A., 2, 95–6
Arendt, H., 54–5, 56, 96
Aristotle, 27
Aronowitz, S., 1
articulation, 136, 137–8, 140, 141, 152, 174
associational politics, 75–6, 77, 89, 90n
Aughey, A., 193
Augusteijn, J., 192
Australia, 55–7, 69–71, 72n
autonomy *see* self-determination
axiology, 6, 7

Badiou, A., 134
Baehr v. *Lewin case* (1993), 39
Bakhtin, M., 145, 154, 156

Balibar, É., 93. 109, 106
base-superstructure topography, 113, 117–19, 121
Beasley, C. and Bacchi, C., 85
Belfast Agreement (1998), 180–1, 187, 189, 191, 193, 194, 195, 196, 197n
Bellamy, R., 161, 163
Benjamin, W., 154, 155
Bennett, J., 6, 26
Bew, P., 193
Bey, H., 145
Bloch, E., 21
body politics, 74, 84–9
Bologna, S., 148
boundaries, 67, 121, 175–6
Bourdieu, P., 78–9, 83
Bourke, R., 188
Bretton Woods system, 114, 116, 123, 128
bribery, 29
Brown, J., 170, 174
Bush, President G. W., 40
Butler, J., 4, 5, 26, 27, 33, 73–89, 112, 201
  body politics, 85–7
  ethics of non-violence, 88–9
  normative violence, 86–7
  same-sex marriage, 38–9, 38–50, 41, 42–8, 80
  universality, 34–8, 40–1, 46, 48

California, 40
Canada, 16
capitalism, 1, 122–4
Card, C., 42, 50n
carnivalesque, 145
Castoriadis, C., 154
catachresis, 27, 28
chain of equivalence, 127–9
Chatterjee, P., 146
Chesters, G. and Walsh, I., 149
Christodoulidis, E., 60
churches, 104, 105
citizenship, 61, 63, 64, 68, 76
  articulating principle, 136, 137–8
  Australia, 69
  body politics, 85
  equality, 162
  rights, 40, 55, 117, 129
  United States, 173–4
  without community, 109

227